BEHAVIORAL ETHICS IN PRACTICE

This book is an accessible, research-based introduction to behavioral ethics. Often ethics education is incomplete because it ignores how and why people make moral decisions. But using exciting new research from fields such as behavioral psychology, cognitive science, and evolutionary biology, the study of behavioral ethics uncovers the common reasons why good people often screw up.

Scientists have long studied the ways human beings make decisions, but only recently have researchers begun to focus specifically on ethical decision making. Unlike philosophy and religion, which aim to tell people how to think and act about various moral issues, behavioral ethics research reveals the factors that influence how people really make moral decisions. Most people get into ethical trouble for doing obviously wrong things. Aristotle cannot help, but learning about behavioral ethics can. By supplementing traditional approaches to teaching ethics with a clear, detailed, research-based introduction to behavioral ethics, beginners can quickly become familiar with the important elements of this new field. This book includes the bonus of being coordinated with Ethics Unwrapped – a free, online, educational resource featuring award-winning videos and teaching materials on a variety of behavioral ethics (and general ethics) topics.

This book is a useful supplement for virtually every ethics course, and important in any course where incorporating practical ethics in an engaging manner is paramount. The content applies to every discipline – journalism, business ethics, medicine, legal ethics, and others – because its chief subject is the nature of moral decision making. Because the book is research-based yet accessibly written with interesting studies, it could be used in high schools, colleges, graduate schools, and industry.

Cara Biasucci is Creator of Ethics Unwrapped, and Director of Ethics Education for the Center for Leadership and Ethics, University of Texas at Austin. For more than a decade, she made films for (among others) American Public Television, Discovery Times, New England Patriots, National Gallery of Art, and Johns Hopkins.

Robert Prentice has for 40 years taught business law and ethics at the McCombs School of Business, University of Texas at Austin. He is also Chair of the Business, Government & Society Department and Faculty Director of Ethics Unwrapped.

BEHAVIORAL ETHICS IN PRACTICE

Why We Sometimes Make the Wrong Decisions

Cara Biasucci and Robert Prentice

LONDON AND NEW YORK

First published 2021
by Routledge
2 Park Square, Milton Park, Abingdon, Oxon OX14 4RN

and by Routledge
52 Vanderbilt Avenue, New York, NY 10017

Routledge is an imprint of the Taylor & Francis Group, an informa business

© 2021 Cara Biasucci and Robert Prentice

The right of Cara Biasucci and Robert Prentice to be identified as authors of this work has been asserted by them in accordance with sections 77 and 78 of the Copyright, Designs and Patents Act 1988.

All rights reserved. No part of this book may be reprinted or reproduced or utilised in any form or by any electronic, mechanical, or other means, now known or hereafter invented, including photocopying and recording, or in any information storage or retrieval system, without permission in writing from the publishers.

Trademark notice: Product or corporate names may be trademarks or registered trademarks, and are used only for identification and explanation without intent to infringe.

British Library Cataloguing-in-Publication Data
A catalogue record for this book is available from the British Library

Library of Congress Cataloging-in-Publication Data
Names: Biasucci, Cara, 1964– author. | Prentice, Robert, 1950– author.
Title: Behavioral ethics in practice : why we sometimes make the wrong decisions / Cara Biasucci and Robert Prentice.
Identifiers: LCCN 2020022516 (print) | LCCN 2020022517 (ebook) | ISBN 9780367341633 (hardback) | ISBN 9780367341657 (paperback) | ISBN 9780429324246 (ebook)
Subjects: LCSH: Decision making—Moral and ethical aspects.
Classification: LCC BJ1419 .B53 2021 (print) | LCC BJ1419 (ebook) | DDC 170—dc23
LC record available at https://lccn.loc.gov/2020022516
LC ebook record available at https://lccn.loc.gov/2020022517

ISBN: 978-0-367-34163-3 (hbk)
ISBN: 978-0-367-34165-7 (pbk)
ISBN: 978-0-429-32424-6 (ebk)

Typeset in Bembo
by Apex CoVantage, LLC

BEHAVIORAL ETHICS IN PRACTICE

Why We Sometimes Make the Wrong Decisions

Cara Biasucci

Robert Prentice

CONTENTS

Introduction   1

PART I
Why it's hard to be the kind of person your dog thinks you are   5

1 Making moral judgments   11

2 How emotions influence ethics   21

3 Moral action decisions and moral reasoning flaws   31

4 Obedience to authority   37

5 Conformity bias   45

6 Overconfidence bias   53

7 Self-serving bias   61

8 Framing   71

9 Incrementalism   81

10 Loss aversion   89

viii Contents

11	Role morality	97
12	Moral equilibrium	105
13	Tangible and abstract	113
14	In-group bias	121
15	Implicit bias	129
16	Cognitive dissonance	135
17	General situational factors	143
18	Temporal factors	155
19	Fundamental attribution error	163

PART II
How to improve your chances of living a life you can be proud of — **169**

20	Being your best self	175
21	Rationalizations and other mechanisms of moral disengagement	187
22	Giving voice to your values	203
23	Creating a culture that makes it easier to do the right thing	219

Notes — *231*
Index — *261*

Illustrated by
Buddy Hickerson

INTRODUCTION

> "A strong and wise people will study its own failures no less than its triumphs, for there is wisdom to be learned from the study of both, of the mistake as well as of the success."[1]
> – Theodore Roosevelt

Scientists have long studied the varied and complex ways we humans make decisions. But only recently have researchers begun to focus specifically on ethical decision making. Work done by behavioral psychologists, neuroscientists, evolutionary biologists, primatologists, and many others has contributed to a new and exciting research field: *behavioral ethics*. Behavioral ethics is "the study of why people make the ethical and unethical decisions that they do."[2]

Behavioral ethics is descriptive – it explains the many factors that influence how we make ethical decisions rather than telling us what we should do or think about various ethical issues. This research is exciting because the dominant approach to teaching ethics has been normative or prescriptive ethics – it focuses on deciding how we *should* act in given situations.[3] Much ethics education concentrates on discussing issues that Aristotle, Socrates, Plato, and others were wrestling with 2,000 years ago. In at least some areas, little progress has been made since then.

It is certainly valuable for students (of all ages) to learn ethical frameworks to help resolve their moral dilemmas. The world is full of new and challenging moral questions arising from developments in cloning, artificial intelligence, autonomous vehicles, and the like. However, most people who get into ethical trouble have in fact decided to do an obviously wrong thing – it's not that they haven't read enough philosophy. Aristotle cannot help; behavioral ethics can.

The truth is, white collar criminals don't typically go to prison because they mistakenly thought it was okay to participate in insider trading, tax evasion, money laundering, bribery, or fraud. They go to prison because they made terrible ethical choices. In one recent study, the authors

> looked at 30 recent editions of *The Wall Street Journal* and read the first 5 pages, looking for cases of moral failure or corruption. Every day there was at least one case of moral failure, sometimes more, for a total of 47 cases of scandal and corruption. After reviewing these 47 cases, though, not a single one . . . was a [moral] dilemma. Every case, at least on the surface, seemed to be black and white, right or wrong. People just chose wrongly. These included lying to a grand jury, destroying evidence during a Securities and Exchange Commission investigation, rigging bids to steal from customers, or purposely misstating earnings during reporting season. Not a single case seemed to be a choice between two principled rights or between two principled wrongs.[4]

In addition to focusing (misguidedly) only on stubborn moral dilemmas, there is some evidence that traditional ethics education can be detrimental. It can leave students overconfident regarding their ability to act ethically, particularly as compared to their peers.[5]

This new field of behavioral ethics reveals the insidious influences – of external pressures, internal biases, and situational factors – that interfere with our judgment and decision-making. Learning about behavioral ethics has the potential to improve moral judgments, moral decisions, and moral actions. Psychologist Tomlin and colleagues believe that "[i]mprovement [in ethics education] may be realized by shifting away from traditional ethics toward curricula that focus on behavioral ethics."[6] Business professors Park and Elsass similarly argue:

> The growing attention to the theory and business practices of behavioral ethics scholarship represents a promising trend that encourages management educators and their students to move away from a focus on ethical challenges as intellectual problems (i.e., that could be solved simply by coming up with the most convincing argument in a classroom) to addressing ethics and values-driven leadership in terms of intellectual rigor, a moral perspective, and personal skill development.[7]

Unfortunately, as business ethics scholar Mark Schwartz noted recently:

> a review of the more popular business ethics textbooks finds that most tend to ignore any discussion of the impediments to ethical behavior, other than possibly a brief mention of the moral rationalization process. A review of business ethics course curricula reveals that while the ethical decision making process is often taught, it does not necessarily include discussion of the specific elements of behavioral ethics.[8]

Thus the need for this book, *Behavioral Ethics in Practice: Why We Sometimes Make the Wrong Decisions*. Our goal in writing it is to supplement (not replace) traditional approaches to teaching ethics with an introduction to behavioral ethics that we hope will be clear, accessible, reasonably detailed, and research-based. This book is a stand-alone resource; however it also includes the bonus of being coordinated with Ethics Unwrapped – a free, online, educational resource featuring award-winning videos on a variety of behavioral ethics topics (and general ethics topics). Between the 130+ videos on the Ethics Unwrapped website and this book, beginners can quickly become familiar with the important elements of behavioral ethics.[9] There are suggestions for Ethics Unwrapped videos and case studies that reinforce and extend learning (and teaching) of the chapter's concept (and related ideas) at the end of each chapter.

On the Ethics Unwrapped website, videos and case studies are augmented by discussion questions, teaching notes, lists of additional resources, and a blog. All of the educational materials are available in English and Spanish at EthicsUnwrapped.UTexas.edu, and the videos can also be found by searching YouTube. This robust and valuable ethics resource is offered at no cost by the Center for Leadership and Ethics at the McCombs School of Business at The University of Texas at Austin. In fact, the authors of this book are the Creator (Cara Biasucci) and the Faculty Director (Robert Prentice) of Ethics Unwrapped.

One other important point to make before we get this show on the road. A respectable number of experts distinguish between "ethics" and "morals," but we follow what we believe to be the majority approach and use the words interchangeably in this book. In our view, if you are acting ethically, you are acting morally, and vice versa.

PART I
Why it's hard to be the kind of person your dog thinks you are

Introduction

Your moral self is, in many ways, your essence. If your brain falters and your memory fades, your friends will say that you just can't remember things as you used to. If you suffer a brain injury and begin to have fits of anger, your friends will say that your moods have changed. But if you suffer a brain injury that affects your moral self, your friends will tend to say that *you are just not you anymore*.[10]

Studies demonstrate that your moral character is what forms others' impressions of you.[11] When people judge their closest peers, morality is the most important factor. It's more influential than being competent or friendly.[12] In other words, morality counts! And learning to improve your moral life will be worth any effort you put into it.

Behavioral ethics

Behavioral ethics is the study of how and why people make ethical and unethical decisions. Its roots lie deep in related research fields, including behavioral psychology, evolutionary biology, cognitive science, and primatology. It demonstrates that humans are simultaneously complex, somewhat irrational, and yet generally well-intentioned beings. Indeed, if you're a typical human being, you want to be a good person. But, like all typical human beings, you've probably done things you wouldn't want your mother to know about, or to see splashed across the headlines of the newspaper (even though most people don't read newspapers anymore).

The general point of *Behavioral Ethics in Practice* is to introduce and explain various factors and forces that can make it difficult for you to be a good person – an honest, reliable, fair, open-minded, trustworthy type of person. It's not our goal to tell you what you should believe about the most controversial moral issues of the day – abortion, the death penalty, climate change, artificial intelligence, genetic engineering, and so forth. Rather, we'd like to help you live up to your *own* moral standards. To do that, you must avoid three types of influences that can create a gap between who you want to be and how you actually act. These influences are:

- Social and Organizational Pressures (External Pressures)
- Psychological Biases and Mental Shortcuts (Internal Biases)
- Situational Factors (Circumstances)

These mostly unconscious influences limit human beings' ethicality – our ability to act with integrity, honesty, and transparency. As much as we might think we act logically and with integrity – and are therefore ethical – the truth is that we all lie a little and cheat a little every day,[13] sometimes in response to one or more of these influences. And, even though it may be illogical to act unethically (given the consequences), none of us are perfectly rational thinkers.

In fact, economists and other academics used to assume in their models (and sometimes still do) that people are perfectly rational – logical in their thinking, choices, and actions. But research by psychologists Daniel Kahneman and Amos Tversky demonstrates that human rationality has definite limits. People are only boundedly rational. Kahneman and Tversky's research, as well as the research of dozens of their academic followers, shows that these boundaries (or limits) apply to all peoples' decision making about all things – including when they make ethical choices. In other words, as human beings, we are both boundedly rational and *boundedly ethical*.

Behavioral ethics in practice: why we sometimes make the wrong decisions

This book focuses on some (but not all!) of the many biases and influences described by behavioral ethics research that often serve as a trap for the unaware. We do this to educate you and make you wary, in the hopes that you'll be less likely to fall into ethical traps. We also agree with psychologists Isaac Smith and Maryam Kouchaki, who argue that "recognizing one's own moral fallibility is a key aspect of *moral humility*, and an important step toward closing any gaps between a person's espoused values and their enacted behaviors."[14] In other words, if we succeed in showing you how easy it is to screw up in the ethical realm (and you take this message to heart), you'll be a giant step closer to being the good person you want to be.

In Part I, we discuss the influences and forces that make it difficult for all of us to live up to our own moral standards. Each chapter examines a pressure, bias, or factor that can induce people to make ethical errors. In Part II, we discuss more generally the steps that people can take to prevent and correct ethical mistakes (so they may live a life of which they can be proud). We also give you tools to more successfully avoid ethical pitfalls and more reliably and effectively stand up for what you believe to be right. And we give you some tips to shape your organizations so that it's easier to do the right thing.

Importantly, the material in this book is evidence-based. We reference research and cite scores of studies (empirical, experimental, and more) from many different academic disciplines. Our discussion of behavioral ethics provides real world examples, too, to supplement and bolster the points made in most of the academic studies referenced here.

However, keep in mind that behavioral ethics is a new field. What we think we know is ever-evolving, and it pays to be skeptical.[15] This is especially true because some fields (such as psychology) have suffered a "replication crisis" where important findings from one experiment sometimes don't show up in the next experiment in the same area.[16] So, while your authors are confident in the big picture painted here regarding the field of behavioral ethics, we are equally confident that some concepts may be expanded and described quite differently at some later point (if this book has a second edition). Better-designed studies will debunk some of the finding we report. Science will march on!

ETHICS UNWRAPPED RESOURCES

Videos

Behavioral Ethics
Series: Ethics Defined

Intro to Behavioral Ethics
Series: Concepts Unwrapped

Bounded Ethicality
Series: Ethics Defined

Bounded Ethicality
Series: Concepts Unwrapped

Ethics
Series: Ethics Defined

Case Studies

The CIA Leak

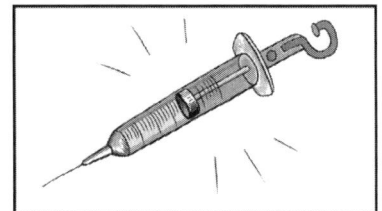

*Healthcare Obligations:
Personal vs. Institutional*

1
MAKING MORAL JUDGMENTS

> "Across all demographic groups, levels of education, ethnicities and both genders, people judge moral dilemmas similarly. . . . However, across all demographic groups subjects were remarkably bad at justifying their reasoning . . . Even a majority of subjects who reported exposure to moral philosophy were unable to provide a sufficient justification of their actions."[17]
>
> – Neil Levy

Introduction

Immanuel Kant, one of history's most brilliant philosophers, thought carefully about masturbation. Don't ask your authors why. We're not sure we want to know.

Everyone knows, Kant said, that masturbation is immoral: "That such an unnatural use (and so misuse) of one's sexual attributes is a violation of one's duty to himself and is certainly in the highest degree opposed to morality *strikes everyone upon his thinking of it*." He acknowledged it was difficult to explain *why* masturbation is immoral, but ultimately argued that "[a] man gives up his personality (throws it away) when he uses himself merely as a means for the gratification of an animal drive."[18]

Now it's unlikely that the average 15-year-old boy is going to find this argument persuasive, and frankly, neither do we. But if one of the best philosophers of all time is this unconvincing in supporting his moral judgments, what hope is there for the rest of humanity? The answer is: Not much, unless we really work at it.

In fact, people are generally bad at moral reasoning (Kant probably thought he killed it with that "gives up his personality" argument!). When we make moral judgments, it seems to us that we're thinking logically and carefully and reaching sound conclusions. But the science shows that we often choose poorly.

This mismatch between our actual ability and our self-perceived ability makes us close-minded to other points of view or new evidence.

If we can be convinced of the reality that people are bad at moral reasoning, then perhaps we can be persuaded to be open and reflective when we make moral judgments. Rather than just assume that we're getting it right, we can be thoughtful and ask questions. As ethics professors Rand Park and Priscilla Elsass note, ethics "education has to cultivate moral humility rather than moral confidence."[19]

Moral intuitions

Daniel Kahneman, a psychologist who won the Nobel Prize in economics for his research with psychologist Amos Tversky, demonstrated that the vast majority of our brain's work is done below the conscious level. In fact, most of our decisions are made by what Kahneman calls "System 1" – an emotional, intuitive, and almost instantaneous system in the brain that operates without conscious input. Astoundingly, only about 10 percent of our brain's decisions are made by its more conscious, logical, reasoning "System 2." This is true of how our brain makes moral decisions, too.

Psychologist Jonathan Haidt observes that "[m]oral intuitions arise automatically and almost instantaneously, long before moral reasoning has a chance to get started, and those first intuitions tend to drive our later reasoning."[20] In other words, when we feel we are reasoning our way through a moral problem, often all we are doing is creating *rationalizations* for decisions that the emotional parts of our brain have already embraced. This doesn't mean we never use the reasoning parts of our brain in moral decision making.[21] If we think carefully, we can summon System 2 to override many of the conclusions made automatically by System 1. Unfortunately, we seldom do this.

Whether these all-important moral intuitions are primarily emotional in nature (as Haidt suggests) or primarily rational (as Kant suggests) is one of the key topics of inquiry in ethics.

Sentimentalism

Sentimentalism, also called *emotionism*, is the view that our moral judgments and decision making are largely grounded in moral sentiments (also called *moral emotions*).

To illustrate, consider the emotion of disgust. Many studies show that if researchers trigger the emotion of disgust in people – by putting them in a filthy room, by using fart spray (yes, there really is such a thing), or even by hypnotizing them – people will make much harsher moral judgments than if they are not feeling disgusted.[22] Although people won't realize the impact that disgust is having on their moral judgments, the effect (though it's not huge) is consistent and easily replicated.

Human beings are confabulators. Our minds make sh*t up! We are notoriously bad at explaining why we have done many things, including making particular moral judgments. In one experiment, participants were hypnotized to feel disgust when they read the word "take." Then they were shown one form or the other of the following scenario:

> Dan is a student council representative at his school. This semester he is in charge of scheduling discussions about academic issues. He [tries to take/ often picks] topics that appeal to both professors and students in order to stimulate discussion.

Those participants whose scenario was worded "often picks" didn't think Dan had done anything wrong. But those whose scenario included the "tries to *take*" language felt disgust (as they had been hypnotized to do). They judged Dan harshly. When asked to explain *why* they felt Dan had acted immorally, their brains invented reasons for their conclusion, but they were not very convincing. The participants said:

- "It just seems like he's up to something."
- "It just seems so weird and disgusting."
- "He seems like a popularity-seeking snob."
- "I don't know why it's wrong, it just is."[23]

In another study, psychologists triggered people's disgust by having them watch a video clip from the movie "Trainspotting" that featured a filthy, repulsive toilet. Again, people's moral judgments became more extreme. But once they were given the opportunity to wash their hands (lessening the disgust emotion), their moral judgments softened.[24]

Clearly, emotions play a significant role in much of our moral decision making.

Rationalism

A more traditional view of ethics (the one Kant subscribed to) is *rationalism*. Rationalism is the idea that our moral judgments are mostly the product of careful, reasoned judgment. This is obviously not true.

Contemporary philosopher Joshua May, a strong rationalist, admits that "[c]learly, both reason and emotion play a role in moral judgment."[25] Hanno Sauer, also a modern rationalist philosopher, concedes that the evidence of behavioral ethics research reveals that "conscious reasoning of the kind that rationalists put such high hopes on does little work; emotions and unconscious influences carry the day."[26] That said, Sauer argues that moral "reasoning figures in the acquisition, formation, and maintenance of those moral intuitions."[27] In other words, Sauer believes that the thinking and studying you do in this ethics course, and the life lessons you gain through experience, will mold your moral intuitions – the intuitions that unconsciously and immediately arise when you face future moral questions.

So the argument between the sentimentalists and the rationalists is largely a matter of degree. Both sides admit that emotion *and* reason play a role in our ethical decision making and actions. Both sides agree there are unconscious and conscious processes involved. But there is disagreement as to which one rules. No matter which it is, though, human moral decision making is often less than optimal.

Values

In 2016, San Francisco 49ers quarterback Colin Kaepernick refused to stand at the beginning of an NFL football game when the "Star-Spangled Banner" was played. He was protesting racial discrimination in the United States, especially as manifested in police violence against young black men.

Kaepernick faced fierce criticism. Many critics echoed a theme struck in one letter to the editor: "What he has done is choose to disrespect all of the millions of men and women who have served our great nation over the centuries. And disrespect all that they believed in, fought for, and in some cases, died for."[28]

Kaepernick's supporters argued, to the contrary, that what the men and women in our armed services have fought for is the Constitution, including the First Amendment's right to free speech, which Kaepernick was exercising. As one supporter wrote: "Without her heroes and heroines who dared to say 'No,' America would be the lesser. Like the Alabama bus-sitter, Rosa Parks, Mr. Kaepernick stood up for America by sitting down."[29]

These two strong opposing views of the morality of Kaepernick's actions are embodiments of the differing *values* that people often hold. Indeed, ethical issues often begin with (or boil down to) values conflicts.

Philosopher Hanno Sauer claims that "[m]oral intuitions are not deduced from first principles."[30] In other words, our moral intuitions or moral beliefs are not produced by rational System 2 thinking. Rather, we develop our moral intuitions from our particular culture's beliefs and value systems. Psychologist Jonathan Haidt argues that politically liberal people tend to value three moral foundations, or moral principles:

- The Care foundation, which causes people to be sensitive to suffering and need, and to condemn people who harm others in the in-group.
- The Fairness foundation, which causes people to want to punish cheaters.
- The Liberty foundation, which causes people to hate tyranny and oppose oppression.

Haidt further argues that liberals are unable to understand why anyone would vote Republican because they don't relate to three additional moral foundations that tend to influence politically conservative people:

- The Loyalty foundation, which causes people to stand with their in-group.
- The Authority foundation, which causes people to obey tradition and support authority (and oppose subversion).
- The Sanctity or Purity foundation, which causes people to hate disgusting things. It also can make people invest objects with illogical and sometimes extreme values, which can help bind groups together.[31]

So, while liberals tended to see Colin Kaepernick as a person who was exercising his free speech rights under the Constitution, and calling for fairness and compassion for black Americans, conservatives tended to see Kaepernick as someone who was subverting traditions, not standing with his team, and degrading the patriotic symbolism of the national anthem and the American flag.

Because liberals and conservatives begin by applying different values, they tend to leap to different conclusions. Then they speak (or often shout) past each other, and there is little actual reasoning going on. These two political groups don't disagree with each other because one side reasons more effectively than the other. They disagree because they are unknowingly coming from different places. Consequently, both groups are typically unable to construct arguments that persuade the other side.

Sacred values

For many of us, certain values become so important that they are called *sacred values*. Often, we will defend sacred values at any cost. Given the name, it's not surprising that religious beliefs are generally considered sacred values. Anthropologist Tanya Marie Luhrmann observes:

> [S]cholars have determined that people don't use rational, instrumental reasoning when they deal with religious beliefs. . . . [S]acred values are immune to the normal cost-benefit trade-offs that govern other dimensions of our lives. Sacred values are insensitive to quantity (one cartoon can be a profound insult). They don't respond to material incentives (if you offer people money to give up something that represents their sacred value, they often become more intractable in their refusal). Sacred values may even have different neural signatures in the brain.[32]

Sacred values, and their resistance to reason, extend well beyond religion. For many conservatives in America, gun rights have become a sacred value. Both pro-abortion and anti-abortion advocates tend to treat the abortion debate as a matter of sacred values. Ditto the debate over physician-assisted suicide.

Sometimes, when our moral beliefs are focused on outcomes, such as equal pay or fair taxes, these beliefs can be swayed with new facts and logical arguments. However, when our beliefs are based on sacred values, new facts and new explanations tend not to change our opinions, or even to moderate them.[33]

Moral socialization

Scientists often use the term *moral socialization*,[34] or sometimes *automatic norm following*,[35] when speaking specifically of the moral standards that human beings adopt. In general, we tend to take our cues as to how to act and think from our peers. As an evolutionary survival technique, this is a sound strategy generally speaking.

In fact, our geographic location has more influence on our beliefs than the neurons in our brains. If you take a minute to think about what people raised in Tuscaloosa generally believe, what people raised in Riyadh generally believe, and what people raised in Beijing generally believe, you'll see that people tend to believe that X is right and Y is wrong because the people around them tend to believe the same thing. In other words, we tend to believe that things are right and wrong because our group's moral standards tell us so, not because those things are necessarily right and wrong in any lasting, objective sense. Indeed, most groups' moral standards evolve substantially over time.

Because our own group's standards make sense to us, things seem "naturally" right and wrong to us. Even when we engage in moral reasoning, that reasoning typically has its roots in our group's values; we are usually applying the norms that are common in our society. Our group's values might not be the ones we'd adopt if we had open and rational debate about them in the first place. But we adopted those values because they seemed "right" to us because they were our community's values.

All of this means, among other things, that we should carefully examine our own values and belief systems. And we should always be open-minded about other people's values, especially when we enter moral debates, since values are largely the product of our environment. This does not mean, in your authors' opinion, that there is no way to know moral truths – also known as *moral relativism* – , so anything goes.[36]

ETHICS UNWRAPPED RESOURCES

Videos

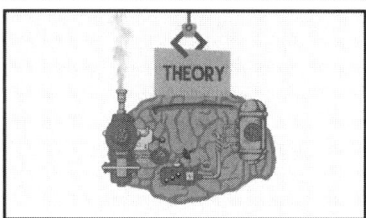

Moral Reasoning
Series: Ethics Defined

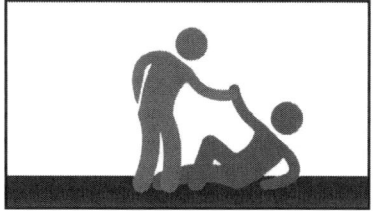

Morals
Series: Ethics Defined

Values
Series: Ethics Defined

GVV Pillar 1: Values
Series: Giving Voice to Values

Related Videos

Rationalizations
Series: Ethics Defined

Moral Emotions
Series: Ethics Defined

Social Contract Theory
Series: Ethics Defined

Moral Relativism
Series: Ethics Defined

ETHICS UNWRAPPED RESOURCES

Case Studies

Edward Snowden: Traitor or Hero?

Responding to Child Migration

Bullfighting: Art or Not?

2
HOW EMOTIONS INFLUENCE ETHICS

> *"As a social primate species, we modulate our morals with signals from family, friends and social groups with whom we identify because in our evolutionary past, those attributes helped individuals to survive and reproduce."*[37]
>
> – Michael Shermer

Introduction

Human emotions have evolved to do important work in keeping us on the straight and narrow. One theory (that makes sense to your authors) states that as human beings evolved, they lived in bigger groups and needed members of the group to adhere to social rules. Rule-following enabled the group and its members to survive, reproduce, and prosper. Certain emotions were co-opted to motivate members to follow the group's rules.[38]

One way to sort *moral emotions* is into the following four categories: self-conscious emotions, other-condemning emotions, other-praising emotions, and other-suffering emotions.[39]

Self-conscious emotions

Self-conscious emotions make us feel bad if we do not follow our group's moral and social norms. One of these emotions is *guilt*, an unpleasant feeling we get when we violate group norms. Even if no one ever finds out about our transgression, the guilty feeling lingers for most of us. We generally follow our group's moral standards to avoid this uncomfortable feeling. Psychologist Tina Malti has noted that "[m]oral guilt is healthy, good to develop. It helps the child refrain from aggression, antisocial behavior."[40] Indeed, studies confirm that guilt reduces unethical behavior.[41] In fact, the more intense our sense of guilt, the more trustworthy we tend to be.[42] Guilt can even induce us to agreeably help others.[43]

Shame is another unpleasant self-conscious emotion that we feel when people learn we have strayed from the group's moral standards. While guilt is an internal process, shame is the result of others' external judgment of us. Shame is reinforced by *embarrassment*, which is not quite as extreme an emotion as shame, but it still carries enough punch to encourage many of us to follow the rules.

Other-condemning emotions

The second category of moral emotions is other-condemning emotions, which are reciprocal to the self-conscious emotions. For example, *contempt* is what we often feel towards those who have violated moral norms. Likewise, *anger* and *disgust* are other-condemning emotions that we often feel toward rule violators.

Unlike self-conscious emotions, which are internal states we mostly generate ourselves, other-condemning emotions are external to us. These emotions – anger, contempt, disgust – that are generated by other people will cause us to feel emotions such as shame and embarrassment. Sometimes just anticipating how we will feel in the face of others' contempt can encourage us to follow group norms.[44] Neurological scientist Robert Sapolsky supplies an example of how other-condemning emotions can trigger self-conscious emotions, hopefully leading to better future behavior.

> [In 1999,] more than a dozen healthy, strapping football players at UCLA were discovered to have used connections, made-up disabilities, and forged doctors' signatures to get handicapped parking permits. Their privileged positions resulted in what was generally seen as slaps on the wrist by both the courts and UCLA. However, the element of shaming may well have made up for it – as the players left the courthouse in front of the press, they walked past a phalanx of disabled, wheelchair-bound individuals jeering them.[45]

A more recent example is the Varsity Blues college admissions scandal of 2019 where famous actors, hedge fund managers, and other wealthy folks were publicly shamed for having paid bribes to enable their children to enter colleges like Harvard, Yale, and The University of Texas.[46] Their shame should cause other parents to second guess whether they wish to cheat on their children's behalf in such a manner, too.

Psychologist Jonathan Haidt thinks that Glaucon, a character in Plato's *Republic*, got it right when he suggested that "the most important principle for designing an ethical society is to *make sure that everyone's reputation is on the line all the time*, so that bad behavior will bring bad consequences."[47]

This, ultimately, is what these other-condemning moral emotions help to ensure.

Other-praising emotions

The third category of moral emotions is other-praising emotions, which are the feelings we get when we feel thankful and admire others. *Gratitude* is one other-praising emotion that often spurs us to act morally. If we are grateful for another person's actions, or the actions of the group, we will probably respond by being thankful and showing appreciation. If someone has been kind to us, for example, our gratitude for that kindness may cause us to be kind in return.

Moral elevation, also known as *moral awe*, is another other-praising emotion. It is the inspiring feeling we often get when we see other people act as moral heroes. That feeling can spur us to act morally, too, as we will see in more detail in Chapter 5 when we discuss the *conformity bias*.[48]

Other-suffering emotions

The fourth category of moral emotions is other-suffering emotions. Sympathy, compassion, and empathy are other-suffering emotions which describe the feelings we get when we see other people hurting or in need. *Sympathy* is a basic concern for the welfare of others.[49] Closely related to sympathy is *compassion*, which "is characterized by feelings of warmth, concern and care for the other, as well as a strong motivation to improve the other's well-being. Compassion is feeling *for* and not feeling *with* the other."[50]

Empathy is probably the most important of these other-suffering emotions. Substantial psychological evidence demonstrates a link between empathy and prosocial behavior.[51] Empathy involves feeling *with* the other person. Psychologist Paul Bloom defines empathy as "the act of coming to experience the world as you think someone else does."[52] In other words, when we walk a mile in another's shoes or wear someone else's skin for a while (so to speak) we feel empathy. In fact, empathy "is responsible for some of humankind's most socially beneficial sentiments and noblest acts."[53]

Bloom makes a decent case that moral reasoning often leads to better outcomes than those produced by blind empathy,[54] but your authors contend that people often don't summon moral reasoning to reexamine their moral intuition. That seems, at least to us, more like wishful thinking. It is clear, though, that a lack of empathy (as found most extremely in psychopaths) is responsible for much of humanity's ills.

Moral emotions and their role

Experts have studied many other emotions that impact our moral judgments such as trust, forgiveness, vengeance, righteous anger, remorse, fear, and more.

Some experts wonder if "morality is even possible in the absence of anger and guilt."[55] Historian Michael Shermer writes that moral emotions give us

> true and genuine morality even if we don't always live up to our own or society's moral standards. Without such moral emotions, our actions would be nothing more than a simple selfish moral calculation. . . . Morality is a real, biologically-based phenomenon, and the desire for moral justice is as concrete an emotion as love.[56]

Moral dumbfounding

If you happen to know any professors of moral reasoning, they are likely no more moral in their actions than anyone else.[57] A review of moral identity research found: "Empirical research shows that the strength of association between moral reasoning and moral action is small or moderate, meaning that other mechanisms must be involved in moral functioning."[58] In fact, moral emotions are the most important of these other mechanisms.

As psychologist and business ethics researcher Nina Strohminger and colleagues note:

> Many processes underlying moral judgment are not accessible through introspection. Moral intuitions and other "gut feelings" represent an output whose underpinnings are introspectively inaccessible; the reasons that a person gives for them are often little more than a *post hoc* confabulation. Moral judgment is at least partly a product of these fast, automatic, affective, and often unconscious cognitive processes – though deliberative, slow, flexible, controlled processing also plays a role.[59]

In other words, moral intuitions underlie most of our moral judgments, whether they are primarily based on emotions or have a more reasoned footing. But often, we cannot provide rational reasons to support our moral judgments. This experience is known as *moral dumbfounding*. A popular scenario used to illustrate moral dumbfounding goes like this:

> Rex and Sarah were brother and sister, both in their late 20s. They had always been close. One evening, after they watched a movie in Rex's apartment, they decided to have sexual relations, reasoning that it would make their relationship even closer and more special. They took all necessary precautions to protect against pregnancy. They never chose to have sex again. Did they act immorally?[60]

Your authors, students, and most groups of people quickly and intuitively conclude that, yes, Rex and Sarah acted immorally! Of course! How disgusting! How weird! They will regret this!

However, while it may be possible to produce persuasive reasons why Rex and Sarah acted immorally, most of us have difficulty doing so. People can come up with many reasons why incest is weird and disgusting, and reasons why Rex and Sarah might live to regret their actions. But being unwise is not the same as being immoral. Because no one was hurt, and the obvious downside (potential pregnancy) was not a possibility, it is extraordinarily difficult to come up with a persuasive reason why their actions were immoral. Most people resort to saying things like: "Well, I just know in my gut it's wrong."[61]

In fact, most of us find the thought of incest disgusting. We then assume that if we feel disgust, what we are reacting to must be immoral. But that is not the case at all. Philosopher Daniel Kelly argues that the disgust emotion evolved in human beings to keep us from eating poisonous things and from exposing ourselves to germs residing on corpses or feces, for example. The disgust emotion was co-opted, Kelly says, and "became implicated in the psychological systems underlying cognition of social norms and ethnic boundary markers."[62] In other words, evolution roped disgust into fulfilling other functions that keep human beings safe, too, such as encouraging people to follow their group's moral code so they're not cast out of the group (and perish in isolation).

To take moral dumbfounding a step further, consider the famous trolley problem that philosophers and psychologists have puzzled over for decades.[63] Here is a version (from one of many versions):

Trolley problem – first scenario

Denise is standing next to a switching lever near a trolley track when she sees an out-of-control trolley. The conductor has fainted, and the trolley is headed toward five people working on the track. The banks are so steep that the people won't be able to get off the track in time. The trolley track has a side track leading off to the left. Denise can turn the trolley onto the side track by flipping the lever next to her. There is one person, however, working on the side track. Denise can turn the trolley (killing one person) or she can do nothing and let five people die. *Is it morally permissible for Denise to flip the lever, turning the trolley onto the side track?*

Trolley problem – second scenario

Frank is standing on a footbridge over a trolley track. He knows about trolleys and can see that the one approaching the bridge is out of control. Its conductor has passed out. On the track just past the bridge, there are five people. The banks are so steep that they won't be able to get off the track in time. Frank knows that the only way to stop an out-of-control trolley is to drop a very heavy weight into its path. But the only available heavy weight is a large man standing next to Frank, who is also watching the trolley from the footbridge. Frank can save the five people by shoving the large man onto the track, blocking the trolley's path, but this will result in the large man's death. On the other hand, Frank can do nothing and let the five people on the track die. *Is it morally permissible for Frank to push the large man onto the track?*

Because both scenarios involve someone taking an action – either flipping a switch or pushing a person – you would think that the two actions would be judged as equally moral (or immoral). Both actions will take one life in order to save five. However, studies show that most people believe it is morally permissible for Denise to flip the switch, but not morally permissible for Frank to push the big guy. When asked to logically explain why they reached these different conclusions, people tend to experience moral dumbfounding.[64]

From a utilitarian perspective, of course, both actions are morally permissible. Perhaps, even, they are morally required because both actions produce the greatest good for the greatest number. However, people tend to apply a utilitarian calculus to the Denise scenario (focusing on the results) but apply a deontological approach to the Frank scenario, focusing on the rule "Thou shalt not kill." Why the difference?

Although the issue is hotly contested by the experts, emotions seem to be the strongest reason:

- Brain scans show that people have a stronger instinctual reaction to thinking about Frank pushing the big guy than to Denise merely flipping a switch. Denise's action is more clinical, more detached, and therefore less emotional.[65]
- If researchers give people drugs to heighten emotions, and then present those subjects with the trolley problem, they feel the moral difference between Frank's actions and Denise's actions even more acutely. But if subjects are given drugs to depress emotions, then they see the differences between the two actions as less significant.[66]
- People who score relatively high on psychopathy tests are less likely to condemn Frank's actions as immoral. Brain scans show that these people don't feel the emotions stemming from hurting others as strongly as most people.[67]
- Simply changing people's moods by having them watch a funny video before they are given these two scenarios also makes people less harshly judgmental in the Frank scenario.[68]

Some scientists believe that emotions play a much smaller role in people's moral judgments than is painted here. Philosopher Joshua May, for example, argues that reasoning can also occur quickly, implicitly, and unconsciously.[69] He believes those nearly automatic moral judgments we often make may be based on reason as well as emotion.

Whatever the mix of emotion and reason in making moral judgments, there is definitely a role played by the cognitive parts of our brains, too. Many experts believe we should do everything we can to be thoughtful and deliberate in order to increase that cognitive role. Why? In part, because emotions often get it wrong. Why did it take so long, for example, for gay marriage to become widely accepted by most of the population? One reason might be that visualizing the mechanics of homosexual sex triggered the disgust emotion for many people, which led them to conclude (erroneously) that the disgust they felt signaled that the action was immoral. But as we have seen in our incest example with Rex and Sarah, this is not the case. Philosopher Daniel Kelly, who has studied disgust in detail, has this to say: ". . . The fact that something is disgusting is not even remotely a reliable indicator of moral foul play. . . . [T]he moral significance that should be assigned to the fact that people are disgusted is: none."[70]

ETHICS UNWRAPPED RESOURCES

Videos

Moral Emotions
Series: Ethics Defined

Moral Emotions
Series: Concepts Unwrapped

Related Videos

Prosocial Behavior
Series: Ethics Defined

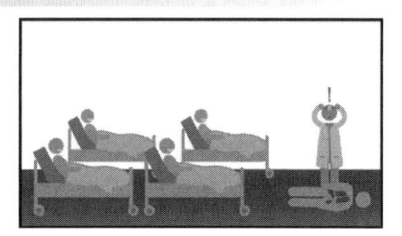

Utilitarianism
Series: Ethics Defined

Deontology
Series: Ethics Defined

Case Studies

Flying the Confederate Flag

Wells Fargo and Moral Emotions

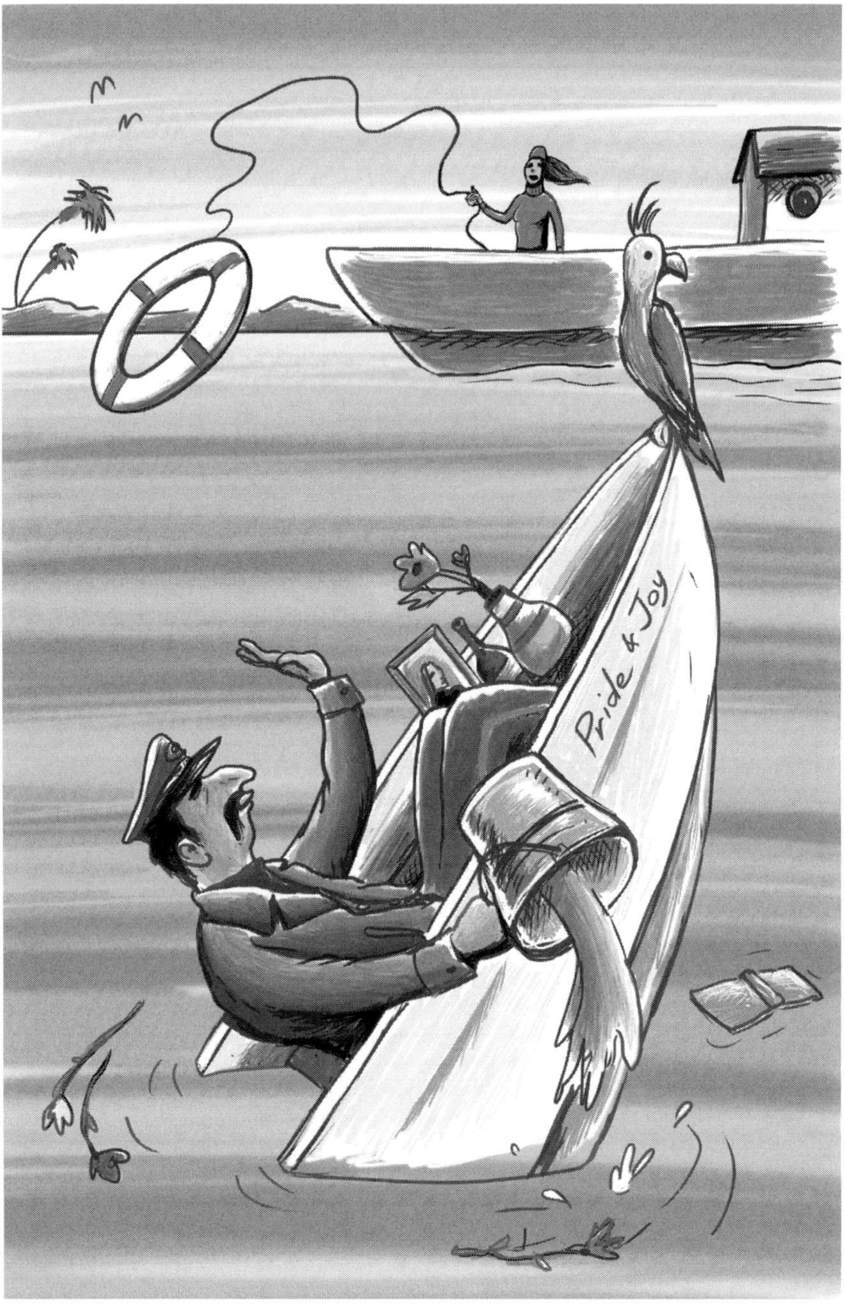
Pride & Joy

3
MORAL ACTION DECISIONS AND MORAL REASONING FLAWS

> *"Moral judgments without emotions are empty, emotions without moral reasoning are blind."*
> *– Hanno Sauer*[71]

To recap, here are the principles of human moral decision making that form the bedrock of behavioral ethics understanding:

- People make most of their moral judgments intuitively and nearly instantaneously.
- There are limits to our ability to think rationally and deliberately when it comes to making moral judgments.
- Our moral judgments are not always correct, or even defensible.
- Emotions are a significant factor in making moral judgments.

Moral judgments versus moral action decisions

There is a significant difference between *moral judgments* and *moral action decisions*. We make moral judgments about *other* people's moral choices and dilemmas. Moral action decisions are the choices we make about how to act when *we* face moral challenges.

Our moral reasoning is different depending on whether we're making a moral judgment ("Is it moral for Denise to flip the switch?" in last chapter's Trolley Problem) or whether we're making a moral action decision ("Should I flip the switch?"). When we make moral action decisions, we are much more likely to deliberate. We imagine, for example, the different consequences that might follow for us from the various choices we're considering.

Psychologist Jonathan Haidt, creator of the "social intuitionist model," suggests that most moral judgments are made intuitively and emotionally. Haidt acknowledges that this model applies primarily to moral judgments, and is less applicable to moral action decisions. Still, Haidt makes three points worth remembering regarding moral action decisions:

- First, we automatically do the right thing most of the time without deliberation. The impact of moral emotions we discussed in the last chapter (guilt, shame, embarrassment, etc.) often herd us automatically toward the right choice.
- Second, when we do deliberate regarding moral action decisions, our thought process will be heavily influenced by various biases (such as the self-serving bias, implicit bias, role morality, incrementalism, moral equilibrium, etc.). These biases, which we will soon study in detail, can lead us down the wrong path.
- Third, even when we engage in our best version of reasoning, there is little doubt that our thought processes are heavily influenced by our emotions.[72]

Moral reasoning flaws

Psychologists and scientists have identified a vast number of forces that get in the way of sound moral decision making and moral action-taking. This book covers but a handful of the many influences that can impede our ability to detect moral issues, to engage in sound moral reasoning, to choose to do the right thing in a given instance, and to act effectively.

The rest of Part I will cover the basic, pervasive forces – the internal biases, external pressures, and situational factors – that impede moral decision making. These psychological biases, mental shortcuts, social and organizational pressures, and situational factors often work in concert with each other – you can think of them as overlapping layers of unhelpful influences. Ethical crises such as the Enron scandal, for example, illustrate how overconfidence bias in leaders, obedience to authority in others, conformity bias among people in an organization, self-serving bias in everyone, and a dose of in-group bias, groupthink, and rationalizations will interact to support a distortion of ethical vision that can impact the moral action decisions of an entire organization. These influences are powerful; don't underestimate them!

Before diving more deeply into these fundamental forces, here is a short list of additional specific biases that get in the way of sound moral reasoning. These influences – like all the ones described in Part I – will help make it clear why it really is a challenge to be the kind of person that your dog (or maybe your best friend) thinks you are. Hopefully, this book will help you face that challenge gracefully and with skill.

The confirmation bias

The *confirmation bias* is the tendency we have to search for information that confirms, rather than falsifies, our beliefs.

So, when our moral intuition leads us to a particular conclusion, we will look for (and find much more convincing) the evidence that confirms our belief rather than the information that challenges it. Regardless of whether the moral intuition is primarily emotion-based or reason-based, our conclusion (and subsequent ethical belief) will not receive the critical analysis it deserves.

The omission bias

We tend to judge harmful *actions* as less moral than equally harmful *omissions*. The reason appears to be that actions are more emotionally impactful to us than inactions.

For example, one study involved a thought experiment where a tennis player, John, was about to face a tough opponent who he knew had a food allergy. If people were told that John recommended food containing the allergen to his opponent, they judged John more harshly than if they were told that John saw the opponent order and eat food with the allergen, but said nothing. Deciding to be silent was also a choice, but it was judged less harshly than choosing to recommend the food.[73]

Moral luck

Moral luck is present when luck affects our moral judgments regarding *other* people's actions.

For example, assume that on Tuesday night Al drove down a dark road going 40 miles an hour over the speed limit. Sam did the same thing on Wednesday night. On Tuesday night, Karen walked across the road two minutes before Al zoomed by. But on Wednesday night, she had the misfortune to cross the road just as Sam sped by. Sam's car struck Karen, and killed her. Most people would blame Sam for speeding more than they would blame Al for speeding. Even though the two men were equal in every way in what they did (only with differing consequences), Al's good luck factors in people's moral judgment of the two men.[74]

Knobe effect

The *Knobe effect* is named for psychologist and philosopher Joshua Knobe, who discovered it.

Assume that a CEO doesn't care one way or the other about the environment. She wants to take a particular action to increase her company's profits, regardless of its environmental consequences. If the action has a *beneficial* impact on the environment, most people will not give the CEO much credit for the beneficial action. But if the action has a *harmful* impact on the environment, people are much more likely to conclude that the CEO acted intentionally to harm the environment and judge her harshly.[75]

Indelible victim effect

When we oppose things on moral grounds, we feel a need to think of those things as being bad.[76] To be bad, those things must cause harm. This phenomenon is called the *indelible victim effect* or *dyadic completion*.

For example, because Kant believed masturbation to be bad, he felt the need to manufacture a harm that it caused ("Oh my God! I gave up my personality!"). Similarly, people who oppose gay rights often make up a harm ("They're child molesters!") with no scientific basis to justify their moral position. These "harms" are an example of *rationalizations*, which help to justify our moral actions and beliefs. Rationalizations are key to unethical decision making; they help us disengage from the moral dimensions of issues. Both rationalizations and *moral disengagement* are covered in greater detail in Chapter 21.

Just world hypothesis

Many of us seem to have a psychological need to believe that the world is a just place. Otherwise, it can be a tough place to inhabit.

So when something bad happens to someone, we tend to conclude that the person deserved it, even if the person was the victim of a crime or an accident. This attitude helps give us a sense of safety. We can assume that we're good people who don't deserve to be harmed, and in this way, a just world hypothesis protects us.[77]

The "blame the victim" mentality is stronger in people who have *binding values* as contrasted to people who have *individualizing values*. Individualizing values (such as care and fairness) tend to be emphasized by politically liberal people. Binding values (such as loyalty, obedience, and purity) tend to be emphasized by politically conservative people. Studies show that the more intensely people hold to binding values, the more likely they are to consider victims of crimes as responsible for their own injuries.[78]

Conclusion

One final point. Although we've emphasized that emotional reactions can miss the mark in matters of moral decision making, it is still wise to pay attention to our gut, which often can help us keep ethical matters in our frame of reference. As psychologists DeSteno and Valdesolo note: "One answer can be found in a simple gut check. When faced with a moral decision, take a few seconds to pause and listen to your inner voices. Is there a hint of guilt, a hint of shame, a gut feeling of unease? If so, don't ignore it."[79]

ETHICS UNWRAPPED RESOURCES

Videos

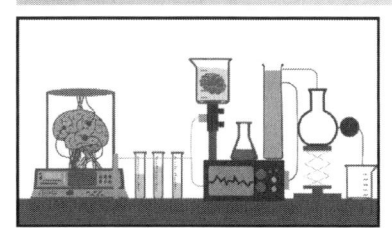

Moral Cognition
Series: Ethics Defined

Moral Psychology
Series: Ethics Defined

Rationalizations
Series: Ethics Defined

Related Videos

Moral Emotions
Series: Ethics Defined

Moral Agent
Series: Ethics Defined

Case Studies

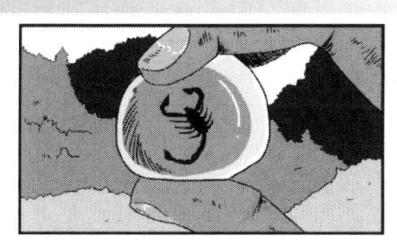

Myanmar Amber

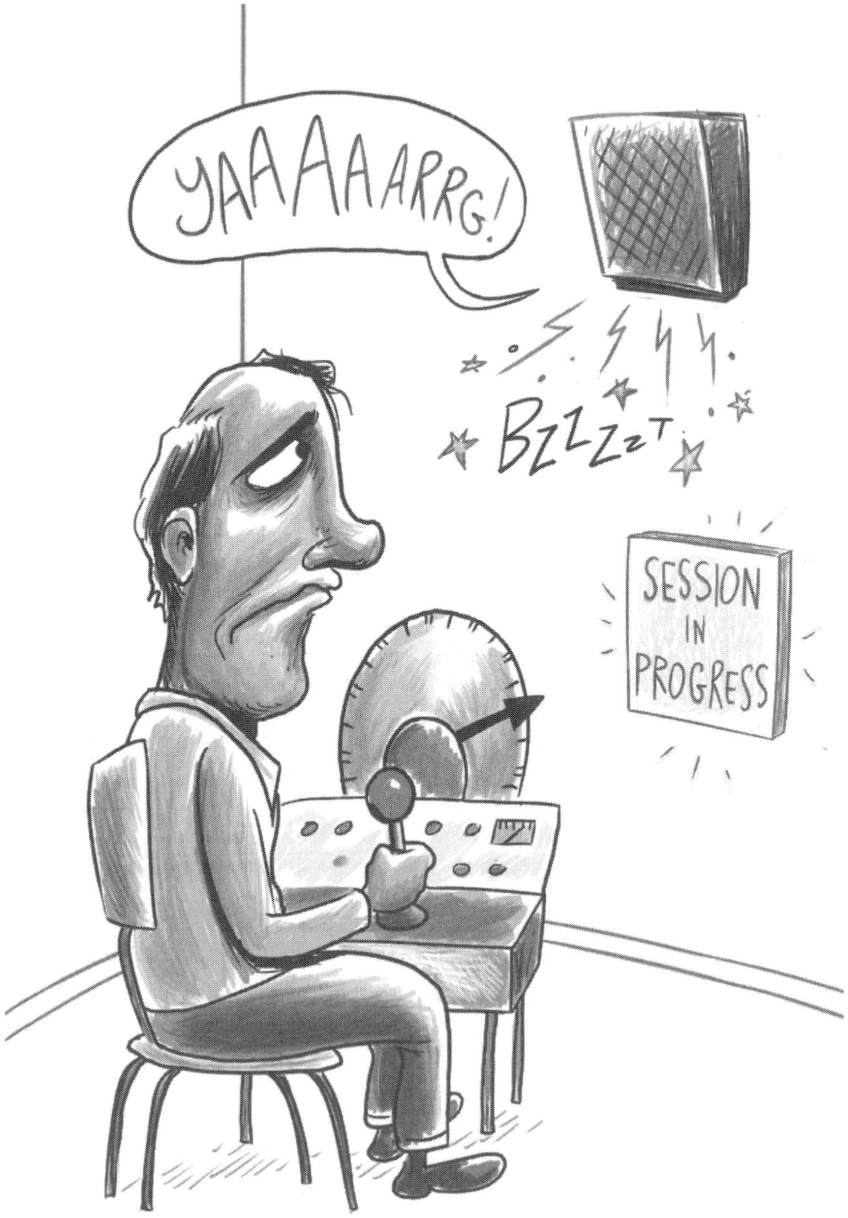
YAAAAARRG!
BZZZzzT
SESSION IN PROGRESS

4
OBEDIENCE TO AUTHORITY

> *"One of the most consistent findings in human psychology is that people tend to do what they are told to do."*[80]
>
> – Lynn Stout

Introduction

As noted in Chapter 1, when we make moral judgments and act on moral choices, we are frequently influenced (and often not in a good way) by external pressures – social pressures and pressure created by organizational structures. Most of us are familiar with "peer pressure," but in fact there is a whole range of social and organizational pressures that can negatively affect people's moral choices and actions. Two of the most pervasive and influential of these forces are explored in this chapter and the next: *obedience to authority* and the *conformity bias*.

Let's begin with obedience to authority. Are you a "pleaser"? Most of us, most of the time, are inclined to be obedient. We learn from an early age that there are benefits to pleasing parents, teachers, preachers, police officers, and similar authority figures.

In fact, societies are more orderly (and typically safer) when people obey authority. But obedience to authority is not always good. Authority figures can be corrupt or selfish. People in power may (intentionally or accidentally) ask people who work for them to do something unethical. Being a pleaser can get you in trouble if you don't listen to your own moral sense.

The Milgram experiment

One of the most famous experiments in all of psychology was undertaken by Stanley Milgram. Like many others after World War II, Milgram wondered how perfectly normal Germans (who presumably went to church on Sunday and had families they loved) could become part of Hitler's death machine. Was there something unique about the German character that made them particularly susceptible to following the orders of authority figures? Even if those authority figures asked for horrendous acts?

Milgram's experiment worked roughly like this:

> A person in a lab coat – the experimenter – would welcome two people into a lab and thank them for helping with an experiment on learning. The experimenter would explain that the two of them were to play the roles of "teacher" and "student." The "student" (always secretly in cahoots with the experimenter) would be selected to be hooked up to electrodes, and would be led away into the next room. The door would shut.
>
> The "teacher" (who was the real subject of the experiment) would be seated at the control panel of an impressive-looking machine. It had buttons and knobs labeled "Slight Shock," "Moderate Shock," "Strong Shock," "Very Strong Shock," "Intense Shock," "Extreme Intensity Shock," "Danger: Severe Shock," and finally "XXX." The "teacher" would be told that his job was to administer shocks when the "student" missed a question.
>
> The experimenter, in the room with the "teacher," would then begin asking the "student" questions over an intercom. When the "student" missed, the experimenter would instruct the "teacher" to administer a slight shock. The "student" was not actually shocked, but he would pretend to be, and over the intercom he would say "ouch." As the student missed more questions, the dial on the machine was turned up. The student would complain more vigorously each time he was shocked, saying that he wanted to quit, that this really hurt, that he had a heart condition, and the like. Most "teachers" quickly became uncomfortable with continuing to administer the shock, saying things like: "Hey, we're hurting this guy. I think we should stop." But the experimenter would respond with: "The experiment must continue" or something similar.

When this experiment was described to people before it was run, only a tiny percentage of people thought that Americans (unlike Germans) would administer apparently very painful shocks to another person just because some stranger in a lab coat told them to. And yet, approximately two-thirds of the "teachers" kept administering the shock all the way to "XXX" – even though it appeared that the "student" had passed out from the pain! And virtually 100 percent of the "teachers" continued very far up the scale (even though they were obviously distressed) before refusing to go on. This was true even though the experimenter had no true authority over the "teacher" and the "teacher" received no additional compensation for continuing the experiment.[81]

Although it would be very difficult to run such a study in the United States today due to current rules on human experimentation, its results have been widely duplicated over the many decades since. After 90 percent of Polish subjects were obedient to authority in a 2015 re-creation of Milgram's experiment, the experimenters noted that "the original explanations proposed by Milgram [that most "normal" people are exceptionally obedient to authority], are difficult to refute, and – significantly – relatively stable over time."[82] A psychologist who replicated Milgram's findings in 2006 also noted that these "obedience studies are a dramatic demonstration of how individuals typically underestimate the power of situational forces when explaining another person's behavior."[83] The innate desire to please authority is one such force.

Obedience to authority outside the lab

Often, problems resulting from blind obedience to authority are found in the real world. Some people have traced American soldiers' mistreatment of prisoners at the Abu Ghraib prison in Iraq in part to the obedience to authority phenomenon.[84] When one of the key figures in that scandal, Private Lynndie England, was asked about the impact of her superiors' approval, she said: "Well, at the time I didn't really think about it. Cause like I said, it was a job. You knew it was wrong deep down inside, but if they're saying it's okay, then, hey, well. . . ."[85]

The Enron scandal – which resulted in the largest bankruptcy in American history (at the time) and the collapse of one of the largest accounting firms in the country – has been traced in part to ". . . the 'cult-like' atmosphere at Enron. Specifically, Enron employees reported being 'fanatically loyal' to the CEOs. . . . One Enron employee explained: '[E]verytime [CEO Jeff] Skilling spoke, I'd believe everything he'd say.'"[86]

There are many other examples:

- Toshiba employees were pressured both directly and indirectly into fudging earnings by $1.2 billion, as desired by their bosses.[87]
- Engineers who worked on the Ford Pinto knew that the car had dangerous safety problems, but were intimidated by the bluster of Ford's president, Lee Iacocca, into putting the car on the market anyway.[88]
- In the more recent Volkswagen emissions scandal, supervisors at VW asked an engineer to create software that would defeat government emissions tests: "The engineer was profoundly uneasy about the assignment, but he did as he was told."[89]

Indeed, the instinct to be obedient to authority can lead us to do the most horrific things. Psychiatrist Robert Jay Lifton interviewed a German physician who (reluctantly) became an active participant in a killing center in World War II. Why did he do it? After interviewing the doctor, Lifton wrote:

> Generally speaking, the encounter evoked his long-standing impulse toward obedience – an impulse inculcated during his rural childhood,

40 It's hard to be who your dog thinks you are

especially by his civil-servant father. And when [the doctor] inquired of [his superiors] whether he could discuss the matter with an older respected friend, he was told quite sharply that 'the entire matter was top secret.'"[90]

So the doctor went along.

Sometimes we are obedient to authority because we fear the consequences of not being obedient, even though we know something is wrong. During the dot-com boom in the late 1990s, for example, New York investment banks hired research analysts to supposedly rate various company stocks fairly. But the New York banks also wished to secure the investment banking business of those same companies. If their analysts were dissing the companies' stocks, the banks worried that they wouldn't get the companies' investment banking business. Emails between analysts made it clear that they felt pressure from supervisors to positively rate company stocks that they thought were "POS" (pieces of you-know-what). Even though the analysts could see what was happening, they lacked the courage to stand up for the right thing. They knowingly knuckled under to their bosses' pressure because they didn't want to jeopardize their bonuses or their jobs.

And the analysts weren't the only ones. Employees of ratings agencies such as Standard & Poor's and Moody's also succumbed to superiors when asked to positively rate crappy financial instruments. As one employee said in an internal e-mail, "We rate every deal. . . . It could be structured by cows and we would rate it."[91]

Perhaps more worrisome than knowing wrongdoing is the fact that sometimes we become so focused on pleasing the boss that we don't see the ethical issue facing us. We screw up before we even notice that there may be a problem, we're so intent on performing and looking good to our superiors.

An example of this comes from the infamous Watergate scandal that ended Richard Nixon's presidency. Egil "Bud" Krogh was a young lawyer working in the White House. One of President Nixon's top aides, John Ehrlichman, asked Krogh to take a leadership role in a secret Special Investigations Unit aimed at (among other things) discrediting whistleblower Daniel Ellsberg. Ellsberg had leaked the "Pentagon Papers" – documents that made it clear that the government was lying to the American people about the progress being made in the Vietnam War (maybe you saw Meryl Streep and Tom Hanks in the 2018 movie *The Post* about publishing the Pentagon Papers?).

Bud Krogh enthusiastically focused on carrying out his assigned mission. This included breaking into the office of Ellsberg's psychiatrist to look for disparaging information, and using a team of men who would later become infamous as the "Watergate burglars." Later, Krogh said that he was so focused on his assignment (and, no doubt, on pleasing his superiors) that he completely missed the ethical ramifications of what he was doing. It wasn't until arrests started happening all around him that he applied his own moral compass to what he'd been asked to do. Then, Krogh realized he'd made a huge mistake. He pled guilty, cooperated with prosecutors, and has spent much of his life trying to make up for his wrongdoing.[92]

Related to obedience to authority is something called the *acceptability heuristic*[93] – a heuristic being a mental shortcut. In the context of business organizations, the acceptability heuristic may cause us to become more concerned with whether or not the decision we make is acceptable to our bosses than whether it is, indeed, the best (most ethical) decision. When decision-makers begin to focus more on pleasing their boss than on doing the right thing, the acceptability heuristic has come into play. It's scary to think that we can become so focused on pleasing our boss that we don't even see what should be glaring ethical issues, but this *ethical fading* can easily happen (especially when we like our boss).

Absolving ourselves from responsibility

The obedience to authority phenomenon is also powerful because we can psychologically absolve ourselves of responsibility for our actions and their consequences. We transfer that responsibility to the authority figure. Stanley Milgram himself suggested:

> The most common adjustment of thought in the obedient subject is for him to see himself as not responsible for his own actions. He divests himself of responsibility by attributing all the initiative to the experimenter, a legitimate authority. He sees himself not as a person acting in a morally accountable way, but as the agent of external authority.[94]

This same rationalization was invoked by Eric Fair, a U.S. interrogator at Abu Ghraib who tortured prisoners. Recalling his frame of mind at the time, he wrote: "I think about following [my superior's] instructions. It's not my interrogation. It's not my sin."[95]

It shouldn't surprise us, then, that research shows junior staff pressured by senior staff to "cook the books" are more likely to do so than underlings who are not so pressured.[96] When chief financial officers fudge the numbers, it's more likely that they're succumbing to CEO pressure rather than acting out of a desire to put money in their own pocket.[97] This is the power of our inclination to be obedient to authority.

Importantly, the obedience to authority phenomenon is – along with all the other influences and forces discussed in this book – an *explanation* for why good people do bad things. It is not an *excuse*. As philosopher Jonathan Glover observes in his moral history of the 20th century:

> The excuse of 'obedience to orders' has been discredited because of its use by Nazis, notably Adolf Eichmann. Pressure to conform is no more impressive as an excuse. *But there are hard questions about when to stand out against obedience and conformity, and about how much we can reasonably expect of people.*[98]

ETHICS UNWRAPPED RESOURCES

Videos

Obedience to Authority
Series: Ethics Defined

Obedience to Authority
Series: Concepts Unwrapped

Related Videos

Ethical Fading
Series: Ethics Defined

Role Morality
Series: Ethics Defined

Moral Muteness
Series: Ethics Defined

Moral Muteness
Series: Concepts Unwrapped

Case Studies

Stangl & the Holocaust

Krogh & the Watergate Scandal

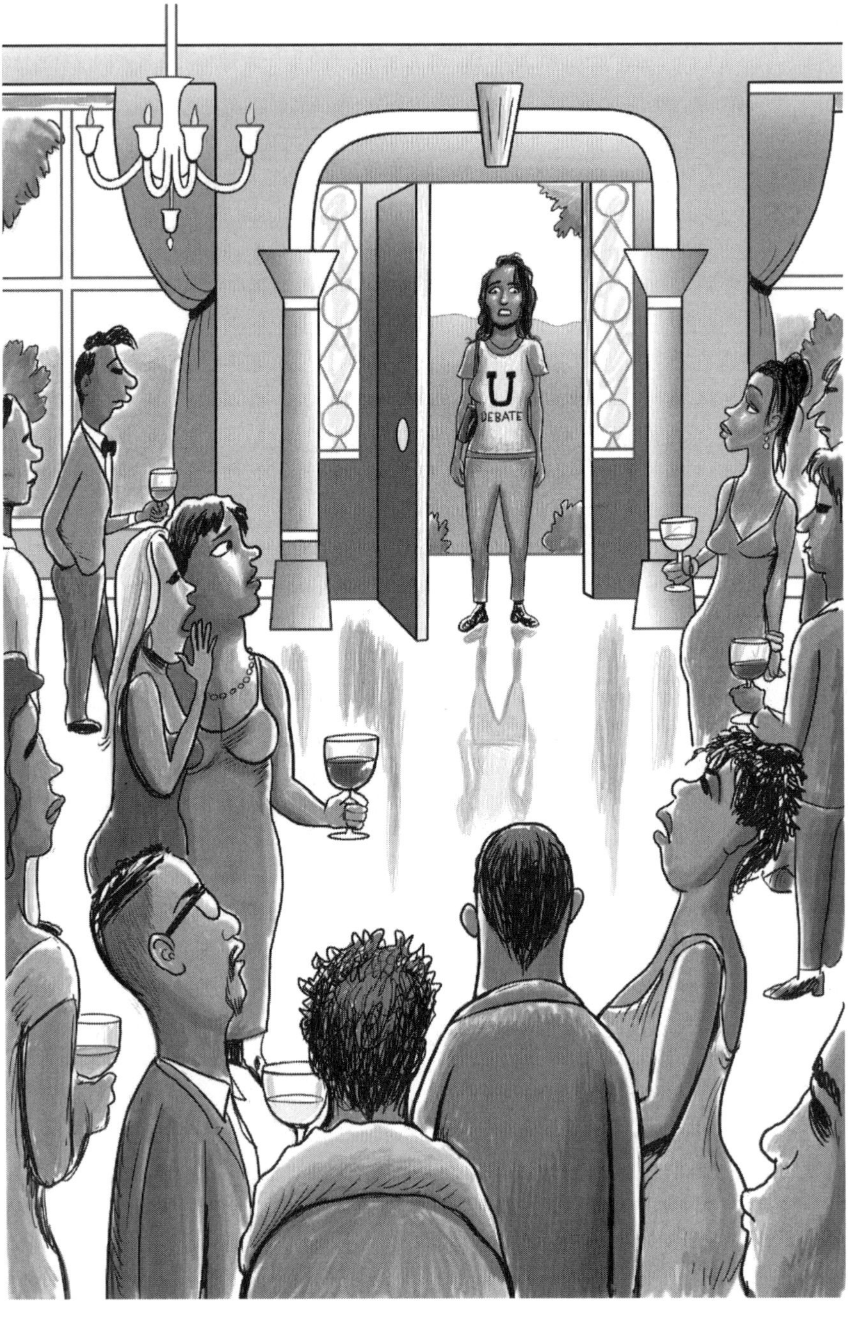
U
DEBATE

5
CONFORMITY BIAS

"Among all psychological processes influencing the ethics of groups, conformity is the most basic and pervasive."[99]

– *Thomas Oberlechner*

Introduction

One of you authors, Robert Prentice, grew up on a farm in the middle of Kansas where (at suppertime) one fork always seemed to suffice. Why would you need more? But in his sophomore year at the University of Kansas, Prentice was invited to a fancy restaurant where, lo and behold, he was confronted with three forks. Even a country bumpkin like Prentice was able to deduce that proper etiquette probably required certain forks be used for certain purposes. But which one for what course?!

If you have ever found yourself in a similar situation, we suspect you did exactly what Prentice did: hide and watch. He took his time, observed what other people did with their multiple forks, and followed along. This tendency to take our cues for proper behavior from others in our peer group is called the *conformity bias.*[100]

An old TV series, *Candid Camera,* and its movie version, *What Do You Say to a Naked Lady?*, featured host Alan Funt playing tricks on people while recording them with a secret camera. In the movie, Funt put a help wanted ad in a newspaper. A man responding to the ad was directed to a waiting room containing three of Funt's accomplices. At one point, for no apparent reason, all three accomplices stood up and took off all their clothes. The poor fellow, who thought he was applying for an actual job (and was not in on the joke), looked uncomfortable for a while. Finally, he took his own clothes off and stood there buck naked with the others, waiting for whatever came next.[101]

Our tendency to conform probably has an evolutionary basis.[102] This tendency is shared by other primates[103] and in human beings develops at a very young age.[104] Learning from others and following their lead seems like an evolutionarily sound strategy. But if those other folks choose not just the wrong fork, but the wrong ethical fork in the road, then we can get ourselves into a lot of trouble.

The Asch experiment

Consider psychologist Solomon Asch's famous experiment. Like Milgram, Asch was interested in why regular German citizens did horrible things in the service of Hitler's Nazi regime.

Asch's experiment presented participants with two boxes drawn on a piece of paper. The first box contained one line, and the second box contained three parallel lines labeled A, B, and C. Compared to the line in the first box, line A was a bit shorter, line B was a bit longer, and line C was exactly the same length. When Asch asked people which of the three lines (A, B, or C) matched the line in the first box, virtually every person in the experiment had no difficulty identifying line C as the correct answer. So far, so good.

In a second iteration of the study, Asch put a subject in the company of several accomplices who appeared to also be subjects of the experiment. When those accomplices all gave an obviously wrong answer (such as line A), the real subject would often answer line A, too. At some point in the experiment, about two-thirds of the participants gave an obviously wrong answer.[105]

The correct answer was right there in black and white. If the participant had been alone, she or he would undoubtedly have given the right answer. But we are so conditioned to take behavioral cues from people around us that we will give clearly wrong answers just to fit in. Why? Well, brain scans indicate that asserting independent judgment rather than conforming to those around us exacts a psychic cost – an emotional and cognitive burden – on us.[106] It is much more psychologically comforting to go along with other members of the group, even if they are running over a cliff as lemmings are said to do.[107]

In a later version of Asch's study, neuroscientist Gregory Berns and colleagues not only found a similar result but also looked at participants' brain scans for insight. They discovered that those who gave wrong answers in order to conform to a group's wrong decision "showed less activity in the frontal, decision-making regions and more in the areas of the brain associated with perception. Peer pressure, in other words, is not only unpleasant, but can actually change one's view of a problem."[108] Sometimes we are not just pretending to believe something in order to fit in; rather, our beliefs actually change as a result of the conformity bias.

Conformity bias in the real world

Given the strong influence of the conformity bias, you won't be surprised to learn that advertising agencies (which have used the research generated by behavioral psychology for a long time) regularly employ the conformity bias to flog their products. Nothing seems to make consumers more eager to try a particular brand than to learn that it is "America's favorite," or "the fastest growing."[109] This is a widespread phenomenon. As legal scholar Cass Sunstein observed: "Social norms have an independent effect; whether people smoke cigarettes, exercise, buckle their seat belts, text while driving, eat healthy foods, or enroll in a retirement plan is significantly influenced by the perceived norm within the relevant group."[110]

Psychologist Dacher Keltner and colleagues have similarly observed:

> From laughter, blushing, and voting patterns to destructive health habits, feelings of anxiety, and expressions of gratitude, nearly all manner of social behavior is potentially contagious, spreading to others in rapid, involuntary fashion. . . . Humans are a highly mimetic species, disposed to imitate and take on the tendencies of others in their surroundings and social networks.[111]

Conformity bias and ethics

As you may have guessed by now, the conformity bias is not relevant just when Frito-Lay persuades you to buy Cheetos. It also is very important in ethics, because we often tend to adopt the crowd's moral beliefs and actions and then simply *ignore our own moral judgment*. This often ends badly.

The unfortunate fact is that if everyone else is committing a particular wrong, it may seem right. Although parents usually don't accept the "everyone else is doing it" excuse from their children, this is a common defense raised by white collar criminals.[112] And they are not necessarily making it up. If everyone around us is doing something, it may truly seem like it's a fine thing to do. For example, because cyclist Lance Armstrong believed that all the other cyclists in the Tour de France were doping, he told Oprah Winfrey that it didn't feel wrong for him to dope, too: "[Lance] regarded the use of performance-enhancing substances as a normative practice in the fiercely competitive culture of professional sports."[113]

The conformity bias is a strong influence and can affect whether or not we engage in unethical activity. In one study, researchers found that the most significant factor in determining the level of cheating in a school was how much cheating students believed their peers were doing: "Academic dishonesty not only is learned from observing the behavior of peers, but . . . peers' behavior provides a kind of normative support for cheating."[114] In another striking study, students who saw cheating by another student were more likely to cheat themselves, especially if the cheating student was wearing a sweatshirt from their school. Cheating actually went down if the student who was observed cheating was wearing a sweatshirt from a rival school. In other words, we take our behavioral cues from our in-group members, not from out-group members.[115]

In yet another case, a student chastised for illegally downloading music easily rationalized her actions in light of her peers' actions: "I don't think me [sic] alone is making that much of a difference by downloading. When you think about it, everyone downloads."[116] This is the conformity bias in action.

In another example, when officials at the Petrified Forest in Arizona faced increased pilfering by tourists who wanted souvenirs of their visit, they posted a sign reporting the high rate of stealing. They asked guests not to take items. The sign's impact? Pilfering went up, not down. It *tripled!*[117] If everybody else is doing it, it must be okay.

What is true on a bicycle, or in school, or in a national park is also going to be true in the workplace.[118] Unfortunately, this means that if employees observe their coworkers acting unethically, they are much more likely to act unethically themselves than if they had not received this signal.[119] In fact, a corporate code, written in bold print on the finest paper, is meaningless when it runs up against a corrupt corporate culture. The corporate culture will win every time.[120] "The moral authority of the normative reference group – in this case, fellow employees – far outweighs authority inscribed in organizational behavioral codes or societal laws and regulations."[121]

Consider Enron. It had a fine corporate code of ethics, the RICE code. The letters stood for Respect, Integrity, Communication, and Excellence. They just didn't stand for reality.[122] The culture that CEOs Ken Lay and Jeff Skilling cultivated had everything to do with innovation and profit making and almost nothing to do with ethics. As one Enron employee said:

> If your boss was [fudging earnings], and you never worked anywhere else, you just assume that everybody fudges earnings. . . . Once you get there and you realize how it was, do you stand up and lose your job? It was scary. It was easy to get into "Well, everybody else is doing it, so maybe it isn't so bad."[123]

The conformity bias also contributed to the rash of bogus tax shelters that were created around the turn of the 21st century:

> The view among many tax professionals that shelter activity was unproblematic was reinforced by the fact that other prestigious firms were involved. For some participants "everyone else is doing it" meant that as a practical matter their firm could engage in wrongdoing without being penalized. For many others, however, the fact that other elite accounting firms – KPMG, Ernst & Young, Arthur Andersen, BDO Seidman – were marketing tax shelters was a clear indication that there was nothing illegal or unethical about the activity."[124]

Business scholars and researchers Lamar Pierce and Jason Snyder found that as workers move from less ethical to more ethical environments (or vice versa), their own personal ethical practices tend to change. Employee behavior quickly begins to mirror the ethical or unethical behavior of their new workplace.[125]

The good as well as the bad

It's not just that we will do wrong when people around us do wrong, though that is the biggest problem. It's also that we will refrain from doing good when those around us refrain from doing good.[126] Moreover, the conformity bias often causes us to condone corrupt behavior within our group or organization: "When group concerns are made salient, people align their personal views with [the] group consensus."[127]

In an interesting set of experiments, social psychologists John Darley and Bibb Latané had an assistant (their accomplice) lead a participant into a room and then leave. The assistant would then, apparently, have an accident in the next room. There would be a loud crash followed by her crying, "Oh my God, my foot. My ankle! I can't get this thing off me." If the participant was alone in the room, he or she went to help the assistant 70 percent of the time. However, if another person (another accomplice of the researchers) was also in the room with the participant, and did *not* respond to the cries, the participant would only go help the assistant a mere seven percent of the time![128]

Darley and Latané called this the *bystander effect*. It's a form of what has also been called *diffusion of responsibility*.[129] In another experiment, Darley and Latané had a "thief" steal an envelope full of cash from the front of a classroom full of students. Most students in the class didn't do anything. They fidgeted, because they had seen the thief and probably felt that they *should* do something. But when no one else in the room did anything, they didn't either.[130]

We'll see more of this potent external influence in the discussion of *in-group bias* in Chapter 14. For now, it's enough to point out that human beings are social animals whose survival depends on staying connected to the group. Our fear of being cast out of the group is a powerful motivator, and our desire to conform can be overwhelming:

> Ostracism makes individuals feel they lack purpose, have less control over their lives, are less good moral beings, and lack self-worth. . . .
>
> This is so fundamental a part of our evolutionary makeup that it is strong enough to make us give the wrong answers to questions, as in Asch's line of experiments, and *strong enough to make us disregard the moral lessons we've learned and absorbed since childhood*. The carrot of belonging and the stick of exclusion are powerful enough to blind us to the consequences of our actions.[131]

ETHICS UNWRAPPED RESOURCES

Videos

Conformity Bias
Series: Ethics Defined

Conformity Bias
Series: Concepts Unwrapped

Related Videos

Diffusion of Responsibility
Series: Ethics Defined

In-group/Out-group
Series: Ethics Defined

Case Studies

German Police Battalion 101

College Admissions Scandal
Scandals Illustrated

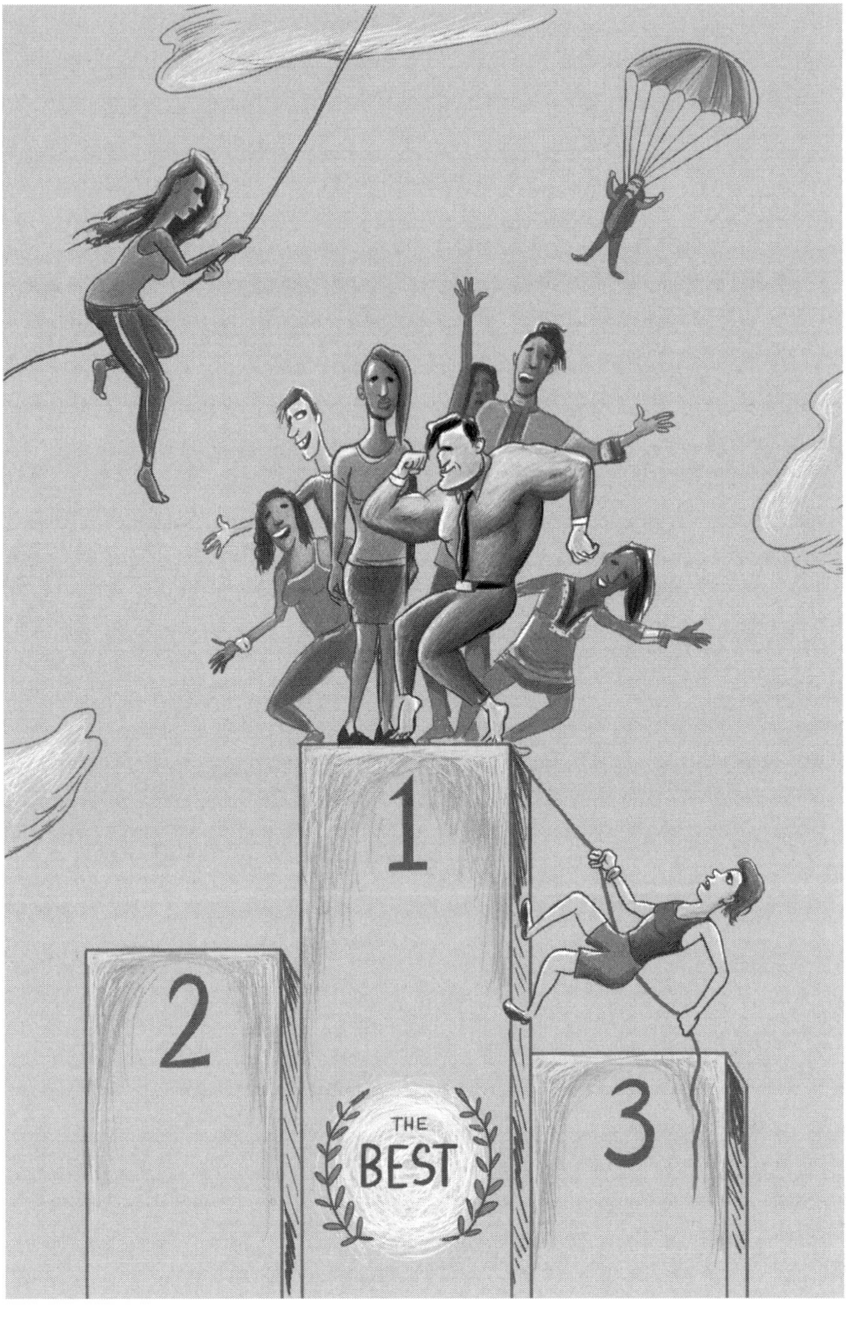
1
2
3
THE
BEST

6
OVERCONFIDENCE BIAS

"It's likely that most of us overestimate our ethicality at one point or another. In effect, we are unaware of the gap between how ethical we think we are and how ethical we truly are."[132]
— *Max Bazerman & Ann Tenbrunsel*

Introduction

The next 11 chapters will focus on the many internal biases and mental shortcuts that affect our moral decision making. Biases in our thinking and outlook on the world, called *cognitive bias* or *psychological bias*, along with *cognitive heuristics* – which are "rules of thumb" or shortcuts that our brains use to simplify the world – are useful in some settings. But these internal psychological influences cause all sorts of mischief as well.

We'll start with the *overconfidence bias*. Evolutionary biologist and political scientist Dominic Johnson has argued that nations are irrationally confident regarding their own virtue and their ability to control events. They suffer positive illusions. According to Johnson, this explains (at least in part) why nations go to war.[133]

Irrational overconfidence has a major impact on individuals as well. Cultural and political journalist David Brooks writes that "the human mind is an overconfidence machine,"[134] and the evidence supports his assertion. Mathematically speaking, no more than 50 percent of people can be above average in any given category, but we all seem to believe that we are living in the fictional town of Lake Wobegon where, according to radio personality Garrison Keillor, "all the children are above average."

Academic research indicates that "[w]e have a largely unconscious tendency to see ourselves in a positive light."[135] For example, you probably have friends whom you would just as soon not ride with, even though they think they are fabulous drivers. It probably won't surprise you to discover that, when surveyed, roughly 80 percent of people claimed that they were above-average drivers.[136] In one study, even drivers who had been hospitalized because of car accidents *they caused* tended to remain convinced that they were above-average drivers![137]

Indeed, when surveyed, impossibly high percentages of people also described themselves as above average in playing chess,[138] investing,[139] and negotiating.[140] An astounding 94 percent of college professors rate themselves "above average" when compared to their peers.[141] And in one study, doctors believed that they had made the correct diagnosis four times as often as they actually did.[142] In similarly impossible proportions, studies show that people believe they are above average in various admirable qualities such as cooperativeness, rationality, health, and intelligence,[143] as well as attractiveness, friendliness, and athletic ability.[144]

Interestingly, people do recognize that overconfidence may present a problem, but they usually recognize the danger only in other people, *not in themselves!*[145]

Overconfidence and ethics

Not only do we tend to think that we are more attractive, smarter, wiser, and more rational than other people, we also tend to believe that we are above average in these morally tinged qualities:[146]

- Considerateness
- Cooperativeness
- Fairness
- Generosity
- Kindness
- Loyalty
- Selflessness
- Sincerity

Studies also show that people tend to *underestimate* their own morally tinged negative qualities: belligerence, deceitfulness, laziness, impoliteness, and meanness.[147]

The bottom line is that human beings tend to be overconfident in their own ethicality.[148] As ethicist Marianne Jennings notes:

> Recent studies indicate that 74 percent of us believe our ethics are higher than those of our peers and 83 percent of us say that at least one-half of the people we know would list us as one of the most ethical people they know. An amazing 92 percent of us are satisfied with our ethics and character.[149]

In fact, surveys indicate that physicians,[150] auditors,[151] and businesspeople in general[152] all believe that they are more ethical than their peers and/or competitors. In one study, people believed that they were *twice* as likely to follow the Ten Commandments as other people.[153] And in yet another survey, a majority of people thought that they were more likely to go to heaven than Michael Jordan, Princess Diana, or even Mother Teresa.[154]

Of course, the worry here is that we may just *assume* that we will naturally do the right thing when the time comes, and this irrational overconfidence can lead us to make important ethical decisions without serious reflection. Disaster can follow. Psychologist John Darley, one of the research giants regarding ethical decision making, captured the key notion of overconfidence bias:

> In our conventional way of thinking about ourselves, we are confident that we would know in advance that to do some set of actions would be morally wrong, and that this realization, occurring prior to the actions, would prevent us from taking them. These comforting thoughts turn out not to be true.[155]

Ethical overconfidence in action

The world appears full of examples that support Darley's warning. One study, for example, found that auditors' overconfidence in their ability to execute an accurate audit can actually lead them to take shortcuts that may well look unethical in retrospect.[156]

Once again, Enron serves as an example. It was repeatedly named the "most innovative" company in America. Its employees had a reputation for being the "smartest guys in the room."[157] Enron was led by one of Houston's most visible philanthropists, CEO Kenneth Lay. The company spent a lot of money putting together its "RICE" (Respect, Integrity, Communication, Excellence) code of ethics. With all that, and a good dose of normal human overconfidence, Enron employees were simply stunned when evidence of the company's financial wrongdoing (and its imminent collapse) began to surface. They initially expressed shock that anyone would question the morality (let alone legality) of the company's actions. People who questioned Enron's actions were told that they "just didn't get it."

Likewise, Mark Watson, partner at accounting giant KPMG, became involved in promoting bogus tax shelters (in part) because he "really did not want to believe that my partners at a Big Four accounting firm would get into something that would be illegal."[158] His overconfidence in the morality of his peers, and his organization, led to his criminal indictment.

In Chapter 4 we described Stanley Milgram's famous "shock" experiment to demonstrate people's tendency to obey authority. When a professor at the Harvard Business School asked his class how they would respond to Milgram's experiment, *every single student* responded that he or she would stop applying shocks at a lower voltage than the average member of the class.[159] This is ethical overconfidence in action. Author Prentice has received similar (though not quite as overconfident) responses when surveying his own business students at The University of Texas at Austin.

Why does this happen?

Why are we so overconfident regarding ethics? One reason is that we tend to dramatically underestimate the impact that mechanisms of moral disengagement, social and organizational pressures, psychological biases, cognitive heuristics, and other situational factors will have upon our ethical decision making.[160]

Business scholar Eugene Soltes, whose research focuses on corporate misconduct, was interested in white collar crime. He developed relationships with many of the most infamous white collar criminals of the past 20 years when writing his book, *Why They Do It: Inside the Mind of the White-Collar Criminal*. Many of his interviews revealed the perils of overconfidence:

> "What we all think is, when the big moral challenge comes, I will rise to the occasion," argued Steven Garfinkel, the former chief financial officer of DVI. Garfinkel believed that he would successfully handle difficult and complex situations when they came his way as an executive. But now, with the benefit of hindsight, he sees how this confidence was misplaced. "There's not actually that many of us that will actually rise to the occasion," lamented Garfinkel. "I didn't realize I would be a felon."[161]

In fact, most leaders feel it should be easy to be ethical. But as Soltes notes in his book:

> Invariably, new CEOs rank "setting the right moral tone" as one of the easiest aspects of management. "They all feel deeply secure in their own moral compass," [Nitin Nohria, dean of the Harvard Business School] explained. "They have a sense that they are a people of extraordinary moral character and that it is very unlikely that they are going to do anything in their organization to lead either the organization astray or do something that will get them in the front pages of the newspapers."[162]

The more successful people become, research shows, the more overconfident they are likely to be. CEO Dennis Kozlowski of Tyco International, who went to prison for taking $81 million in unauthorized bonuses, had this to say: "We believed our own press. . . . With myself and others – even the board – you become consumed a little by your own arrogance and you really think you can do anything."[163]

Indeed, Soltes saw the corrosive impact of the overconfidence bias over and over again. Most of the white-collar criminals he interviewed thought of themselves as "good" right up until (and sometimes well after) they were arrested:

> Virtually every one of the former executives I spoke with pointed out, even complained, that it was not he who was the true villain – it was always someone else.

Beneath the irony of this defense, there is an interesting truth. We all confidently believe we would have behaved differently if placed in the shoes of an executive engaging in malfeasance. However, this confidence is artificial.[164]

Overoptimism

Irrational overconfidence is often reinforced by irrational optimism, another common human trait. Studies show that we lean toward overoptimism in many settings. For example, although newlyweds know intellectually that roughly 40 percent of all marriages end in divorce, almost all newlyweds place their own chance of ever getting divorced at exactly zero.[165] Likewise, people who smoke tend to believe that cancer will not affect them individually.[166] This tendency to believe that the divorces, illnesses, car wrecks, bankruptcies, and other adverse events that happen to other people will not happen to us is sometimes called the *illusion of hope*.[167]

Both overconfidence and overoptimism can be evolutionarily adaptive.[168] "Irrational optimism can be great; it is why only about 15 percent instead of 99 percent of humans get clinically depressed."[169] However, overoptimism (like overconfidence) has a dark side. It can also undermine our thoughtful moral decision making. We can hear stories from friends who got caught up in difficult ethical environments at companies they worked for, and read of ethical train wrecks on the internet. But if we don't seriously believe that these moral mistakes might happen to us, then we are likely to be unprepared when we do face a true moral challenge.

Legal scholar Donald Langevoort suggested that in many cases of corporate disclosure fraud, officers and directors were not deliberately lying but were, instead, victims of their own irrational optimism about how well the company would do.[170] A subsequent empirical study strongly supported Langevoort's conclusion.[171] But whether misleading financial statements are intentionally misleading, or the product of irrational overoptimism, the damage to investors is the same.

Moderating overconfidence

Some research shows that the overconfidence bias may be lessened under certain circumstances. Some classroom studies, for example, suggest that reducing student overconfidence in their mastery of a subject can improve learning performance. Students' accuracy on quizzes improved as their overconfidence declined,[172] in part because overconfidence undermines a student's incentive to study.

In other research, people were asked to generate reasons against a decision (before making predictions of their success). Doing so, under some circumstances, reduced the impact of the overconfidence bias.[173] In other words, if we think of specific reasons why we might *not* be successful, our confidence regarding our success will likely be tempered. Other studies have found similar debiasing success by requiring participants to generate counterfactual scenarios to the ones they hope will occur[174] (e.g., "If I approve the sale of this product despite the fact that it flunked safety tests, it's unlikely that any customers will be seriously hurt, so this seems ok. *But what if someone is hurt? Would it be ok then?*").

Despite this sampling of promising studies, it is safe to say that overoptimism is widespread and resilient.[175] And when it reinforces the overconfidence bias, the best among us will fall into a trap of our brain's own making.

ETHICS UNWRAPPED RESOURCES

Videos

Overconfidence Bias
Series: Ethics Defined

Overconfidence Bias
Series: Concepts Unwrapped

Jack & Overconfidence Bias
Series: In It To Win

Case Studies

Dennis Kozlowski:
Living Large

Approaching the Presidency:
Roosevelt & Taft

Theranos' Bad Blood
Scandals Illustrated

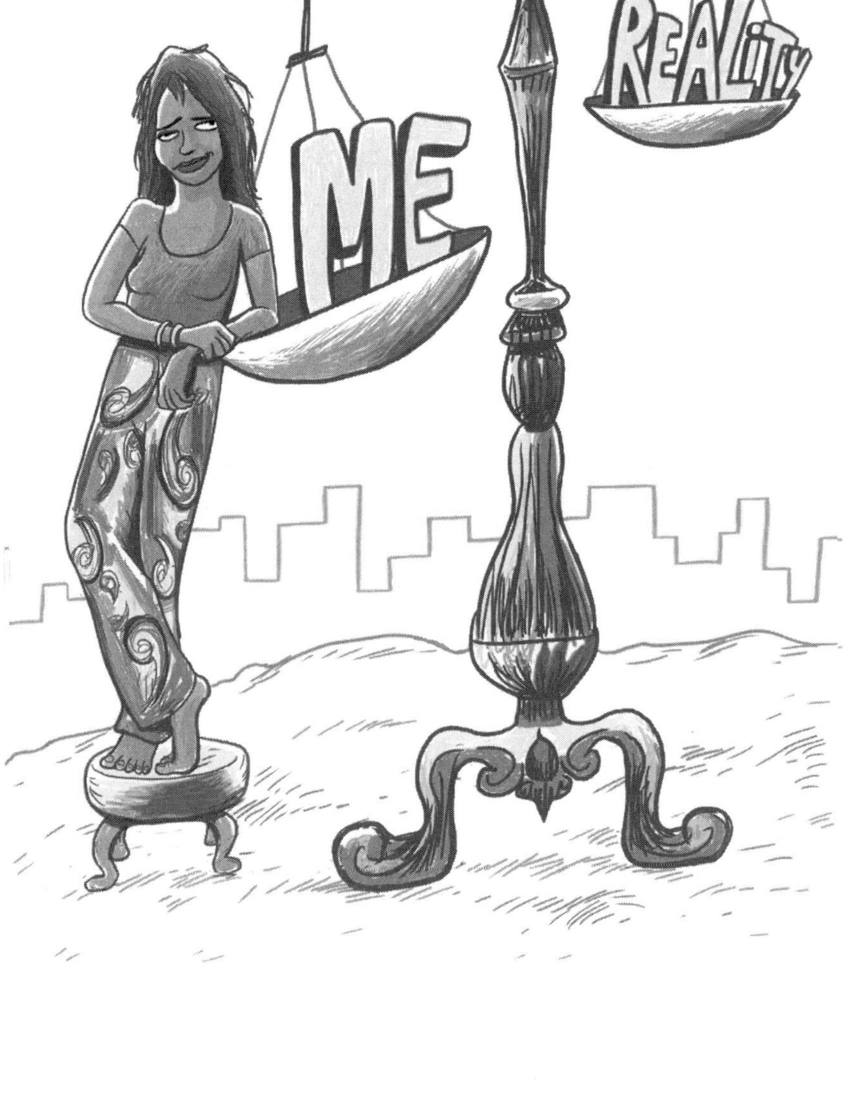
ME
REALITY

7
SELF-SERVING BIAS

> *"People tend to confuse what is personally beneficial with what is fair or moral."*[176]
> – Max Bazerman

Introduction

The *self-serving bias* is the tendency we have to interpret the world and make decisions in such a way as to confirm our preexisting beliefs and to advance our perceived self-interest. Needless to say, we often intentionally choose to act in our own naked self-interest.

But the self-serving bias often manifests on an unconscious level and is therefore one of the most intractable ethical traps discussed in this book. It encompasses the tendency we have to:

- Gather, process, and even remember information in ways that support positions we have already taken or that are beneficial to us.[177]
- Conflate what is "good" with what is "good for me."[178]
- Attribute to ourselves more positive qualities or contributions to a successful outcome than is objectively justified.[179]

Self-serving ways we gather, process, and remember information

Your authors love to hear that they are kind and brave and smart and other wonderful things. Don't you? We are all more likely to listen to our mothers who tell us how fabulous we are than to our teachers who tell us that we are underperforming. And we want to hear that we are right.

It's not surprising, therefore, that Americans of a certain political persuasion tend to watch mostly Fox News. If they are of a different political persuasion, they tend to watch mostly MSNBC for their political news. In fact, studies indicate that as people access the internet, they tend to simply skip over the stories that contain information or viewpoints that they don't already agree with.[180]

An example of how the self-serving bias manifests when gathering information was given by a British civil servant who was tasked with helping his government build the case for invading Iraq in 2003:

> The speeches I drafted for the Security Council and my telegrams back to London were composed of facts filtered from the stacks of reports and intelligence that daily hit my desk. As I read these reports, facts and judgments that contradicted "our" version of events would almost literally fade into nothingness. Facts that reinforced our narrative would stand out to me almost as if highlighted, to be later deployed by me, my ambassador and my ministers like hand grenades in the diplomatic trench warfare.[181]

Not only do we tend to seek out information that serves our own perceived interests and preexisting beliefs, we also tend to process the information we gather in a self-serving way.

In one experiment, for example, participants were shown slides of two phony studies on capital punishment, and were told that the studies had used two different methodologies. When asked to evaluate the methodologies, participants who supported capital punishment rated the study concluding capital punishment discouraged crime as superior. The other participants (who opposed capital punishment) favored the methodology of the study finding that capital punishment did not deter crime. In essence, people with different initial beliefs evaluated the same empirical results differently in order to support their preexisting views.[182]

In another classic study, fans of two college football teams watching a matchup tended to disagree completely regarding which team was responsible for the rough play in the game.[183] Each group thought that players from the *other* team were at fault. If you've ever watched a football game in a bar containing fans of both teams, you'll be familiar with such disagreements.

Likewise, when informed that a piece of legislation is being put forward by their own political party, people are much more likely to agree with the legislation than if they're told that an *identical* piece of legislation is being advanced by the opposing party.[184] In another study, when shown a film of protestors, people who believed in the protesters' cause were much less likely to believe that the protestors "went too far" than did people who didn't agree with their cause.[185]

Even people who are trained to be objective, such as auditors and scientists, tend to find information more persuasive when it is consistent with their self-interest or their previously drawn conclusions. For example, when academics evaluate the methodologies of various studies, they tend to be unconsciously affected by whether or not the studies' conclusions are consistent with their preexisting beliefs.[186]

People even tend to remember information in a self-serving way.[187] In one study, believers in extrasensory perception (ESP) more accurately recalled information from apparently successful ESP demonstrations, as compared to apparently unsuccessful ESP demonstrations.[188]

Factors that reinforce the self-serving bias

As noted in earlier chapters, our mental shortcuts and internal psychological biases readily support unethical decisions and blind us to ethical blunders. The self-serving bias is fertile ground for many of these other biases to also flourish. For example:

- The *confirmation bias* is the tendency we have to seek out information that confirms our original beliefs or our desired outcome.

  In one study, participants were told to test for a particular disease by putting a piece of paper in their mouths. Although the paper was a sham, half of the individuals were told that no change in the paper meant that they did *not* have the disease. Those people put the paper on their tongue, looked at it, got the answer they wanted, and went on their way. The other half were told that no change meant they *did* have the disease. When these people put the paper in their mouths and saw no change, they put the paper back onto their tongues multiple times, hoping the result would change.[189] We are motivated to seek the answers that we want to hear, which are generally the answers that best serve our self-interest.
- *Motivated reasoning* is the tendency we have to use a variety of mental means to arrive at a desired conclusion while appearing, at least to ourselves, to be using unbiased reasoning. Because motivated reasoning is unconscious, our claims that we are unaffected by bias or self-interest can be sincere, even as we make decisions that are in reality self-serving.

  For example, many physicians think that they're immune from any monetary influence. Yet recent studies show that accepting industry hospitality and gifts has a significant subliminal effect on patient-care decisions.[190] Literally scores of studies show that if financial incentives shift for doctors, their diagnosing and prescribing behavior often shifts as well. If compensation rises for C-sections versus natural births, C-sections will increase. If compensation goes up for CT scans, doctors more frequently conclude that CT scans are medically indicated. Most of these doctors are presumably not consciously prioritizing their own financial best interest over their patients' health, but their behavior tends to change nonetheless. As psychologists Bazerman and Tenbrunsel note: "Most smart, well-educated doctors are puzzled by the criticism against them, as they are confident in their own ethicality and the 'fact' that they always put their patients' interests first."[191]
- *Belief persistence* is the tendency we have to hold on to beliefs long after the basis for those beliefs has been substantially discredited, especially when those beliefs serve us in some way.[192]

For example, when William Harvey discovered how the human circulatory system works, overturning Galen's 1,500-year-old theories, many physicians resisted the evidence, saying that "they would rather err with Galen than proclaim the truth with Harvey."[193] Their patients probably had a different point of view!

In a more recent example, people who worked in the asbestos and tobacco industries (and initially believed that their products were essentially harmless) had great difficulty accepting the (eventually overwhelming) evidence that these substances cause cancer.[194]

- The *causal attribution bias* is the tendency we have to attribute to ourselves more skill, intelligence, or contributions to a successful outcome than is objectively justified. This, again, is self-serving and can cause us to make choices that objective third parties view as unfair or unfounded.

For example, when four authors of an article are asked what percentage of the credit they deserve for the article's successful publication, their answers should add up to 100 percent. But studies show that the answers tend to add up to 140 percent or more, even when the authors are trying to be fair and accurate.[195]

Conflating what is good

Conflating what is "good" with what is "good for me" often happens at an unconscious level. Nonetheless, it happens. Indeed, the self-serving bias is often placed in sharp relief when someone's interests change and their moral views follow along. In early 2013, for example, family-values Senator Rob Portman of Ohio (Republican) announced that he had switched from opposing gay marriage to supporting it. Why? Because his son had announced that he was gay.[196]

Similarly, surveys demonstrate that people who believe that it is terribly unethical for an American clothing company to source from suppliers using child labor will tend to ignore the ethics of the company if they discover cute clothes that they really want to buy in the company's catalogue.[197]

Likewise, people who have an opportunity to save money by evading taxes don't judge tax evasion as harshly as people who do not have such an opportunity.[198] As behavioral finance scholar David Solomon has said, "Nobody is ever the villain in their own narrative. So if someone takes actions that threaten to paint them as a bad person, they are more likely to change their opinion of what's right and wrong, rather than change their opinion of themselves."[199]

Complicating factors

Several factors, including size and wiggle room, can easily exacerbate the impact of the self-serving bias on our ability to see ourselves clearly, and to make well-defined moral judgments.

Magnitude

Unsurprisingly, the larger the incentive, the more likely we are to react in a self-serving manner, whether consciously or unconsciously. Studies show that the higher the percentage of compensation CEOs are paid as stock options, the more likely CEOs are to fudge numbers to keep stock prices up.[200]

Enron provides a classic case of a rewards system that created an ethical swamp:

> When Enron employees valued proposed deals, which affected the numbers Enron could put on its books, which in turn determined whether or not employees met their bonus targets, which in turn determined whether millions of dollars in bonuses were paid to the very people who were deciding what the numbers should be, even assuming good faith (and at least some of the Enron officers must have been acting in good faith), the self-serving bias must have had an impact. This is especially so because Enron employees were often not choosing between legitimate Option A and legitimate Option B; rather [according to former Enron employee Brian Cruver] the "prices were pulled from someone's ass . . . because there was nowhere else to get them!"[201]

Ambiguity and complexity

The more ambiguous a situation is, the more room there is for the self-serving bias to rear its ugly head. In such a setting, all arguments become more plausible, and self-serving decisions are easier to rationalize. One study found that people are less generous when their actions occur in a morally ambiguous situation.[202]

Ambiguous *and* complex situations give rise to conflicts of interest, where what's in our own best interest is not in the best interest of our employer (or client or customer or someone to whom we owe a duty of loyalty). Conflict of interest and the self-serving bias mingle in this example from Wall Street:

> Research done with brokerage house analysts demonstrates how conflicts of interest can unconsciously distort decision making. A survey of analysts conducted by the financial research service First Call showed that during a period in 2000 when the Nasdaq dropped 60%, fully 99% of brokerage analysts' client recommendations remained "strong buy," "buy," or "hold." What accounts for this discrepancy between what was happening and what was recommended? The answer may lie in a system that fosters conflicts of interest. A portion of analysts' pay is based on brokerage firm revenues. Some firms even tie analysts' compensation to the amount of business the analysts bring in from clients, giving analysts an obvious incentive to prolong and extend their relationships with clients. But to assume that during this Nasdaq free fall all brokerage house analysts were consciously corrupt, milking their clients to exploit this incentive system, defies common sense.

Surely there were some bad apples, but how much more likely is it that most of these analysts believed their recommendations were sound and in their clients' best interests? What many didn't appreciate was that the built-in conflict of interest in their compensation incentives made it impossible for them to see the implicit bias in their own flawed recommendations.[203]

Subconscious influences

So, we are often heavily impacted by the self-serving bias and yet do not realize it. We make moral judgments, or take actions, that objective third parties question, yet we believe ourselves to be ethically pure.[204] Sometimes, this happens because the self-serving bias operates at a subconscious level. And sometimes it happens because we are just so darned good at rationalizing our actions!

In truth, there are serious difficulties with recognizing a bias that largely operates at an unconscious level. An unconscious, self-serving bias likely explains the following testimony before the SEC of a top official in the American Institute of Certified Public Accountants in 2000, just before the Enron-era scandals broke out (amid a tidal wave of busted audits): "We are professionals that follow our code of ethics and practice by the highest moral standards. *We would never be influenced by our own personal financial well-being.*"[205]

Really?! Accountants are never influenced by their own financial well-being? We suggest a more plausible assessment is the following:

> The majority of professionals are unaware of the gradual accumulation of pressures on them to slant their conclusions, a process we characterize as moral seduction. Most professionals feel that their conclusions are justified and that they are being unfairly maligned by ignorant or demagogic outsiders who raise concerns about conflicts of interest. Given what we now know generally about motivated reasoning and self-serving biases in human cognition, and specifically about the incentive and accountability matrix within which auditors work, we should view personal testimonials of auditor independence with skepticism.[206]

The self-serving bias is a devilishly difficult problem for those of us who wish to choose the right path and act ethically. Psychologist Ann Tenbrunsel notes that "our morality is constrained in systematic ways that favor self-serving perceptions, which in turn can result in behaviors that contradict our intended ethical standards."[207]

Truthfully, the results of studies attempting to counter the self-serving bias are discouraging.[208] Still, we must try. Because we can easily see how *other* people are affected by the self-serving bias, one key is to convince ourselves that we are *not* special . . . that this insidious bias affects everyone, including us.[209] Studies show that informing people of racial bias in their actions can help them

Self-serving bias 67

reform their behavior,[210] so maybe the same sort of education can work for the self-serving bias as well:

> A starting point is to teach people that bias typically operates outside of conscious awareness. Doing so can help people to recognize their susceptibility to bias by preventing them from relying excessively on introspective evidence of bias. Furthermore, it can reduce the bias blind spot by helping people to realize that they are not likely to be any less biased than those around them. It can also inspire people to engage in efforts to overcome their biases. Research . . . has suggested the promise of this strategy.[211]

It's also important that we pay close attention to our profession and/or our company's codes of conduct. Codes of conduct are commonly focused (to a significant degree) on the types of *conflicts of interest* that provide opportunities for the self-serving bias to wreak havoc. By complying with such professional codes, we can stay away from the biggest temptations.

ETHICS UNWRAPPED RESOURCES

Videos

Self-serving Bias
Series: Ethics Defined

Self-serving Bias
Series: Concepts Unwrapped

Jack & Self-serving Bias
Series: In It To Win

Conflict of Interest
Series: Ethics Defined

Case Studies

A Million Little Pieces

Cheney v. U.S. District Court

Countrywide's Subprime Scandal
Scandals Illustrated

OxyContin: Whale Watching
Scandals Illustrated

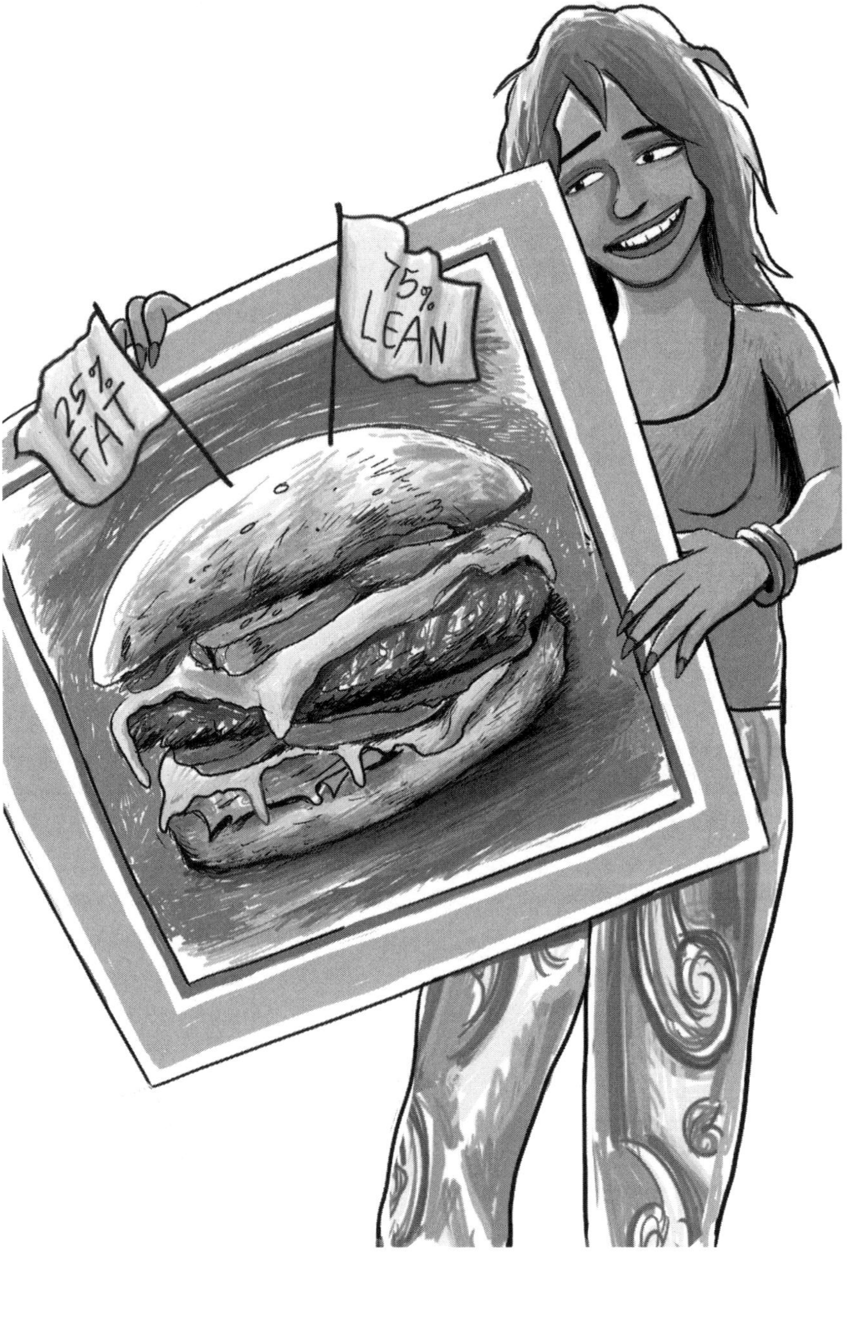
75% LEAN
25% FAT

8
FRAMING

"Our biggest mistakes in ethical decision making are mistakes in framing."[212]
— *Ronald Howard & Clinton Korver*

Introduction

People often say: "It all depends on how you look at it." And that's correct. How we look at things has a huge impact on how we judge things and on the actions we take. If we frame things one way, we may make one choice. If we frame them another way, we often make a different choice. According to psychologists, "Frames make us view the world from one particular and thus necessarily limited perspective. They have blind spots."[213] Importantly, sometimes people frame things for us, and our judgments, choices, and actions are thereby affected in ways that we don't even realize.

It's fun to be a psychologist – you get to think up amusing experiments that show how people's minds really work. In one interesting study regarding framing, experimenters presented participants with identical hamburgers. Some were labeled "75% lean ground beef" and others were labeled "25% fat ground beef." As you might imagine, people generally chose the burgers labeled "75% lean" over those labeled "25% fat," even though they were identical. This is why we'll see "95% fat free" on potato chip bags at the grocery store, but almost never "5% fat."[214]

Psychologists have also demonstrated that the amount of risk we are willing to assume in financial investments is often very much more influenced by the way that investment is framed than by our own natural risk preferences. For example, in one experiment people tended to roll the dice on riskier opportunities when the possible outcomes were explained to them in terms of absolute values (when the possibility of losing money is made less obvious) rather than a rate of return.[215] Other studies show that by manipulating reference points,[216] time horizons,[217] and/or presentation formats,[218] investment professionals can materially affect the investment choices of their customers.

Framing also affects our health choices. Nobel Prize winning psychologist Daniel Kahneman and his coauthor Amos Tversky (also a psychologist)[219] presented study participants with two choices of treatment for lung cancer: surgery or radiation therapy. One group of participants was presented with the options worded in a "survival frame":

- Surgery: Of 100 people having surgery, 90 live through the post-operative period, 68 are alive at the end of the first year, and 34 are alive at the end of five years.
- Radiation: Of 100 people having radiation therapy, all live through the treatment, 77 are alive at the end of one year, and 22 are alive at the end of five years.

People in the second group were presented with exactly the same options, but worded in a "mortality frame":

- Surgery: Of 100 people having surgery, 10 die during surgery or the post-operative period, 32 die by the end of the first year, and 66 die by the end of five years.
- Radiation: Of 100 people having radiation therapy, none die during treatment, 23 die by the end of one year, and 78 die by the end of five years.

Because these choices are mathematically the same, we wouldn't expect the differences in wording to have an impact on people's choices . . . unless we've studied framing! In the survival frame, only 18 percent of participants favored radiation. But in the mortality frame, 44 percent favored radiation. This is a huge difference. The same significant framing effects were found whether the people responding were patients, business students, *or even experienced physicians.*[220]

Framing and ethics

This is all very interesting, you say, but what does it have to do with ethical decision making? Well, as in all these chapters, the answer is that framing hugely impacts our moral judgments and action choices, sometimes in major ways, and often in ways that we don't anticipate (and even don't realize at the time). Studies show that people will make different decisions if viewing a choice through an "ethical frame" rather than through a "managerial frame."[221]

Think about Kahneman and Tversky's study just described for a second. Physicians who are familiar with this study can gently "nudge" their patients toward one alternative or the other, while pretending to present treatment options in a completely neutral manner. Would that be ethical?[222]

The key message of this chapter is that framing affects our ethical judgments and moral action decisions in large part by involving other psychological forces, some of which are featured in other chapters.

Framing and ethical fading

The concept of *ethical fading* is relevant here. Often our choices are framed so as to focus our attention completely on monetary or other practical considerations. Or perhaps we are focusing intently upon pleasing our higher-ups, getting along with our coworkers, or meeting performance goals. In such a setting, ethical issues can completely fade from view and not be considered at all, which can be disastrous.[223]

Promisingly, experiments show that when psychologists prompt people to think of cooperation, they make more prosocial decisions than when they are prompted to think of competition.[224] What is in our frame of reference at the time we make a decision tends to affect the outcome of our decision.

Framing in the real world

You may be thinking: "How relevant to me are a bunch of studies involving college sophomores done in a psychology lab?" That's a reasonable question, especially since at least one meta-study found that (overall) the framing effects demonstrated in psychologists' laboratories are fairly mild.[225] However, real world examples substantially bolster the conclusion that framing effects must be carefully monitored.

For example, a day care center in Israel was having trouble encouraging parents to pick up their children in a timely manner at the end of the day. In an attempt to reduce late pick-ups, the center began charging a late fee. But the fine actually *increased late pick-ups substantially.* Why? Before the fee, the parents probably felt guilty when they made the staff stay late. There was an ethically and socially tinged relationship that encouraged the parents to try really hard to be on time. Imposing a fee caused parents to reframe the arrangement as a strictly monetary one, where they were simply buying the staff's time when they were late. They no longer felt guilty that they were doing something wrong. Less guilt = more tardy.[226]

In another example, when NASA contemplated launching the space shuttle Challenger in chillier conditions than it had ever been tested in, Morton Thiokol's engineers who had designed the ship's solid rocket boosters recommended against it. When NASA pushed back, one of Morton Thiokol's executives told another to "take off his engineer's hat and put on his manager's hat," reframing the issue from one focusing on safety to one focusing on the dollars and cents that would be lost by rescheduling the launch. Once the executives decided they were facing a "management issue," they overruled the engineers and approved the launch. The Challenger exploded, killing seven astronauts.[227]

In fact, there's no end to the real-world examples of framing affecting people's moral actions:

- Some energy traders at Enron manipulated energy markets (causing no end of inconvenience and cost to consumers) by framing their actions as mere "marketing."[228] A conversation between two traders went like this:

    Greg: "It's all how well you can weave these lies together, Shari."
    Shari: "I feel like I'm being corrupted now."
    Greg: "No, this is marketing."
    Shari: "OK."

- Experts have traced the Volkswagen emissions scandal to a relentless focus by VW Chairman and CEO Ferdinand Piëch on market domination by all means necessary.[229] Total focus on market domination doesn't leave much room in one's frame of reference for considerations of right and wrong.

Related considerations

In addition to ethical fading, other psychological factors affect the framing of decisions, including our aversion to loss, role morality, and the use of euphemisms in our language.

Loss aversion

Some of the studies on financial investment mentioned earlier in this chapter, as well as the Kahneman and Tversky study on medical care options, implicate loss aversion's role in framing our decisions.

Loss aversion is the tendency we have to dislike losses more than we like gains and, therefore, to take bigger risks to avoid losses. Ethics gets involved with loss aversion because when we focus on a potential loss that we are facing, we are more likely to take unethical actions to avoid that loss than we'd take to achieve a similar-sized gain. Whether the decision is framed to focus on a potential gain or a potential loss can make a substantial difference in our choices.

We'll discuss loss aversion in detail in Chapter 10.

Role morality

At other times, framing effects implicate *role morality*. Role morality describes the phenomenon where we feel that we are playing different roles in life and will apply different ethical standards as we play those different roles. For example, in the role of "loyal employees," we may make different ethical choices in an attempt to help our company than we would to help ourselves or to benefit our families.

For instance, how could average folks take part in the atrocities committed by the Nazis in World War II? Framing helped many of them. After the war, Albert Speer, Hitler's Minister of Armaments and War Production, explained that he was able to play his part in Hitler's death machine by framing his job as that of an "administrator." As a mere administrator, he felt no responsibility for the horrific human consequences of the policies he helped to execute.[230]

We'll discuss role morality in depth in Chapter 11.

Euphemisms

Often, we manage to give ourselves permission to do bad things by labeling those things so they appear harmless, or even beneficial. These misleading labels are called *euphemisms*. For example, people may call laying off employees "rightsizing," or mass genocide the "final solution."[231]

Euphemisms in language can be used to frame a choice in such a way as to lead to poor ethical decisions. As psychologist Celia Moore and behavioral economist Francesca Gino note:

> Empirical studies confirm that euphemistic labels can psychologically sanitize unethical practices, facilitating our participation in them. In part, this is because language signals how a decision ought to be understood, which in turn changes the appropriate choice in that particular context. For example, framing a social dilemma in economic terms ("invest in a joint investment fund") results in less cooperation than framing it in cooperative terms ("contribute to a social event"). Likewise, framing a prisoner's dilemma in economic terms ("Wall Street game") results in higher rates of defection than framing it in communal terms ("community game").[232]

The example of Timothy McVeigh, the Oklahoma City bomber, gives us something to consider. As described by psychologist John Gibbs, a little role morality mixed with euphemisms enabled McVeigh to frame his actions so he was the good guy (in his own eyes) in the horrific mass murder of 168 people (including 19 children):

> McVeigh used the military phrases he had learned as a soldier in the U.S. Army. As he prepared to bomb, he was "in a combat mode." "If he seemed devoid of feelings and sensitivity," then, "that was because he was a soldier" preparing for an "act of war," with a "duty to carry out a . . . mission." His "positive offensive action" against the government would need to generate a large "body count" if it was to make its point.
>
> The military metaphor, then, enabled [McVeigh] to minimize the enormity of the crime with euphemisms. The dead among the "body count" who were peripheral to the evil empire were "collateral damage."[233]

Interestingly, framing effects tend to disappear when people are communicating in a foreign language.[234] Of course, it's not practical to speak in a foreign language all the time (for most of us), so if we're to live up to our own ethical standards, we must be aware of the prevalent and adverse impact improper framing can have on our thinking and choices.

Promising research in the field of negotiation reveals that people can be taught to pay attention to framing effects so as to spot and resist them.[235] By combining such training with a little self-monitoring, we might be able to reduce the likelihood that ethical issues are missing from our frame of reference when we make important decisions. Psychologists have discussed how dieters can more effectively avoid temptation by refocusing their attention from the concrete qualities of the temptation ("Boy, that brownie looks yummy!") to its abstract qualities (thinking of the brownie as if it were a mere picture of a brownie, for example). Regarding ethics, scholars go on to suggest:

> In the domain of ethical decision making, when people are faced with a decision, they may be able to enact the "should" self [in other words, establish an ethical frame for their decision] by similarly focusing on the high-level aspects of the situation. For example, consuming limited natural resources can be thought of as an intergenerational tradeoff. When the decision is framed as such, people can take the long-term harm of consumption to the collective – including future generations – into account. . . . In ethical dilemmas, we should envision two choices before us – the ethical choice and the unethical choice. Doing so allows us to see that in choosing the unethical action, we are not choosing the ethical act. Not doing so allows the ethical choice to hide in the background and helps to fade just how unethical the unethical choice is.[236]

ETHICS UNWRAPPED RESOURCES

Videos

Framing
Series: Ethics Defined

Framing
Series: Concepts Unwrapped

Jack & Framing
Series: In It To Win

Related Videos

Ethical Fading
Series: Ethics Defined

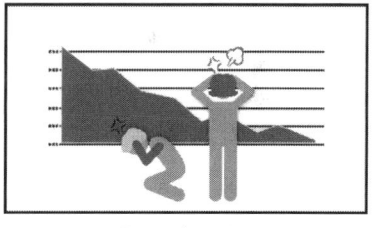

Loss Aversion
Series: Ethics Defined

Role Morality
Series: Ethics Defined

78 It's hard to be who your dog thinks you are

ETHICS UNWRAPPED RESOURCES

Case Studies

Selling Enron

Arctic Offshore Drilling

Dr. V's Magical Putter

Collapse at Rana Plaza
Scandals Illustrated

Armstrong's Doping Downfall
Scandals Illustrated

BEGINS...

ENDS!

9
INCREMENTALISM

> *"Well, you know what happens is, it starts out with you taking a little bit, maybe a few hundred, a few thousand. You get comfortable with that, and before you know it, it snowballs into something big."*[237]
>
> – Bernard Madoff

Introduction

At first blush, *incrementalism* may sound like some obscure, mystical practice. Actually, it's just another name for the slippery slope. You've probably heard that if you throw a frog into a pot of boiling water, it will hop out. But if you put the frog in a pot of cool water and slowly turn up the heat, it will boil to death. If this amphibian story were true, it would be a vivid illustration of incrementalism. But it's just an urban legend so we aren't going to try to disprove it (and besides, we like frogs).

Change blindness

What is not an urban legend is that human beings are not particularly adept at noticing small (and sometimes even big) changes in their environment. This has led to a number of very interesting experiments regarding what scientists call *change blindness*, which is our failure to notice an obvious change.[238]

One such study is "The Door Study" by two psychologists named Daniel – Daniel Simons and Daniel Levin.[239] In a video of the experiment, an accomplice of the experimenter approaches a stranger on the street, handing him a map and asking for directions. As the helpful bystander is consulting the map and pointing around in the process of giving directions, two fellows come down the sidewalk carrying a door. They walk between the accomplice and the helpful bystander (who is the subject of the experiment) and, as the door passes, the accomplice swaps places with the door-carrier. Even though the two men were far from identical twins, only half of the subjects noticed that the accomplice (the person asking them for directions) had been replaced by another person.

In another experiment,[240] a clerk in a store ducks down below the counter (apparently in order to pick up something) and an entirely different person stands back up and continues the conversation with the customer. In about half the cases, the customer doesn't notice this change either.

Yet another video[241] shows a still picture of an outdoor scene. Over the course of about ten seconds, a not insubstantial plant turns into a rock, yet most people don't notice the incremental change in the picture until it's pointed out to them.

There are many more such videos on the internet. You may well be saying: "I'll check some of these out, but what does incrementalism have to do with ethics?" As in earlier chapters, the answer is: a whole bunch!

As we proceed through life, we mentally compare our conduct with our moral standards and monitor whether we're living up to those standards. The fact is, most of us want to be good people; we have moral standards. We believe that we shouldn't kill, we shouldn't lie, we shouldn't steal, and so forth. But incrementalism can drastically undermine our ability to self-monitor effectively. The problem is not a visual limitation, as with change blindness, but it's a form of blindness nonetheless.

Two varieties of incrementalism

Incrementalism comes in two major varieties. In the first version, if we do not notice small degradations in our moral standards, our conduct may degrade and still seem perfectly fine because it matches our new (lower) moral standards. In this case, we end up with both lower moral standards and worse moral conduct.

Consider what happens, for example, in wartime when standards for treating the enemy start eroding. In trying to explain how the My Lai Massacre in Vietnam could have happened, where American soldiers murdered 347 *civilians*, one soldier said that the unnecessary killing

> started with just plain prisoners – prisoners you thought were the enemy. Then you'd go on to prisoners who weren't the enemy, and then the civilians because there was no difference between the enemy and civilians. It came to the point where a guy could kill anybody.[242]

In the second variety of incrementalism, if we don't notice small changes in our conduct, we may not realize that it no longer conforms to our moral standards (which may not have degraded). We end up with the same moral standards but worse moral conduct, though we still feel quite good about ourselves. Some experts argue that the key problem is that we use past actions as the benchmarks for new actions.[243] The new, degraded actions now represent the norm. We fail to check our new actions against our moral standards because they just seem routine. Through routinization, the need to make any ethical judgments is eliminated,[244] and "[a]ny ethical coloration is lost."[245]

Unless we are psychopaths (which only about 1 percent of the population is[246]), our brains generally send us negative emotional responses – such as a feeling of guilt – when we do something that is inconsistent with our moral standards. However, we often excuse ourselves for very small deviations – after all, what's the harm if it's just a tiny slip? We then become desensitized to the deviations, as psychologists Debra Comer and Gina Vega note:

> Over time, however, if people violate their moral standards in response to situational pressures, they may gradually become inured to substandard behavior and desensitized to the intensity of moral encounters. Just as virtuous character develops through habitual good acts, dishonorable character may develop as individuals habituate to performing immoral deeds of incrementally greater intensity. Through a process of desensitization, we could grow accustomed to acting in ways we once thought we never would or could.[247]

Moral disengagement (which receives substantial attention in Chapter 21) describes how we put psychological distance between ourselves and our actions and therefore do not feel as guilty or responsible for those actions.[248] Because it's easier to rationalize small changes than large changes, incrementalism can facilitate moral disengagement.[249]

A group of psychologists uncovered a biological mechanism that helps explain the slippery slope phenomenon. Studies found that when people lie, their amygdalas (a region of the brain that controls our sympathetic nervous system and is designed to keep us safe) appear to receive a negative signal. But the more people lie, the weaker that signal becomes. After a while, peoples' brains don't generate the original strong negative signal to remind them that lying is bad.[250]

Prominent behavioral ethics researchers Max Bazerman and Francesca Gino found that ethics violations in the business world don't happen so much because a group of evil people sit down to hatch a dastardly plan. Rather, manifesting the impact of incrementalism, regular people gradually deviate from normal standards of behavior. According to Gino:

> When people do not perceive small changes, they don't realize the consequences of things accumulating over time and the consequences of their unethical behavior. . . . We showed that with that slippery slope, people do behave unethically, and those who were supposed to monitor them would not notice the changes when they are small ones, just like the situation with the auditors at Enron.[251]

In fact, in a series of four experiments, Gino and Bazerman found that people are much "more likely to accept the unethical behavior of others if the behavior develops gradually (along a slippery slope) rather than occurring abruptly."[252]

Sliding down the slippery slope in the real world

Overbilling clients is much too common among lawyers. Federal District Judge Patrick Schiltz has warned young practicing lawyers regarding this widespread practice, and his description is incrementalism embodied:

> Let me tell you how you will start acting unethically: It will start with your time sheets. One day, not too long after you start practicing law, you will sit down at the end of a long, tiring day, and you just won't have much to show for your efforts in terms of billable hours. It will be near the end of the month. You will know that all of the partners will be looking at your monthly time report in a few days, so what you'll do is pad your time sheet just a bit. Maybe you will bill a client for ninety minutes for a task that really took you only sixty minutes to perform. However, you will promise yourself that you will repay the client at the first opportunity by doing thirty minutes of work for the client for "free." In this way, you will be "borrowing," not "stealing."
>
> And then what will happen is that it will become easier and easier to take these little loans against future work. And then, after a while, you will stop paying back these little loans. You will convince yourself that, although you billed for ninety minutes and spent only sixty minutes on the project, you did such good work that your client should pay a bit more for it. After all, your billing rate is awfully low, and your client is awfully rich.
>
> And then you will pad more and more – every two minute telephone conversation will go down on the sheet as ten minutes, every three hour research project will go down with an extra quarter hour or so. You will continue to rationalize your dishonesty to yourself in various ways until one day you stop doing even that. And, before long – it won't take you much more than three or four years – you will be stealing from your clients almost every day, and you won't even notice it.[253]

WorldCom's bankruptcy was the largest in the history of the world when it filed in 2002 (in the wake of one of the biggest securities frauds in history). Whistleblower Cynthia Cooper pointed to incrementalism's subtle impact in WorldCom's scandal when she wrote: "People don't wake up and say, 'I think I'll become a criminal today.' Instead, it's often a slippery slope and we lose our footing one step at a time."[254]

The U.S. military's mistreatment of prisoners at the Abu Ghraib prison in Iraq is another example of incrementalism in action. As recounted in a *New Yorker* article, incrementalism seems to have played a major role:

> But after four or five nights of running the [Military Intelligence] block of the Abu Ghraib hard site, Davis said, "I just wanted to go home." He felt that what he did and saw there was wrong. "But it was reaffirmed and

reassured through the leadership: We're at war. This is Military Intelligence. This is what they do. And it's just a job," he said. "*So, over time, you become numb to it, and it's nothing. It just became the norm.* You see it – that sucks. It sucks to be him. And that's it. You move on."

Sabrina Harman also said she felt herself growing numb at Abu Ghraib: "In the beginning," she said, "you see somebody naked and you see underwear on their head and you're like, 'Oh, that's pretty bad – I can't believe I just saw that.' *And then you go to bed and you come back the next day and you see something worse. Well, it seems like the day before wasn't so bad.*"[255]

When we look to illustrate the worst of humanity's inhumanity, it's hard to go wrong with an examination of the Nazis in Hitler's Germany. Although many psychopaths no doubt flourished in the SS, it is indisputable that many thousands of Germans (who would have rated in the "normal" range on any psychological profile given today) played significant roles in the Holocaust.[256] Had Hitler swept into power in 1933 and immediately begun the Final Solution, it's probable that there would have been widespread opposition to such grotesquery. But Hitler's decade-long debasement of the Jews – slowly depriving them of their property, their dignity, and their very status as human beings – paved the way for the wholesale murder that was the Holocaust. It required not only the passive acceptance of regular Germans, but also the active assistance of so many regular German citizens.[257] Even those who killed Jews for a living became, because of incrementalism, habituated to the situation.[258]

Many believe that incrementalism has also played a meaningful role in some of the largest business scandals in recent years, including Ford's decision to market the dangerous Pinto;[259] General Motors' handling of defective ignition switches;[260] Nick Leeson's rogue trading that sank Baring's Bank;[261] and prominent accountant Scott London's insider trading.[262] This is certainly plausible. As one C-suite executive (who was convicted of financial fraud) explained from prison:

> I call it increment . . . incrementalization, whether that's even a word. You . . . you get to here so it must be okay to go to here. And if you're here, it surely is okay to go here. It's really fuzzy where you cross the line. [. . .] At what point do you cross the line where the act becomes illegal? I don't know. I don't know.[263]

When the line between ethical and unethical keeps moving (as it does with incrementalism), it's pretty hard to see that we are crossing a line at all.

ETHICS UNWRAPPED RESOURCES

Videos

Incrementalism
Series: Ethics Defined

Incrementalism
Series: Concepts Unwrapped

Case Studies

The FBI & Apple:
Security vs. Privacy

Academic Fraud at UNC
Scandals Illustrated

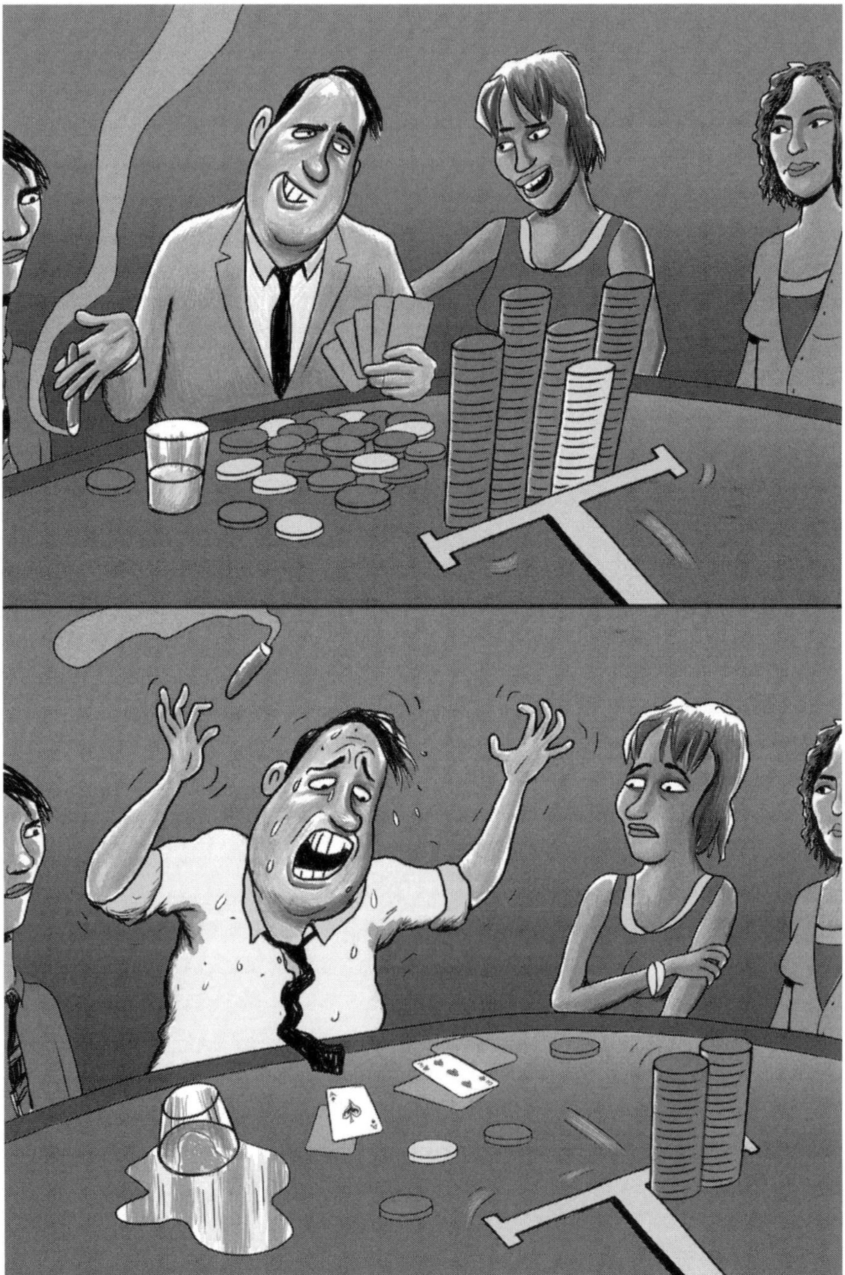

10
LOSS AVERSION

"[Loss aversion] is an underappreciated contributor to many types of unethical behavior."[264]
— *Jessica Cameron & Dale Miller*

Introduction

We tend to hate losses roughly twice as much as we enjoy gains.[265] This is called *loss aversion*. It means that if we go around making bets, we'll probably really enjoy winning a bet of $1,000, but losing $1,000 will suck about twice as much.

Loss aversion is interesting in and of itself, and it has an emotional aspect as well. For example, studies show that negative experiences impact us more emotionally than positive experiences do. The psychic pain of losses outweighs the pleasure of gains.[266] Some neuroscience research traces this phenomenon to the brain's amygdala, which seems to play a major role in processing losses.[267]

Studies of loss aversion

Loss aversion also has significant practical implications for how we make decisions of all types. This was discovered, as was so much else, by psychologists Daniel Kahneman and Amos Tversky.[268] To simplify somewhat, we will make different decisions depending upon whether we see the consequences of our choice as potential gains or potential losses. In general, because we hate losses more than we enjoy gains, we are willing to take more risks to avert a loss than to garner a gain. One study found that companies that have made bad acquisitions (and are therefore facing losses) tend to respond by taking more risks than companies whose acquisitions went better.[269]

Kahneman and Tversky also found that the framing of gains and losses has much to do with the reference points that people use. For example, if we need or want $100 but are looking at a potential gain of only $75, it may seem like a loss. However, if we are fearing a loss of $100, but see an opportunity to lose only $75, it may seem like a gain. If potential gains and losses are of similar size, the losses will tend to loom larger and exert more influence on decision making than will the potential gains.[270]

Knowing how loss aversion works can help everyone set up more effective incentive systems. For example, say you want to encourage people to exercise by taking 7,000 steps a day. Let's assume you intend to pay them $1.40 for each day they reach that goal. You'll have more success if you give them $42 on the first of every month and then *deduct* $1.40 for each day they don't make 7,000 steps, than if you give them $1.40 after each day that they reach the goal. In fact, in a study published in the *Annals of Internal Medicine*, subjects who were paid up front, and therefore faced loss aversion every day, exercised more than the subjects who were simply paid $1.40 per day *after* they did the exercising.[271]

In another study, teachers were more effective at increasing student achievement if they were given bonuses in advance (that they would have to pay back if their students didn't meet performance targets) than if they were promised bonuses only after students hit the targets. Also, students performed better if given rewards ahead of time in an "it's yours to lose" frame of reference.[272] And workers in a Chinese factory were more productive when conditional incentives were framed as losses rather than as gains.[273] Indeed, these real-world results have been replicated in many studies in the lab.[274]

Loss aversion can also push us towards unwise financial decisions. Loss aversion helps explain why people who want to sell their home (but are expecting to receive less than they paid originally) often fail to even list the house for sale. They don't want to suffer a loss even though the economically rational thing to do may well be to sell the house.[275] Investment advisers also report difficulty in inducing clients to sell stocks at a loss, even when it's the best financial strategy.[276]

Loss aversion and ethics

You can see where this is going, right? If loss aversion can cause us to make poor financial decisions, it can also contribute significantly to poor ethical decisions.

Studies show that people tend to judge individuals and companies less harshly if they are motivated to avoid a loss than if they're acting to secure a gain. For example, we'll judge a company as less unethical for laying off employees if it did so to minimize losses it was sustaining than if it were making money at the time and laid off employees to reap even larger gains.[277] If we judge others less harshly for acting to avoid a loss, we'll judge ourselves less harshly, too. We will also more readily whip up a rationalization for our actions that we'll find convincing.

Academic studies

Psychologists Jessica Cameron and Dale Miller set up a study where they rewarded students for solving anagrams. They allowed students to claim their rewards without supervision, giving them a golden opportunity to cheat. Thirty percent of students (appallingly high!) cheated when placed in a gain frame – they could earn $1 for each of the ten anagrams they managed to solve. But 53 percent of students cheated when placed in a loss frame – they started with $10 and were told that they would lose $1 for each anagram they failed to solve.[278] Now we're really talking appalling!

In another experiment, accounting professors found that even in the absence of a direct economic incentive, the study participants were more willing to fudge the numbers to avoid reporting a loss or an earnings decrease. Even people who thought that earnings management was highly unethical were more likely to play that game in order to avoid a perceived loss.[279]

In a similar experiment, people were more likely to tell lies, and to favor gathering illicit insider information, if facing a loss rather than a potential gain.[280] And in another study, people who just "did their best" cheated less than people who set goals – especially if those people found themselves falling just short of meeting their goals, which made their gains seem like a loss.[281]

Loss aversion in the real world

The laboratory evidence is overwhelming that human beings are more likely to cheat to avoid a loss than to reap a gain. In the real world, there are also numerous examples where moral wrongdoing seems to have stemmed from loss aversion. A study of tax professionals, for example, found that they were more likely to cheat in order to please clients if they were worried about losing existing clients, than if they were contemplating gaining new clients.[282]

In another study, professors crunched the numbers and discovered that many of the real-world companies that they studied were more likely to have cheated (even if they had been doing well on an objective basis) if they found themselves falling short of internal aspirations or external expectations. To fall short of these targets felt like a loss, triggering loss aversion, which in turn led to cheating. The more prominent the company (and thus the more it had to lose in terms of reputation by falling short) the more likely the company was to cheat.[283]

In a later study, two business school professors investigated 434 publicly listed companies that had misrepresented their financial statements in a given period and found that the companies were much more likely to have lied when their performance was not keeping up with their peer companies. That also felt like a loss.[284] Writing of the specific companies caught up in the Enron era financial frauds, one observer noted the role of loss aversion:

> My own opinion is that none of the managers of these once successful companies [WorldCom, Qwest, Global Crossing] set out to commit fraud. But as pricing and demand dropped, they did anything and everything to keep their stock up, to buy time to raise more money, or hope demand would return. By doing this, they crossed the line of honesty into fraud. It's a short walk.[285]

Consider these other examples of loss aversion as well:

- Rite-Aid, once the country's largest chain of drugstores, suffered a huge accounting scandal in the late 1990s under CEO Martin Grass. His explanation for participating in the fraud seems to have more than a small element of loss aversion involved: "In early 1999, when things started to go wrong financially, I did some things to try to hide that fact. Those things were wrong. They were illegal. I did not do it to line my own pockets."[286] In fact, rather than admit to financial distress (which would lead to a loss of Rite-Aid's reputation) Grass covered up the losses. He was sentenced to eight years in prison.
- A 2017 documentary, *Disgraced*, tells the story of former Baylor University basketball coach Dave Bliss, who found himself in a bad way. One of his players murdered one of his other players. The deceased player had received illegal payments from the coaching staff. How to account for the cash found by law enforcement? Coach Bliss urged his assistant coaches to lie, and to say that the deceased player was a drug dealer and that's where the cash had come from. Few things seem as low as falsely telling a mother whose son has just been murdered that he was a drug dealer. It's unlikely that Bliss would have told such a despicable lie to get the Baylor coaching job in the first place. But when he was faced with losing his job, he was willing to tell that lie. That's loss aversion in action.[287]
- You may have heard of Raj Rajaratnam, the billionaire who went to jail for insider trading. Not too many billionaires go to jail, and certainly not with an 11-year sentence. One of Rajaratnam's sources for insider information was Roomy Khan, a very successful businesswoman in Silicon Valley. When Khan's career went sideways, she could have tightened her belt. Instead, she began insider trading. She later wrote: "As I reflect back, I am horrified by the choices I made. . . . Over time, the shame of losing my house and status in this society became more important than the unlawfulness of insider trading."[288]

The failure to own our mistakes

One common scenario where loss aversion can cause us to go off the ethical rails looks like this: We make a relatively innocent mistake. We're too proud to admit the mistake and are worried about losing our reputation, our job, and maybe even a lawsuit. To avoid suffering these losses, we do something we would never have done to achieve a gain (like a bonus or a raise) – we lie to cover up the mistake. That lie becomes the first intentional act of wrongdoing, but it can soon lead to moral, reputational, and financial disaster. The headlines are filled with such examples.

Dennis Gentilin, who has thought and written about why good people do bad things ever since he was caught up in an unauthorized trading scandal at National Australia Bank, comments:

There is a driver of behavior within organisations that goes beyond money and power. People within organisations, especially the most senior and powerful, have worked for years to attain a status or title that they become highly attached to, is central to their identity, and defines who they are. When their position is threatened, be it due to poor performance, feelings of incompetence, changes in organizational structure or the risk of having previous maleficence uncovered, the natural response is to go to extreme lengths to defend and protect this position. What is driving this defensive response is the fear associated with the loss of their status and title, and the associated financial rewards and lifestyle the position affords. By extension, what is at stake is their very sense of self and identity.[289]

Other examples of business scandals that fit this mold include:

- General Motors found itself in the middle of a scandal caused by its failure to address a problem with ignition systems in its cars. G.M. initially denied that there was a problem, and then things snowballed. *New York Times* business writer Floyd Norris, who covered the scandal, wrote:

    I suspect that every one of the people involved at G.M. considers himself or herself to be an honest, ethical person. Yet, collectively, they acted in a way that is absolutely stunning in its callousness. . . . Then, as time went on and more evidence piled up, some G.M. officials could have been in the position of fearing that disclosure of their earlier decisions would be embarrassing, or worse, if they belatedly admitted there was a problem. So the easy path was to continue to ignore the evidence.[290]

- Bernie Madoff's huge Ponzi scheme began with an innocent mistake, a loss in trading that he couldn't muster the courage to admit. Rather than own up to his mistake, Madoff covered it up and tried to earn back the losses. But he only got in deeper and deeper. He said: "I refused to accept the fact – could *not* accept the fact that for once in my life I had failed. I couldn't admit that failure and that was a tragic mistake."[291]

Why is it that we repeatedly see "rogue trading" scandals? In part, the explanation lies with loss aversion. Like these other examples, most rogue traders have enjoyed some success and, in exchange, been given some measure of discretion. The trader then suffers a loss of some sort, which threatens her record and her reputation as a "star." But rather than admit to the loss, she hides it, hoping to gain it back before being discovered. If the trader doesn't succeed right away, the losses mount and the trader must take increased risks to hide the problem. The trader doubles down and doubles down again. Pretty soon, a few billion dollars have been lost due to loss aversion (coupled in this case with incrementalism). Observers believe that loss aversion played a role in the sinking of Barings Bank by Nick Leeson,[292] the $2.3 billion loss suffered by UBS at the hands of Keweku Adoboli,[293] and Société Générale's $7.2 billion loss caused by Jerome Kerviel.[294]

An executive with years of experience in human resources once confided to author Prentice that he had fired many people over his years in the industry. He hadn't intended to fire most of these folks. Rather, he'd intended to use the employees' mistakes as learning experiences. But when the employees (fearing the loss of their jobs or their reputations or both) lied to him about their mistakes, then the executive felt that he had no choice but to fire them.

The lesson here is simple: *Own our mistakes*, no matter how hard it is to do.

ETHICS UNWRAPPED RESOURCES

Videos

Loss Aversion
Series: Ethics Defined

Loss Aversion
Series: Concepts Unwrapped

Case Studies

The Collapse of Barings Bank

Raj Rajaratnam: Insider Trader
Scandals Illustrated

Equifax's Breach of Trust
Scandals Illustrated

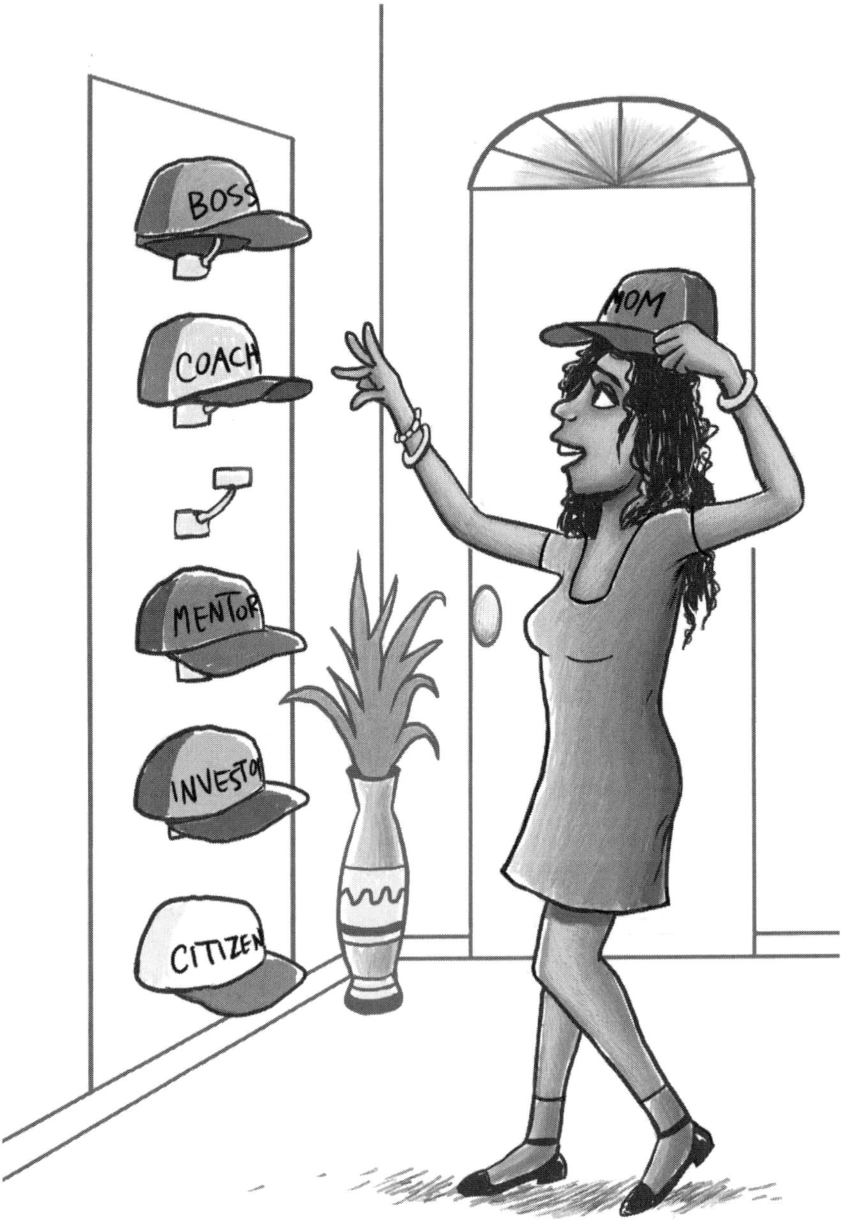
BOSS
COACH
MENTOR
INVESTOR
CITIZEN
MOM

11
ROLE MORALITY

> *"When people switch hats, they often switch moral compasses. People like to think they are inherently moral creatures – you either have character or you don't. But our studies show that the same person may make a completely different decision based on what hat they may be wearing at the time, often without even realizing it."*[295]
>
> – Keith Leavitt

Introduction

Arthur Applbaum, who wrote an influential book on the topic, defines *role morality* as "claim[ing] a moral permission to harm others in ways that, if not for the role, would be wrong."[296] Thus, as you walk down the street, it would be immoral to knock someone over, but if you're a football player on the gridiron, you claim a moral permission to knock people down. In normal life, it would be immoral to kill another person, but if you're a soldier in wartime, or the state-appointed executioner, you claim a moral permission to kill other people while serving in those roles. Other examples of role morality where we have moral permission to cause harm – known as *justified harm* – might include a spy who lies to others while infiltrating a group of terrorists (in order to protect her country's security) or a lawyer who helps a guilty person avoid conviction (while acting as a court-appointed defense attorney).

But playing a particular role does not *generally* give us permission to act immorally. We should always apply (and try to live up to) our own moral code, whether we're in our role as mother at home in the evening or as corporate executive in the office the next morning. In fact, it is morally required that we adhere to our own personal moral code. We shouldn't lie to customers to make a sale in our role as marketing executive for a pharmaceutical company, or inaccurately smear our client's opponent when acting as a political consultant, or illegally dump hazardous waste in a stream in our role as a waste disposal engineer working for a chemical company, or commit financial fraud to keep our corporation afloat in our role as CEO. These actions are almost always morally wrong.[297]

Unfortunately, research shows that some people do choose to act immorally when playing some roles (such as loyal corporate employee) although they would never do those same immoral acts in their other roles as spouse, mother, or citizen in the community.[298] People sometimes, *because of the roles they are playing*, give themselves permission not to live up to their own ethical standards. This is the sense in which we use the term *role morality*.

A famous study

The concept (and impact) of role morality are highlighted in a study in which people were asked to consider the following scenario:

> ABC Drug Company's most profitable drug, its internal studies indicate, causes 14–22 "unnecessary" deaths a year. Competitors offer a safe medication with the same benefits at the same price. If regulators knew of the internal study, they would ban sale of the drug.[299]

The researchers then asked the participants: "*Is it ethical for ABC Drug Co. to continue to sell the drug?*" Ninety-seven percent of people concluded that it was unethical for ABC Drug Co. to continue to sell the drug. Three percent didn't know. Not one person thought it was clearly ethical for ABC Drug Co. to continue selling the drug under these circumstances.

But in a second iteration of the study, researchers presented the same scenario to other people and asked them to deliberate (in groups) as if they were on ABC Drug Co.'s Board of Directors and had just learned of the internal studies. When asked how they would respond, not a single one of the 57 groups of people was willing to remove the drug from the market. An astonishing 80 percent of groups chose to hire lawyers and lobbyists to ensure that ABC Drug Co. could continue to sell the drug, if challenged by regulators or others.[300] That's the pull of role morality!

Role morality and framing

The ABC Drug Co. study illustrates the close connection that role morality has to the concept of *framing* (studied in Chapter 8). When the study subjects played the role of "evaluators" of the company's actions, they framed the issue as an ethical one. But when other subjects played the role of "directors," they framed the issue as a business decision – it was financial in nature, not moral. Because subjects viewed their responsibility as making money for shareholders, they decided to continue with the unethical sales. That's the power of framing.

Unfortunately, role morality is not just a hypothetical concept found only in college psychology labs. Psychologists have found the same phenomenon in field studies as well. Sociologist Robert Jackall did a deep dive into corporate culture, performing a comprehensive examination of a particular company's business environment. Jackall learned that many employees segregated their personal beliefs from the ethics of their workplace. These individuals had a personal code of ethics that they used when playing the role of citizen, of spouse and parent, of churchgoer, of community volunteer. However, when these same people played the role of loyal corporate employee, that personal code of morality went out the window. Tellingly, a company employee told Jackall: "What is right in the corporation is not what is right in a man's home or in his church. What is right in the corporation is what the guy above you wants from you. That's what morality is in the corporation."[301] This employee seemed to be conscious of the fact that he was operating under two separate moral codes, but it is clear from most of the other examples we talk about in this chapter that typically "an individual . . . may not even realize that he/she is engaging in role morality behavior, but may merely feel that he/she is simply carrying out the obligations of the professional role."[302]

In one interesting study, bankers were given an opportunity to answer questions, and then to play a game where they could easily cheat to win a monetary reward. Before playing the game, participants in the control group were asked questions about their television watching habits. Only a few members of that group cheated. But bankers in a second group were asked questions about their *job* before they played the game (thus priming them to think of their profession). More than a quarter of that group cheated! This suggests that when people play the role of finance professional (where the culture may favor dishonest behavior) they will act more dishonestly because they believe that's what is expected of them.[303]

This is unsurprising. Francis Schweigert, who studies businesses' contribution to the public good, has noted that "[w]hatever may be the formal code of conduct in the company, the operative moral code is to be a good team player: Stay versatile and flexible, especially not insisting on one's own strong moral views."[304] In one study, for example, engineers were asked whether U.S. firms should engage in "gifting" to gain a foothold in a new market, even if that activity would violate federal law (such as the Foreign Corrupt Practices Act). One set of engineers were primed to think of themselves primarily as engineers. Of that group, 87.5 percent said that such gifting should never occur. Another set of engineers were asked different questions, primed to think of themselves as working primarily as managers. Of that group, only 46.7 percent said that such gifting should never occur. Clearly, the role these engineers thought of themselves as playing strongly affected their moral judgments.[305]

Role morality and moral disengagement

In addition to being closely identified with the concept of framing, role morality is a method of *moral disengagement* (to be discussed in Chapter 21). With the "help" of moral disengagement, supposedly "good people" may give themselves permission to do a bad thing, and not feel bad about it. Role morality can become a method of rationalizing these illicit actions. Social psychologist Albert Bandura, who created the theory of moral disengagement, gave an example from the Lance Armstrong cycling scandal:

> To blunt self-condemnation of what she was doing, [Emma] O'Reilly [a member of Lance Armstrong's entourage] focused on the methodical efficiency and concealment of the doping rather than the morality of it. "It was just part and parcel of the team's needs at the time. You don't question and analyze it" [she said].[306]

In a recent study, C-suite executives who had been imprisoned for financial frauds of various types were interviewed. One theme that appeared throughout the interviews was that "[e]xecutives' identification with their organizational role, the desire to be successful or to help the company succeed, and even pride, served to induce the executives to engage in accounting fraud in order to meet corporate financial targets."[307]

Altruistic cheating

Speaking of role morality and rationalizations, there is such a thing as *altruistic cheating*, which arises when we tell ourselves that we are acting immorally to benefit someone *else* rather than to benefit ourselves. Parents, for example, are more likely to cheat to help their children than to help themselves.[308] Playing the role of a parent somehow legitimizes the wrongdoing in their own eyes. The Varsity Blues college admissions scandal of 2019 provides several obvious examples of this phenomenon.[309] In other examples, college athletic coaches and academic counselors are more likely to cheat in order to keep players eligible for competition if they can tell themselves that they are doing it *for the student-athlete*.[310] These people pretend that they are not benefiting themselves, but are playing the role of teacher, coach, or mentor.

Other real world examples

Throw role morality into a pot, mix in a little framing (that omits the ethical aspects of decisions), and add a big dash of rationalizations. There you have the recipe for ethical disaster. The following are a few more examples of role morality in action in the real world:

- Mr. Spaulding was seriously injured in a car wreck and sued the driver of the other car. The defendant's insurance company hired a neurologist to examine Mr. Spaulding in preparation for trial. During the course of the exam, the doctor learned that Mr. Spaulding was suffering from a life-threatening aneurism of the aorta that was probably caused by the accident. Rather than inform Mr. Spaulding of his condition so that he could seek treatment, the doctor kept it quiet. The information would, no doubt, disadvantage his client (the insurance company) if it came to light. It seems immoral that the doctor endangered Mr. Spaulding's life in violation of the Hippocratic Oath, but he likely viewed himself as playing the role of an agent of the insurance company rather than the role of a physician whose obligation was to preserve life.[311]

- Kweku Adoboli went to jail as a "rogue trader" who engaged in (and hid) unauthorized trades while he worked in Swiss bank UBS's London office. He lost two billion dollars for his bank, and went to prison for fraud. Both incrementalism and loss aversion played a part in his fraud. So did role morality. In his role of loyal employee, he was able to rationalize what he did: "I don't think at any stage I felt guilty of committing a crime," Adoboli said, "Everything I had done was for the bank and for my colleagues."[312]
- War brings out the best and the worst of humanity. And it's hard to do worse than the Nazis in World War II. Two examples of wartime role morality from Nazi Germany:

  - At Auschwitz, an order from the commandant for two four-retort ovens was bid on by several firms and the winner was I.A. Topf and Sons. Engineers designed ovens to burn 1,500 bodies a day. In 1943, Topf technicians even sought a way to make burning more efficient. They experimented with different kinds of coke and corpses, measuring their combustibility. One of the Topf engineers, Fritz Sander, testified after the war that he had gone so far as to take the initiative in late 1942 to build a better high-capacity crematorium for mass incineration. He had even put in for a patent. [When asked about his actions in light of his knowledge regarding what the furnaces were used for,] Sander replied, "I was a German engineer and key member of the Topf works, and *I saw it as my duty to apply my specialist knowledge in this way to help Germany win the war*, just as an aircraft construction engineer builds airplanes in wartime, which are also connected with the destruction of human beings."[313]
  - Doctors at Auschwitz had to choose daily who lived (for a while, at least) and who died (nearly instantly). They survived their mental turmoil by focusing on their role, on the job they were performing. According to doctors who were interviewed after the war, "*meaning came to lie in the performance of one's daily tasks rather than in the nature of impact of those tasks.*"[314] The doctors often seemed to take pride in the efficiency with which they could "process" large numbers of Jews arriving on trains.

As we can see, role morality can enable us to commit the worst acts imaginable, and also less abominable (but still serious) crimes. It's an influence that all of us well-intentioned people must keep on our radar screens as we adopt and discard our various roles in life.

102   It's hard to be who your dog thinks you are

ETHICS UNWRAPPED RESOURCES

Videos

Role Morality
Series: Ethics Defined

Role Morality
Series: Concepts Unwrapped

Jack & Role Morality
Series: In It To Win

Related Videos

Framing
Series: Ethics Defined

Rationalizations
Series: Ethics Defined

Case Studies

Freedom vs. Duty in Clinical Social Work

Reporting on Robin Williams

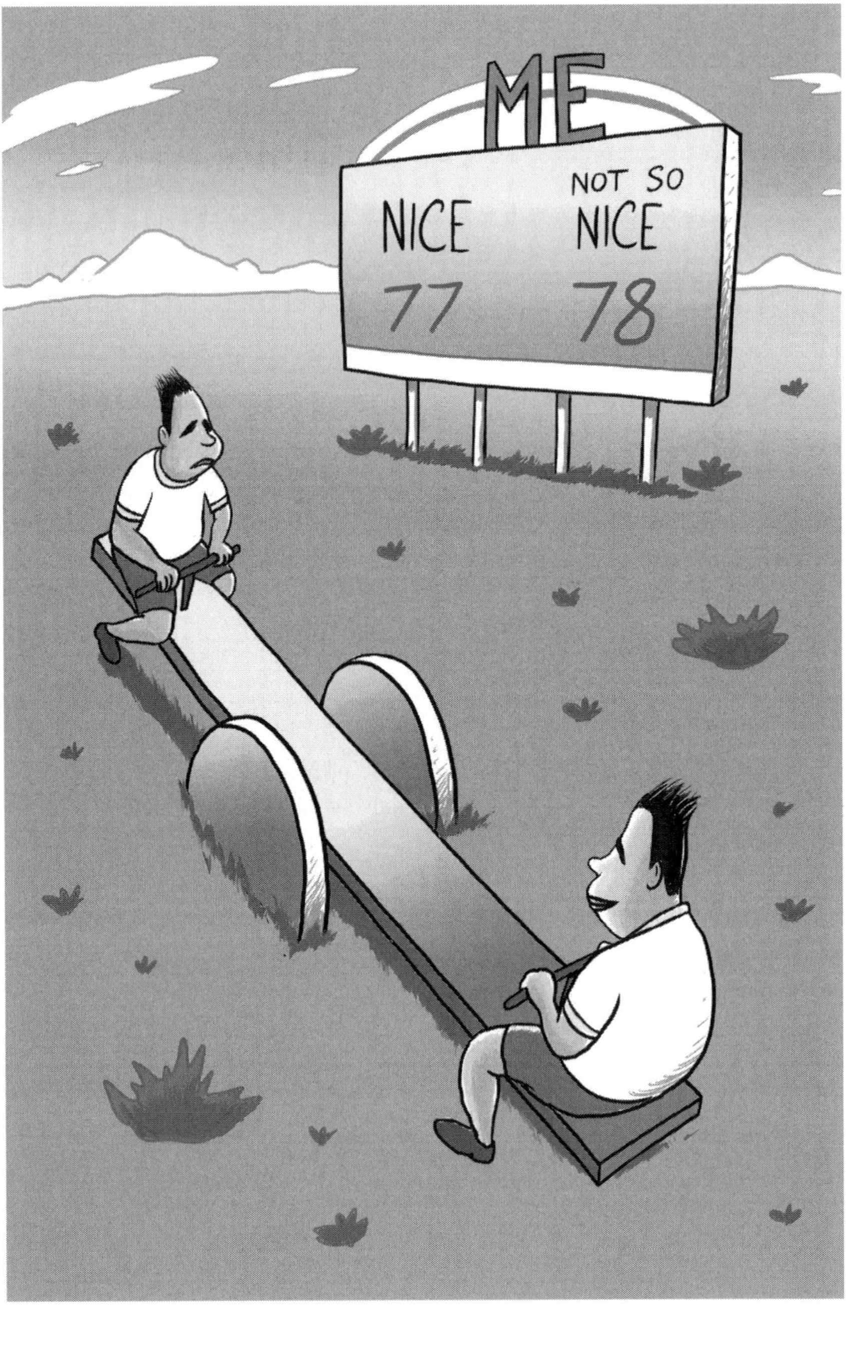
ME
NICE
77
NOT SO NICE
78

12
MORAL EQUILIBRIUM

> *"A research team from Loyola University recently found that people who eat organic food are, on the whole, more likely to be jerks. The lead researcher, Kendall Erskine, chalks his findings up to 'moral licensing.' These folks, he says, 'may feel like they've already done their good deed.'"*[315]
>
> – Hope Reeves

Introduction

Most of us think of ourselves as good people. We also continually keep track of our actions, and mentally compare them to that positive self-image we have of ourselves. This is a big deal. Psychologists Dolly Chugh and Mary Kern argue persuasively that this self-image "(rather than self-interest) is the central driver of ethical decision-making."[316]

In fact, previous decisions – whether good or bad – seem to affect the decisions we're ready to make now. The concept of *moral equilibrium* (also called *moral self-regulation* or *moral balancing*) illustrates this phenomenon. Moral equilibrium has two parts: *moral compensation* (also called *compensatory ethics*) and *moral licensing* (also called *moral self-licensing*).[317]

Moral Compensation + Moral Licensing = Moral Equilibrium

Moral compensation

When we do something we're not really proud of, ethically speaking, our mental scales become unbalanced. Our actions don't match our self-image of being a good person. We then may unconsciously look for something good to do, so that we can rebalance the scales and restore our (mental) moral equilibrium. This is how moral compensation looks in action. The more important it is to us that we perceive ourselves (and be perceived by others) as a good person, the more likely we are to engage in moral compensation.[318]

Even corporations appear to engage in moral compensation. Companies that engage in wrongful acts often quickly engage in acts of corporate social responsibility in order to put the corporate moral scales back into balance.[319] Company employees no doubt have a mental image of their company's relative goodness that is analogous to an individual's self-image. When the organization has (through its employees, of course) acted unethically, its employees may well look for an opportunity for the company to compensate for the wrong.

Moral licensing

Now, consider a situation where we have done something good. Maybe we handled a moral challenge in a way that we *are* proud of. Maybe we did some volunteer work cleaning up a local park or made a generous donation to a local homeless shelter. Such prosocial acts reaffirm our positive moral identity, and therefore might again put our mental scales out of balance – this time on the plus side. If we aren't careful, we may find ourselves thinking: "Look what a good person I am!"

According to some psychologists, "Individuals who have validated or exceeded their ideal moral selves may experience a respite from moral regulatory forces and take ethical liberties in subsequent situations."[320] In other words, after doing something good (and therefore creating a surplus on the good side of our mental moral scoreboard), we may rebalance by giving ourselves license *not* to live up to our own moral standards. Just this once, of course!

As with all psychological tendencies, moral licensing is not a universal phenomenon that happens at every opportunity or with every individual. Still, it's a significant enough factor in allowing good people to give themselves permission to do bad things that it's important to keep an eye on it. Because we may not realize how past decisions affect our current decisions, we may not realize the danger that doing something good puts us in. In fact, giving oneself moral license can be a conscious decision, but more often it will be an unconscious decision (and therefore that much more dangerous!).

Studies of moral equilibrium

The phenomenon of moral equilibrium is "widely documented."[321] For example, in one study psychologists induced some participants to cheat on an exam, but the control group was not so induced. Then both groups were asked to stick around to help grade some questionnaires. The control group volunteered to help for an average of only two minutes apiece. But the cheaters, who may well have been feeling the need to morally compensate for their misdeed, volunteered to help for an average of 63 minutes apiece.[322]

In a series of studies, certain participants (let's call them the moral license group) were given an opportunity to promise to do a virtuous act, such as volunteer at a homeless shelter. Members of the control group were not given such an opportunity. Because the moral license group had committed to do something good, they rated themselves more positively than the control group. But moral equilibrium theory further predicts that the moral license group members will tend to give themselves license not to live up to their normal moral standards *in the future*. And that seems to be exactly what happened in these studies. When both groups were given the opportunity to act prosocially, the moral license group donated less than members of the control group. They also chose more luxury goods over necessities than the control group when given an opportunity to make a purchase. They had committed to do a good thing – they deserved to treat themselves! Of course, none of the participants consciously realized how their previous decisions (e.g., to volunteer or not to volunteer) affected their later actions.[323]

In another study, psychologists prompted participants to write lists of words and think about what those words meant to them. Three different groups were asked to write either (a) neutral words with no moral connotations, (b) positive words (e.g., caring, generous, and fair), or (c) negative words (e.g., disloyal, greedy, and mean). Thereafter, all three groups were given an opportunity to donate to charity. Moral equilibrium theory predicts that those prompted to think about their positive characteristics might well give themselves permission to not donate as generously as they normally would, while those prompted to feel negatively would feel the need to be overly generous. And that is exactly what happened. The participants prompted to think of their positive features gave less than those in the neutral condition, and those prompted to think of their negative characteristics gave more than the neutral group (and five times as much as the positive group).[324]

Another experiment asked participants to recall the many things they had done to help protect the environment. Other participants were asked to recall things they had done to damage the environment. Later, when given the opportunity to support programs to counteract carbon emissions, people in the first group were less willing to do so (they were practicing moral licensing) than were the members of the second group (who were engaging in moral compensation).[325]

In yet another study, participants who self-identified as relatively unprejudiced took a "test" and, no matter how they had actually answered, some participants were told that their responses indicated they were subconsciously racist. Others were told that their responses did not indicate prejudice. As the individual participants left the study site, the experimenters had arranged for them to be asked for a handout by either a black panhandler or a white panhandler. There was no meaningful difference in donations by the two groups, at least to the white panhandler. But the participants who had been told that they were unconsciously racially prejudiced against blacks donated more to the black panhandler, presumably because of their need to engage in moral compensation.[326]

Moral credentialing

In yet another experiment, psychologists gave some participants an opportunity to disagree with a clearly sexist statement. Later, those participants (along with a control group) were asked to make a hiring decision. The people who had been given the chance to disagree with the sexist statement (and therefore to establish their credentials as unprejudiced people) were more likely to favor a man over a woman for a stereotypically male job than were the people in the control group. Another iteration of the study, which involved racial rather than gender prejudice, produced similar results.[327] This form of moral licensing is also called *moral credentialing*.

A different experiment gave participants the opportunity to buy "green" products or regular products. The people who had bought "green" gave themselves license to cheat and steal more than the participants who had chosen to purchase regular products. It seems that after establishing in their own minds their pro-environmental, good-egg credentials, these participants gave themselves permission to depart from their normal moral standards.[328] Indeed, this study provides yet another example of how we can give ourselves license to deviate from our own ethical standards when we feel we've earned our status as morally superior people.

Moral equilibrium outside the laboratory

Moral equilibrium lives in the real world, not just in psychologists' laboratories. In fact, marketers have long been aware of moral equilibrium and have used it to encourage consumers to buy more stuff. You may have noticed, for example, that grocery stores often funnel shoppers first into the fruit and vegetable section. Why? Grocers know that if their customers begin by buying healthy foods, they will often then give themselves license to splurge on some junk food before they leave the store.[329] That's why there are candy bars rather than bananas at the check-out stand (this works on author Prentice almost every time!).

Consider the following examples as well:

- It has been suggested that bankers engaged in enormous philanthropy during (and soon after) the Enron era at a time when banks were engaged in some of the worst moral behavior as moral compensation.[330]
- Oral Suer, who worked relentlessly to raise more than $1 billion for local charities as long-time head of the United Way charity in Washington D.C., fell victim to moral licensing when he "rewarded" himself by appropriating some of those dollars for his personal use.[331]
- Disgraced former New York Attorney General Eliot Spitzer, who relentlessly fought prostitution in his official capacity, was caught visiting prostitutes himself. Psychologists have suggested that moral equilibrium "may also have been partially at play in Spitzer's decision to indulge himself. Didn't all his victories against the scourge of prostitution give him license on some level to enjoy himself in an unsavory act now and again?"[332]

Moral cleansing

Psychologists often use the term *moral cleansing* as a synonym for moral compensation. Moral cleansing describes "the actions people engage in when their moral self-worth has been threatened."[333]

In a narrower sense, moral cleansing ties the concept of moral equilibrium to actual cleanliness. Studies show that if students have showered right before they take a test, they are more likely to cheat on the test. Huh? Strange as it seems, studies show that when we clean ourselves, it is almost as if we've washed away our transgressions, at least in our own minds. Our internal moral scale has tilted back to the good side. Of course, then we are in danger of allowing ourselves to do something immoral. Psychologist Thalma Lobel reports:

> Our study confirmed that those who felt clean on the outside felt "clean" enough on the inside to be able to falsify their test scores and report that they had correctly answered some of the impossible questions. It was as if they felt a "morality surplus" while clean, as if they had moral character to spare and could thus cheat.[334]

Sounds just like moral licensing to us.

Mitigating moral licensing

Studies show that people are more likely to engage in moral licensing if they evaluate their actions from a *utilitarian* (greatest good for the greatest number) approach than from a *deontological* (or rule-based) approach. Let's say, for example, that we detect a dangerous situation and don't simply look the other way. Instead, we make a phone call, write a small check, or call in a favor, and all of a sudden a runaway 14-year-old is off the street and in a safe shelter.

If we focus on the good we did, and how it tips our inner moral scales, we may give ourselves permission to do something that we normally wouldn't do (maybe surf for porn or cheat on a test or our taxes). However, if we say to ourselves, "I'm a caring human being and this is what caring human beings do," then we're more likely to engage in behavior that is consistent with our good deed going forward.[335] In other words, we're building our moral identity. This approach is not bulletproof, but it may be helpful.

Furthermore, studies show that if people think about the good deeds they did recently ("Look at the good thing I just did!"), they are more likely to engage in damaging moral licensing than if they think about the good deeds they did further back in the past ("I'm the kind of person who does good things. I'd like to continue to do good things.") So, it's helpful to maintain a long-term perspective on the trajectory of our moral life.[336]

One final point on moral licensing: Although there is much evidence that doing good things sometimes leads us to give ourselves permission to do bad things, there is also evidence of moral consistency – meaning that doing the right thing can set a precedent that helps us continue to do the right thing. Doing right becomes a habit. Much research addresses the question of under what circumstances is moral licensing triggered, and under what circumstances is moral consistency triggered. And complete clarity on where this line is drawn has yet to be established.[337]

ETHICS UNWRAPPED RESOURCES

Videos

Moral Equilibrium
Series: Ethics Defined

Moral Equilibrium
Series: Concepts Unwrapped

Case Studies

Buying Green: Consumer Behavior

Robert Bentley: A Campaign Affair
Scandals Illustrated

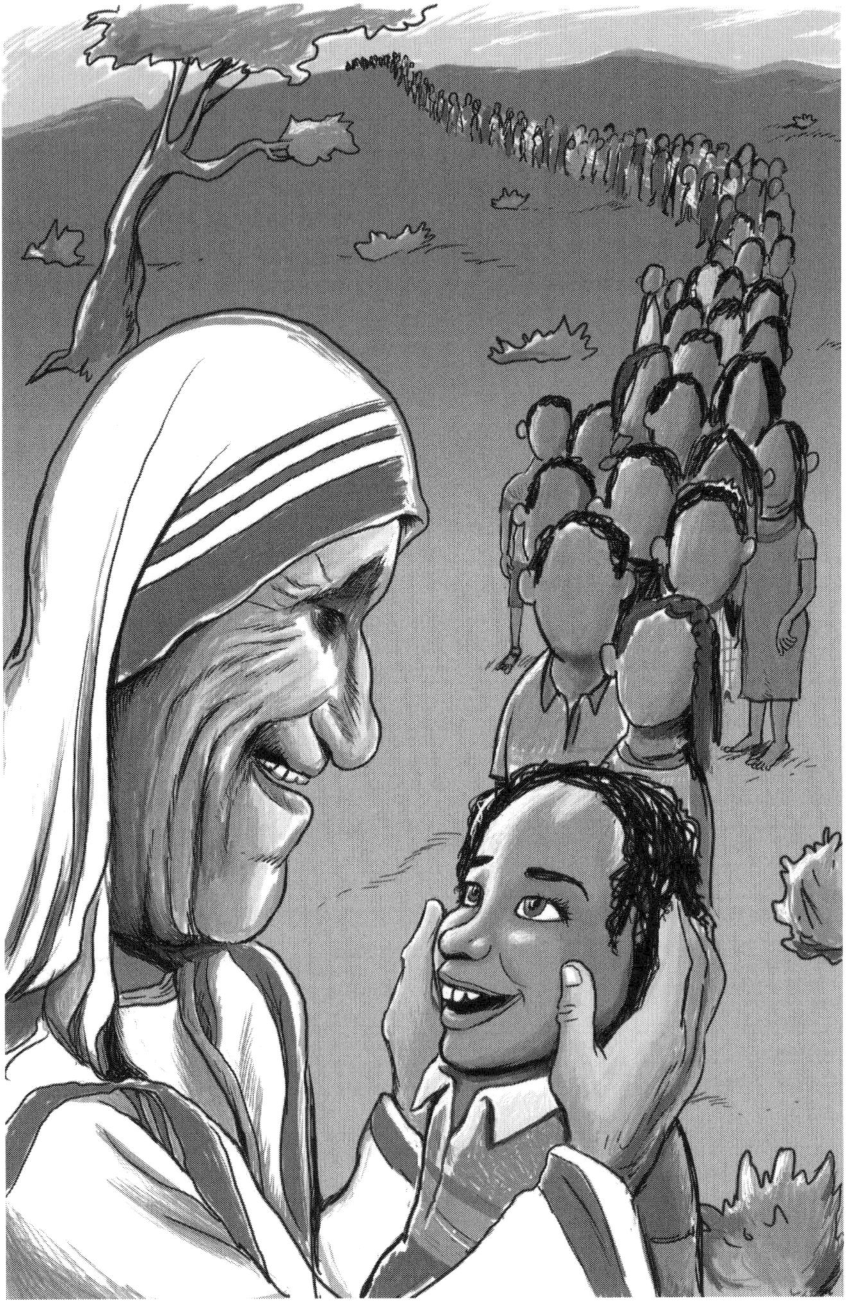

13
TANGIBLE AND ABSTRACT

"If I look at the mass I will never act. If I look at the one, I will."[338]

— *Mother Teresa*

Introduction

As a general rule, our brain cannot efficiently attend to all the stimuli that human senses bring its way. Therefore, it must prioritize. Clearly, vivid factors will have a bigger impact on the brain than bland factors, tangible factors will have more impact than abstract factors, physically close factors will have more impact than distant factors, and contemporaneous factors will have more impact than factors far off in the future.[339] In other words, all things being equal, an unprecedented flood in Houston will be more distressing to Houstonians than to Dallasites, to Texans than to Minnesotans, and to Americans than to Bulgarians. In fact, typically people will be more distressed by relatively minor injuries to their close relatives than by mass murders that occur in a different city, state, or country.[340]

Many readers may not be familiar with a Pulitzer Prize-winning photograph from the Vietnam War era of a small Vietnamese girl running naked down a highway in Vietnam. She is clearly in pain, her clothes burned off by napalm bombs. Americans — who were used to reading bland statistics in newspapers about the numbers of soldiers and civilians killed and injured in the Vietnam War — were all of a sudden able to put a face to the numbers. It had an impact. As the famous social psychologist Albert Bandura wrote:

> This single humanization of inflicted destruction probably did more to turn the American public against the war than the countless reports filed by journalists. The military subsequently banned cameras and journalists from battlefield areas to block the publication of images of death and destruction.[341]

Tangible ethics

In the moral realm, the bias of *the tangible and the abstract* suggests that we tend to overlook the consequences of our actions unless that impact is right in front of our noses. While this tendency is natural (and easily understandable), it can have serious and distressing implications for moral decision making.

The evidence is quite clear that it's easier for people to try to kill someone if they do it remotely (via artillery, airplane, drone, etc.) than if the attempt is up-close-and-personal (via fist, knife, handgun, etc.). Consider what we learned in Chapter 2's Trolley Problem – most people will stand afar and flip the switch to shift the train, but will refrain from pushing the big guy onto the train track. Our distance reduces feelings of responsibility for the harm done, and it also minimizes feelings of empathy and sympathy for any potential victims.[342]

Consider a thought experiment in the business realm rather than in the realm of war (although too often the two worlds have much in common). Assume you are the founder and CEO of a start-up that makes packaged, gluten-free meals that have a long shelf-life even when unrefrigerated. Imagine that a testing lab you hired sends you a report questioning the meals' safety if they have been unrefrigerated for more than nine days. This report has the potential to devastate your company! Its meals were marketed and sold with a shelf life exceeding nine days.

In founding your company, you borrowed heavily from relatives, and convinced several friends to leave their promising jobs to work for your start-up. To recall and destroy all the meals (which is one option) seems impossible for you to even contemplate seriously. It would mean immediate bankruptcy for the firm, devastating financial losses to relatives, and painful layoffs for friends.

On the other hand, while consumers might be injured if they eat the meals, that remains just a possibility. After all, the lab didn't say with 100 percent certainty that the meals will become dangerous to eat on the tenth day. Maybe it's just a ten percent chance, or even less. Furthermore, potential victims are (at this point) nameless and faceless so it's hard to muster a strong emotional reaction when you think of their potential injuries, which (after all) might never materialize. In sum, when you compare the (potential) danger to unidentified future consumers to the vivid images of your family members (who will lose their money), your friends (who will lose their jobs), and your dream (which will be shattered), the danger to customers may seem very slight indeed. This is the bias of the tangible and abstract in operation.

Real world examples

In our highly technological and globally connected business world today, too often "the dash of a pen or the click of a mouse creates a distant and impersonal kind of harm"[343] that will not be adequately considered by those who are making the decision. If we cannot conjure up the faces of the people harmed, or adequately envision those impacts, we'll have great difficulty accurately evaluating the consequences and moral implications of our actions. This differential impact is sometimes called "the 'here-and-now' version of empathic bias [that] favors distressed persons who are immediately present."[344] It's also called the *familiarity bias* because we tend to favor that with which we are familiar over that which seems strange to us.[345]

To put it in real world terms: A manager of a chemical company was presented with the hypothetical choice of (a) disposing of a chemical in a local water source that would kill 20 people out of a million, or (b) spending $25 million of the company's money to spare those lives by properly disposing of the chemical. His response clearly reflected the impact of the tangible and the abstract:

> Is it worth it to spend that much money? I don't know how to answer that question as long as I'm not one of those twenty people. As long as those people can't be *identified,* as long as they are not *specific* people, it's OK to put the chemical in the water. Isn't that strange?[346]

The tangible and abstract phenomenon helps to account for much white-collar crime, too. Mugging someone on the street is pretty darned tangible. But sitting at a computer fudging numbers so that our company can meet its quarterly earnings targets (and thereby avoid a major drop in its stock price) probably doesn't feel so tangible, and the names and faces of individual investors are not top of mind. Often, in fact, employees aren't trying to put money directly into their own pockets; rather, the goal is to help their employer out of a jam. Business scholar Eugene Soltes, who interviewed many of America's most prominent white-collar criminals, notes:

> For most white-collar crimes, the harm created by a dab of a pen or an adjustment on a spreadsheet does not require getting close to individuals. The victims are physically and psychologically distant. In some cases, like insider trading, the victims might not even be identifiable. As a result, perpetrators of white-collar offenses do not experience the same gut feelings of doing harm that kept my interviewees from reaching for my wallet.[347]

Indeed, the abstract nature of intangible harm – not knowing who is harmed or how, or being able to put faces to the harm – exacerbates the ease with which we can rationalize the nature of our wrong. As Soltes observes, "Harming investors or employees is not the intention behind engaging in [white-collar criminal] misconduct but, rather, an inevitable corollary or externality. This distinction is important since it helps explain why, from the standpoint of the executive, misconduct doesn't necessarily lead to the sensation of taking or stealing from anyone."[348]

An attorney for a Ponzi scheme perpetrator made just this point: "[His client] didn't physically print the financial statements depicting the false numbers. It's as though he feels that he didn't perpetrate the fraud and instead was a bystander

116 It's hard to be who your dog thinks you are

to his own decisions."[349] The damage the Ponzi perpetrator was doing to his victims was too intangible to make him to feel guilty enough to stop his scheme.

Consider another example of the tangible and abstract bias from the financial field:

> The story of Noreen Harrington, a Goldman Sachs veteran who was the whistleblower in the mutual fund late-trading scandal, illustrates how depersonalizing the victims of our unethical behavior allows such behavior to be perpetrated. Harrington has said that prior to blowing the whistle on these practices, she viewed them as part of "a nameless, faceless business . . . in this business this is how you look at it. You don't look at it with a face." That view changed, she said, when her older sister asked her for advice on her 401(k) account. Her sister, whom Harrington characterized as one of the hardest workers she knew, was worried that the losses she saw in her retirement account would prevent her from retiring. Suddenly, Harrington "thought about this from a different vantage point," she explains. "I saw one face – my sister's face – and then I saw the faces of everyone whose only asset was a 401(k). At that point I felt the need to try and make the regulators look into [these] abuses."[350]

An unfair stereotype of engineers is that they lack imagination, but all of us tend to have insufficient imagination when it comes to fully considering the impact of our actions on others who are far away in time or distance. Why, for example, did Volkswagen create software that acted as a "defeat device" for government pollution testing? Lots of reasons, of course. But one suggestion is that "[e]ngineers are trained to solve technical problems. They are not always attuned to the collateral damage they may cause."[351] Engineer Deb Grubbe, in speaking about the Piper Alpha fire that killed 167 people on an oil production platform in the North Sea, said:

> As engineers, *we sometimes feel distant or remote from the end result* of what we are working on. If I am working on a product development and I am running into some problems and some things surface that are probably not right *but because I am separated from the end user I might not feel the passion around trying to fix it* because well I'm under a deadline and we're behind and there are money issues. So there's other pressures that I have. I would encourage younger engineers to step back and think about what it would be like if my family or I was going to be using the product that I was working on.[352]

Why did Ford start selling the Pinto car (back in the 1970s) even though it failed all safety tests for a rear end crash? Psychologist John Darley suggests that a major reason was how the (tangible) economic gains of marketing the car overrode the (abstract) danger to potential – but as yet unknown – customers, who hadn't yet bought the car, might never be in a crash, or might be lucky enough to jump out before the car was engulfed in flames. As Darley notes, "Since a good many of the forces that cause people to avoid doing harm to others rely on the salient presence of specific or specifically imagined victims, if such victims are not present then restraining forces are considerably weakened."[353]

How about the mortgage-backed securities crisis that almost crashed the entire world's economy in 2007–2008? Psychologist Dan Ariely hypothesizes:

> Once you've accepted that mortgage-backed securities are the wave of the future, you're at least partially blind to their risks. On top of that, it's notoriously hard to evaluate how much securities are really worth. As you sit there with your large and complex Excel spreadsheet full of parameters and equations, you try to figure out the real value of the securities. You change one of the discount parameters from 0.934 to 0.936, and right away you see how the value of the securities jumps up. . . .
>
> Moreover, you aren't dealing with real cash; you are only playing with numbers that are many steps removed from cash. Their abstractness allows you to view your actions more as a game, and not as something that actually affects people's homes, livelihoods, and retirement accounts.[354]

Author Simon Sinek points out that "[w]hen our relationships with customers or employees become abstract concepts, we naturally pursue the most tangible thing we can see – the metrics."[355] The phenomenon of the tangible and the abstract arguably accounts for the epidemic of cyberbullying across the nation's middle and high schools. Students seem to care more about the number of likes and followers they have than about the harm they cause other students. Sinek notes: "What we've learned is that abstractions can lead people to abhorrent behavior, to act like they're not accountable."[356]

Of course, cyberbullying is bad enough, but it gets much worse. Several scholars have suggested that one reason we keep polluting the planet and ignoring the science on climate change is the fact that the bulk of the harm will be visited upon future generations, who (from today's vantage point) are merely abstract victims.[357] In fact, we are ruining the planet for our children and our grandchildren, but that injury is far enough away that we don't seem to be able to motivate ourselves to make the sacrifices today that are necessary to avoid it. So, the tangible and the abstract bias presents a real danger, and we'd be unwise to ignore its moral implications, especially in our world today.

ETHICS UNWRAPPED RESOURCES

Videos

Tangible and Abstract
Series: Ethics Defined

Tangible and Abstract
Series: Concepts Unwrapped

Case Studies

Climate Change & the Paris Deal

Ebola & American Intervention

Cyber Harassment

Compounding Illness
Scandals Illustrated

Packing Peanuts for Profit
Scandals Illustrated

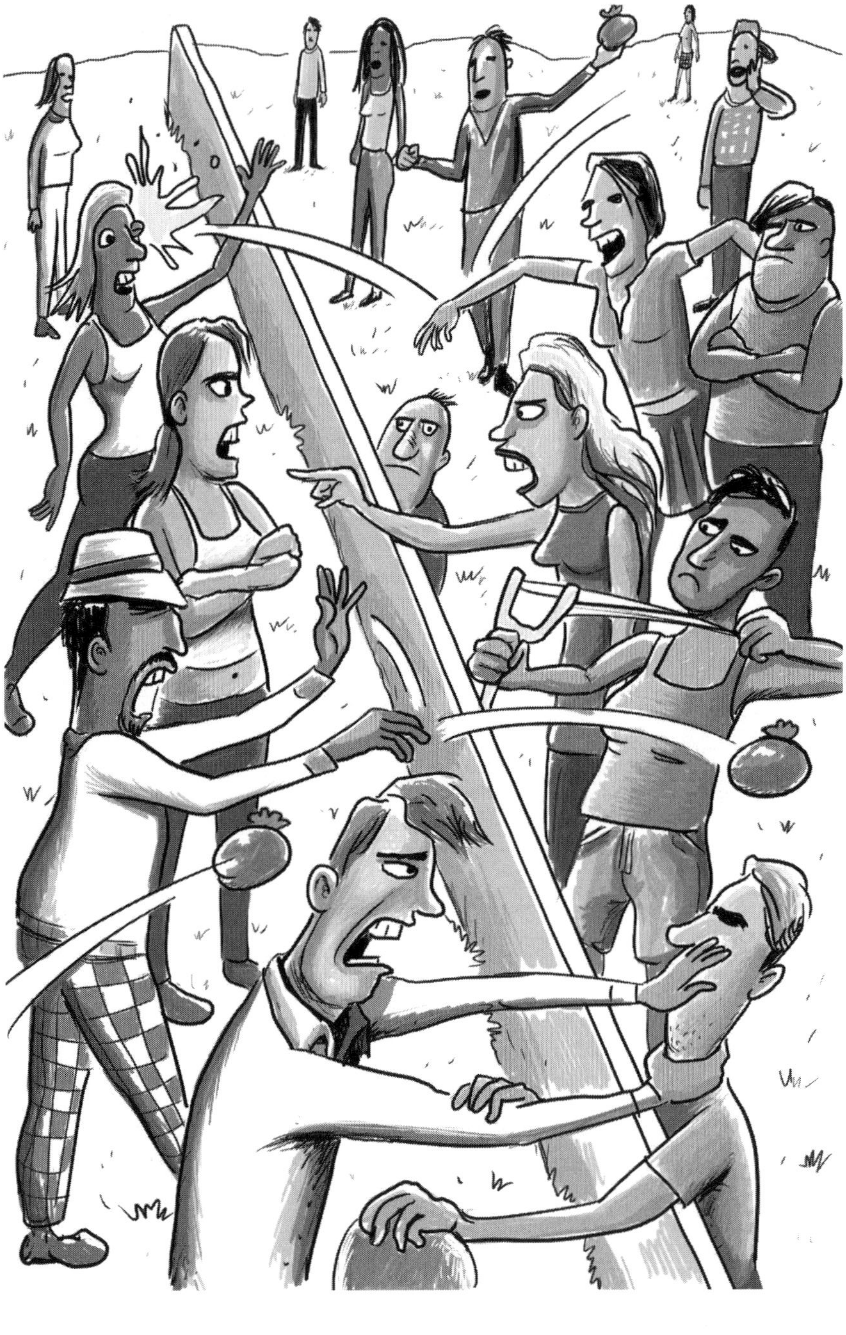

14

IN-GROUP BIAS

"In-group favoritism accompanied by out-group prejudice is one of the best-documented phenomena in all contemporary social psychology."[358]

— *Michael Tomasello*

Introduction

It's pretty amazing how quickly human beings can sort themselves into tribes. And how little it takes to do so. And how significant the consequences of such sorting are for our moral judgments and moral action decisions.

Your authors, being at The University of Texas, hate ALL Aggies – those students and alums from our arch rival, Texas A&M University. Mind you, we've seldom met an individual Aggie whom we didn't find very pleasant and likable, but somehow that doesn't stop us from disliking Aggies when taken as a group. This is a manifestation of *in-group bias*, which causes us to tend to favor people in our in-group over people in an out-group. This unjustified but evolutionarily based favoritism is also called *social identity theory*.

Sorting ourselves into tribes

Psychologist Joshua Greene notes that "our brains are wired for tribalism."[359] For that reason, "in-group favoritism and ethnocentrism are human universals."[360]

One of the most famous experiments in the history of psychology occurred in Robbers Cave State Park in Oklahoma (of all places). Psychologists invited 24 twelve-year-old boys of similar backgrounds (who did not know each other) to a supposed summer camp. The boys were divided into two groups. Each group hiked and swam and bonded over the course of several days, not knowing of the existence of the other group. As they bonded, one group of boys named themselves the Rattlers; the other group named themselves the Eagles. Then, the psychologists brought the two groups together and placed them into competition with each other as they played various games. The two groups of boys battled and antagonized one another with such ferocity that counselors had to intervene to ensure that they didn't hurt each other. It was nearly tribal warfare.[361]

The human inclination to divide ourselves into tribes is likely a product of evolution, which "endowed us with a natural tendency to be kind to our genetic relations but to be xenophobic, suspicious, and even aggressive toward people from other tribes."[362] Over thousands of years, our ancestors survived by banding together to best other groups in competition for resources. As psychologist John Bargh writes:

> So it went, down through the millions of years of our species. We attacked and killed "them" and they attacked and killed "us," at horrific rates by modern standards. Distinguishing us from them, distrusting "them," and helping the others in our own group became things we were born to do. Today, . . . the primordial code still is, Us versus Them, friend or foe, with us or against us.[363]

Author Prentice has occasionally wished aloud for an invasion of aliens from outer space, as in a science fiction movie. It would be traumatic, no doubt, but at least it might bond all people together in joint defense of our planet. Absent such an outside threat, humanity seems destined to continue to divide into rival in-groups – Jews versus Arabs, Democrats versus Republicans, South Koreans versus North Koreans, Liverpool fans versus Manchester United fans, Rattlers versus Eagles. Worse yet, we often sort ourselves into in-groups and out-groups based on the flimsiest of criteria. For example, dressing people in different colors or giving them a common group label, such as "the blue group," can be enough to create that in-group feeling.[364] As long as we continue to divide into rival groups, morally indefensible judgments and morally unattractive behavior seem inevitable.

Moral implications of our tribal sorting

Around the world, there is wide variation among different cultures' moral standards. However, there are a few universal moral values, and one of them has "to do with helping or at least not harming, other people in one's in-group."[365] Too often, when we contemplate what is moral, we're thinking only of our own in-group; we aren't even considering the implications of our actions for out-group members.[366]

As discussed in Chapter 1, because of the *conformity bias*, we tend to adopt the values and views (including the moral views) of our in-group. And, in fact, we often take guidance from out-group members' conduct as to what *not* to do. We also tend to condemn members of out-groups for potentially immoral actions, but give in-group members a pass for doing the exact same things.[367] Indeed, we don't realize that we use different brain circuits to judge in-group and out-group members.[368] These effects tend to be larger in collectivist cultures, as are often found in Asia, rather than in the more individualist American culture,[369] but they are found in the United States as well. Studies show that "[s]uperficial differences grow to be extremely meaningful, leading group members to deny their rivals minds and moral rights."[370]

Because of our in-group biases, "[t]he worst moral offender from an outsider's perspective could be regarded as a moral hero by members of the in-group."[371] For example, because of in-group bias, "for Osama bin Laden, attacking the citizens of the United States seemed like a moral thing to do. A war against terrorism, one that would include the torture of potential terrorists, seemed logical and right to Bush administration officials. Outsiders had different views of all of these moves."[372]

Moral action decisions

In-group/out-group distinctions affect not only our moral judgments regarding others' actions, but also our own moral action decisions. In-group bias, for example, causes us to be drawn to (and wish to help) people who look like us or are otherwise perfectly fitted to be members of our in-group. This can result in "racial inequality without racism," as whites (who hold no conscious bias against blacks) still feel more comfortable spending time around, and bestowing favors upon, those who "look like them."[373]

In general, "people tend to help others in the in-group more than they help people in the out-group."[374] This leads to the phenomenon of *implicit bias*, which we discuss in detail in the next chapter. Research shows that people tend to allocate more resources to in-group members than to otherwise identical out-group members.[375] In one study, students tasked with allocating scholarships between students of their own school and those of another school favored their in-group members.[376]

In Chapter 2, we learned that empathy is one of the most important moral emotions. However, neuroeconomist Paul Zak has noted that "in-group/out-group distinctions can trump empathy and lead to very bad things in part because when we follow the crowd, the dopamine system kicks in, which makes *groupthink* [which occurs when our desire to maintain group loyalty becomes more important than making the best choices] and conformity pleasurable."[377] Also, the beneficial impact of empathy is limited by *empathic bias* (also known as *empathy bias* or *empathetic bias*), which is our tendency to be much more empathetic to members of our in-group than to members of out-groups.[378] Historian Michael Shermer argues that "[o]ur moral nature includes a propensity to be sympathetic, kind, and good to our fellow kith and kin and friends, as well as an inclination to be xenophobic, cruel, and evil to tribal others."[379]

Experiments show that we are more likely to assist someone who has fallen and injured himself if the person is wearing a jersey from the football team we support than if he is wearing the jersey of an opposing team.[380] Behavioral economist Francesca Gino and colleagues have found that in-group loyalty can cause people to cheat more than they would otherwise, in an attempt to advance their group in a competition against out-groups.[381] David Hume, the Scottish Enlightenment philosopher, perfectly described this in-group/out-group prejudice in the 1730s, writing:

> When our own nation is at war with any other, we detest them under the character of cruel, perfidious, unjust, and violent: but always esteem ourselves and allies equitable, moderate, and merciful. If the general of our enemies be successful, 'tis with difficulty we allow him the figure and character of a man. He is a sorcerer: he has a communication with daemons . . . he is bloody-minded and takes a pleasure in death and destruction. But if the success be on our side, our commander has all the opposite good qualities, and is a pattern of virtue, as well as of courage and conduct. His treachery we call policy: His cruelty is an evil inseparable from war. In short, every one of his faults we either endeavor to extenuate, or dignify it with the name of that virtue, which approaches it. 'Tis evidence that the same method of thinking runs thro' common life.[382]

When we dehumanize (or "otherize") out-group members, we free ourselves to act as though they are not *subjects of moral worth*. When we view other people as less than human, very bad things can happen. In one variation of Stanley Milgram's experiment (described in detail in Chapter 4) the participants who heard experimenters speak in dehumanizing terms about "students" who were receiving "shocks" were more likely to escalate the painful shocks when urged to do so by those same experimenters.[383] Genocide almost always involves dehumanization of the victims by the perpetrators.[384]

Minimizing in-group bias

It'll be a wonderful day when members of the human race expand their in-group from the size of small hunter-gatherer bands that wandered across the savanna grasslands to encompass all sentient beings on the planet. Unfortunately, we're still a long way from reaching that ideal state, but there are hopeful signs. A man in New York City, for example, chased down a criminal (who had pushed a woman onto the subway tracks) and held him until the police arrived. He said he did it because "that could have been my mom, it could have been a friend of mine."[385] This man had obviously broadened the circle of people he viewed as being worthy of being treated as in-group members.

Simply being aware of the in-group bias can help us guard against it.[386] Psychologist Jonathan Baron suggests that "[p]arochialism may be reduced by asking people about out-group members as individual people rather than as members of a group."[387] Practicing that should help us UT Longhorns interact more fairly with the Aggies we meet from A&M.

We must also use reason to supplement our natural emotions, such as sympathy. As philosopher Rebecca Goldstein argues, "[r]eason must work to widen the sphere of sympathetic regard, convincing me that what makes the members of my own group worthy of sympathy applies to members of other groups as well."[388]

ETHICS UNWRAPPED RESOURCES

Videos

In-group/Out-group
Series: Ethics Defined

Related Videos

Conformity Bias
Series: Ethics Defined

Implicit Bias
Series: Concepts Unwrapped

Groupthink
Series: Ethics Defined

Subject of Moral Worth
Series: Ethics Defined

Case Studies

*Banning Burkas:
Freedom or Discrimination?*

Welfare Reform

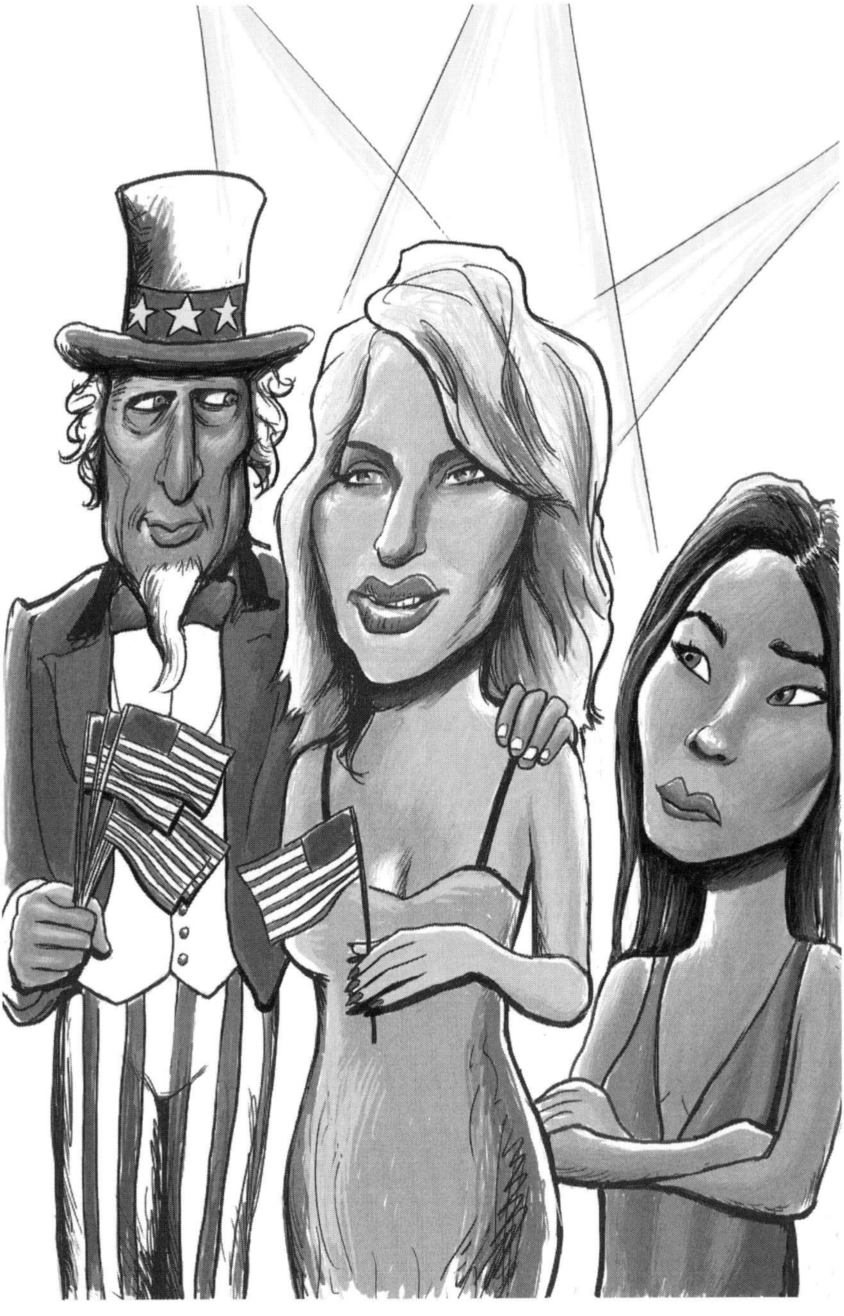

15
IMPLICIT BIAS

> *"[M]any of us are more biased than we realize. And that is an important cause of injustice – whether you know it or not."*[389]
>
> – Keith Payne, Laura Niemi & John Doris

Introduction

Bias undermines fairness – one of the few universal human values – and therefore it can easily lead to judgments and actions that are immoral. As we've seen, effective moral decision making is hampered by many types of internal psychological biases, including overconfidence bias, self-serving bias, role morality, and moral equilibrium. And here's another one: *implicit bias*.

You may be shocked to learn that participants in a study viewed the American-born actress Lucy Liu as less "American" than foreign-born (but Caucasian) Kate Winslet. Perhaps even more shocking, study participants implicitly perceived then-U.S. presidential candidate Barack Obama as less "American" than British-born Tony Blair, then-Prime Minister of Great Britain![390] It's unlikely that most participants would have voted for Winslet and Blair over Liu and Obama on the "Americanism" scale had they put their big brains to work. But reacting instinctively, they did just that.

While it's a good and wonderful thing that *explicit* racial, religious, national origin, gender (and other forms of) bias seem to have abated substantially over time, there has been a regrettable uptick in some of these explicit prejudices in recent years. On balance, however, the trend has been good over the long haul.

Unfortunately, implicit bias – where we *unconsciously* hold prejudices or stereotypes – remains a stubborn factor in ethically-tinged issues.[391] Implicit bias, also called *implicit social cognition*, is deep-seated within the human brain.

We are often culturally induced to be prejudiced (even against our own group) although we generally tend to favor our in-group with positive stereotypes and disfavor out-groups with negative stereotypes.

A disconcerting story

Psychologist Jennifer Eberhardt studies bias and began her book *Biased*[392] with an instructive story. She was on a plane with her five-year-old son, waiting for takeoff. Her son looked around the plane and said, "Hey, that guy looks like Daddy." Dr. Eberhardt checked the fellow out, and he really looked nothing like her husband in terms of age, size, skin color, or hair style. The only commonality was that both men were black. Indeed, this passenger was the only black male adult on the plane. As Dr. Eberhardt prepared to respond, her son blurted out: "I hope that man doesn't rob the plane." Shocked, Dr. Eberhardt asked why he would say such a thing, noting, "You know Daddy wouldn't rob a plane." The boy made a sad face and said: "I don't know why I said that. I don't know why I was *thinking* that." Well, implicit bias may be the reason.

The IAT

You may be saying to yourself: "I'm not prejudiced! I love everybody. There's not a racist (or sexist or ageist or homophobic) bone in my body!" But our implicit prejudices often run counter to our consciously held beliefs, as demonstrated by the Implicit Association Test (IAT) on Harvard University's Project Implicit[393] website. The site contains tests that measure all sorts of implicit biases – e.g., male vs. female, black vs. white, fat vs. thin – and these are available at no cost to all. Give one a try! You'll be asked to associate your selected categories with positive or negative words. The premise is that if you more easily associate positive words with thin people, for example, and negative words with fat people, you are demonstrating an implicit bias against fat people, even if "some of your best friends" are tubby (and you're a little on the chunky side yourself, too).

Now there are limits to how far the IAT can go in conclusively demonstrating the existence and impact of implicit prejudice. The test has been criticized on several grounds,[394] including that people might score differently on different days. Supporters strongly defend the IAT,[395] but even they admit that implicit bias, at least as measured by the IAT, is *relatively minor and generally has only a small impact upon people's real-world actions*. In other words, although there is evidence that implicit bias is widespread, it cannot predict particular behaviors by individual people in a given situation.

Nonetheless, the IAT still indicates how groups of people will act *on average*. For example, the fact that Charlie shows implicit racial prejudice on the IAT does not mean that he will necessarily favor a particular white job candidate. However, it does mean that in a typical job hunt, Charlie and other employers in his position will generally (though unconsciously and modestly) favor a white candidate over an equally qualified black candidate. That is significant and can have meaningful societal impact.[396] Indeed, as well-meaning people, we must be concerned about implicit bias.

Other evidence of implicit bias

Even most critics of the IAT would admit that implicit bias is a real phenomenon. In fact, numerous studies demonstrate biased actions by people who would most likely deny that they are prejudiced in any conscious way. Namely:

- When researchers sent fictitious resumes to help-wanted ads, they found that white-sounding names (Greg and Emily) received 50 percent more callbacks for interviews than black-sounding names (Jamal and Lakisha) *on identical resumes.* This difference was similar across occupations, industries, and employer size.[397]
- In another experiment, would-be clients apparently seeking lawyers received 50 percent more responses if they had white-sounding names than if they had black-sounding names.[398]
- Field studies show that black taxi drivers receive lower tips than white taxi drivers,[399] and that black servers receive lower tips than white servers.[400]
- A study of physicians found no explicit racial bias, but found implicit bias that was correlated with treating white patients (but not identically situated black patients) with thrombolysis.[401]
- Numerous studies show that racial minorities' pain is not treated as aggressively by physicians as is pain suffered by similarly situated white patients.[402]
- A study showed that the more a person implicitly associated good with white faces and bad with black faces, the more likely that person was to shoot unarmed black men (more than unarmed white men) in computer simulation games.[403]
- Data shows that not only are murderers of white people substantially more likely to receive the death penalty than murderers of black people,[404] black defendants whose faces were rated *more* stereotypically black were much more likely to receive the death penalty than black defendants whose faces were rated as *less* stereotypically black.[405]
- In one study, college professors were 26 percent more likely to respond to a student e-mail request to meet in a week when the e-mail was from an apparently white male student as compared to an e-mail from an apparently female or minority student.[406]

Implicit bias, such as the implicit racial bias in the many examples just noted, inevitably causes us to treat some people unfairly based on all sorts of criteria (e.g., race, gender, body mass, sexual orientation) that should be irrelevant to our decision no matter what the context.

In truth, the various behavioral ethics phenomena we've talked about so far – obedience to authority, conformity bias, framing, incrementalism, and the rest – are not universal. These psychological biases don't affect every moral decision made by every person every single time. Usually, they are context specific. But implicit bias is not. And because implicit bias operates mostly at an unconscious level, it's especially difficult to overcome.

People are trying, however. Some research indicates that we may be able to compensate for the effects of implicit bias if we're motivated to do so.[407] There is also research indicating that stereotypes can be unlearned and biases minimized.[408] For example, showing people images of women in positions of leadership[409] or asking participants to imagine what a strong woman is like[410] reduced implicit gender bias in studies. Similarly, the more gay friends we acquire, the less implicit anti-gay prejudice we will likely harbor.[411] Often, these beneficial effects seem not to last too long.[412] However, if we frequently expose ourselves to counter-typical associations, we can certainly improve our chances of acting consistently with our expressed (non-biased) values.

ETHICS UNWRAPPED RESOURCES

Videos

Implicit Bias
Series: Concepts Unwrapped

Case Studies

Meet Me at Starbucks

The Miss Saigon Controversy

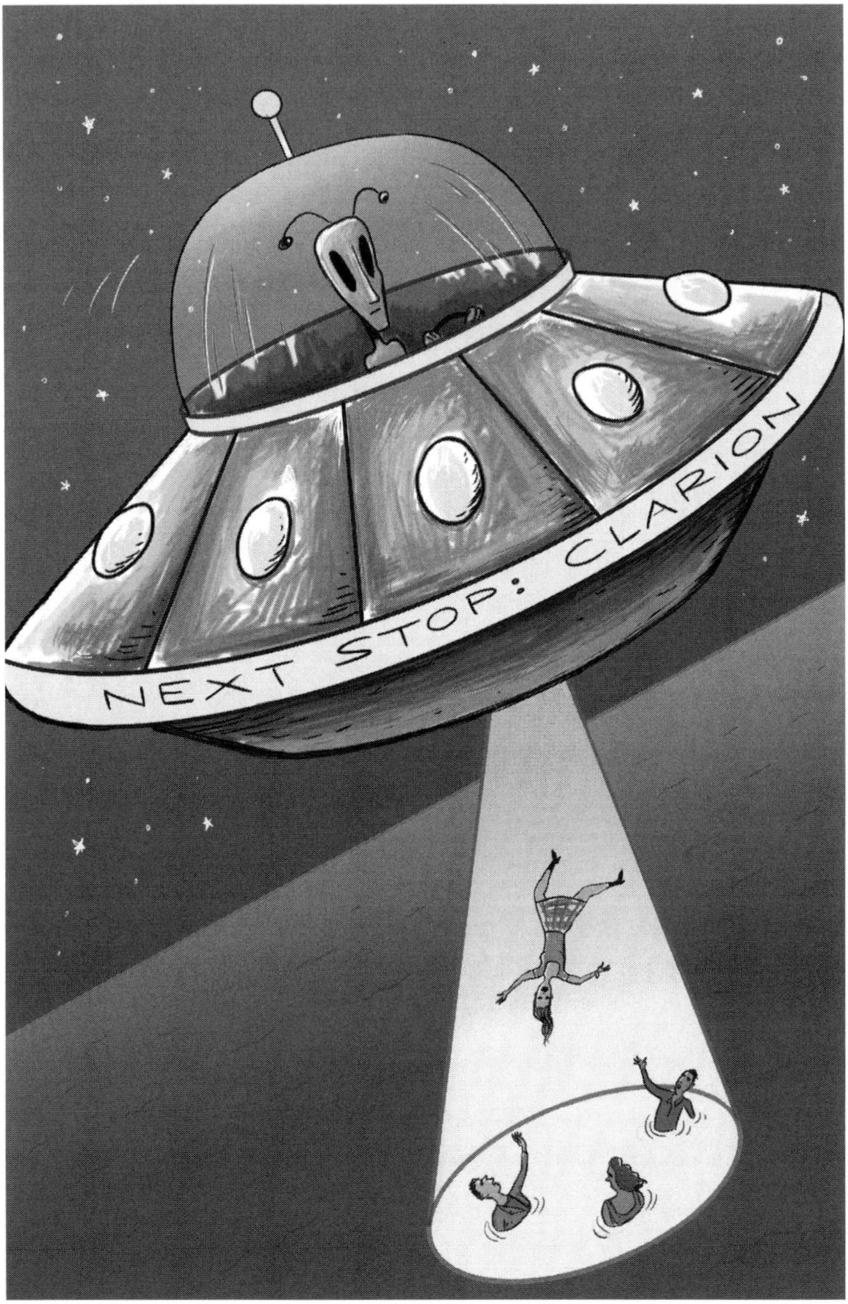
NEXT STOP: CLARION

16

COGNITIVE DISSONANCE

> "Sometimes people hold a core belief that is very strong. When they are presented with evidence that works against that belief, the new evidence cannot be accepted. It would create a feeling that is extremely uncomfortable, called cognitive dissonance. And because it is so important to protect the core belief, they will rationalize, ignore and even deny anything that doesn't fit in with the core belief.[413]
>
> – Frantz Fanon

Introduction

In 1954, Chicago housewife Dorothy Martin (who'd been involved in science fiction writer L. Ron Hubbard's Dianetics movement) announced that aliens from the planet Clarion had informed her that our world was coming to an end. All land masses were going to sink to the bottom of the sea, and a flying saucer would visit the earth and rescue only Dorothy Martin and her followers. This apocalypse was to occur before dawn on December 21, 1954. Martin's followers gave away their possessions in anticipation of the catastrophic event, and gathered outside her house on the appointed day.

As you may have sussed out by now, December 21 came and went with absolutely nothing happening. No sinking of the continents. No appearance of spaceships. Martin's followers sat in stunned silence for several hours until (surprise!) Martin received a *new* message from planet Clarion that the end of the world had been called off, largely thanks to the actions of Martin's spunky little band.[414]

Cognitive dissonance

One would think that when a prophecy doesn't come to pass, followers might lose confidence in their prophet. But no! Instead, Dorothy Martin's followers doubled down; most of them seemed to believe in her even more after the solstice apocalypse hadn't come to pass. Don't be too surprised. This outcome is consistent with the aftermath of numerous end-of-the-world predictions over the centuries.

Psychologist Leon Festinger wrote a book about Martin's cult with two colleagues called *When Prophecy Fails*.[415] In it, and a later book,[416] Festinger firmly established the concept of *cognitive dissonance*. Cognitive dissonance is the psychological discomfort we feel when our minds entertain two contradictory concepts at the same time. For example, we may firmly believe that the world is about to end, but when the world doesn't end at the appointed hour, we'll still wish to believe that there is some explanation (other than our extreme gullibility). Or, perhaps less dramatically, we may believe strongly in our party's candidate for governor, yet learn she has committed a wrong that we'd previously viewed as disqualifying. We still want to vote for our candidate, so our mind may try to find ways to view her wrongdoing as not so bad after all – in other words, we rationalize.

Moral dissonance

When cognitive dissonance has a moral dimension, it's called *moral dissonance*.[417] Moral dissonance often involves a mismatch between our moral values and our (or others') immoral actions.

Other biases may come into play as well to stimulate moral dissonance. For example, assume you're part of a group whose members wish to do something that you would normally find morally questionable. Because of the conformity bias, you want to get along with the group. But the clash between your moral beliefs and your desire to get along with the group may cause you to suffer moral dissonance. And studies show, in fact, that you may resolve that dissonance by aligning your views with the views of the group's majority.[418]

Some years after the failed Planet Clarion prophecy, one of Leon Festinger's students – psychologist Elliot Aronson – wrote:

> If a modern Machiavelli were advising a contemporary ruler, he might suggest the following strategies based upon the theory and data on the consequences of decisions:
>
> - [1] If you want someone to form more positive attitudes toward an object, get him to commit himself to that object.
> - [2A] If you want someone to soften his moral attitude toward some misdeed, tempt him so that he performs that deed;
> - [2B] conversely, if you want someone to harden his moral attitudes toward a misdeed, tempt him – but not enough to induce him to commit the misdeed.[419]

Pharmaceutical companies have learned the first lesson well. By paying physicians to give talks about how effective certain drugs are, companies sway those physicians to more frequently prescribe those drugs themselves.[420] Presumably (viewing themselves as good people), the doctors can make the talks, and accept the money, only by convincing themselves that the drugs really do work. Psychologists Janet Schwartz and Dan Ariely interviewed sales reps from pharmaceutical companies, and found:

> [The reps would hire] physicians to give a brief lecture to other doctors about a drug they were trying to promote. Now, the pharma reps really didn't care about what the audience took from the lecture – what they were actually interested in was the effect that giving the lecture had on the speaker. They found that after giving a short lecture about the benefits of a certain drug, the speaker would begin to believe his own words and soon prescribe accordingly.[421]

Lesson 2A from Elliot Aronson is also reinforced by solid research. Philosopher and legal scholar David Luban noted: "In situation after situation, literally hundreds of experiments reveal that when our conduct clashes with our prior beliefs, our beliefs swing into conformity with our conduct, without our noticing that this is going on."[422] In other words, we may think that adultery (or tax evasion or insider trading) is a terrible deed, until we do it ourselves. Then we may well think of a whole bunch of reasons why (at least in our particular circumstances) these activities aren't so bad after all. These reasons help us resolve our moral dissonance.

Lesson 2B also makes sense. If we've managed to resist temptation, we will probably conclude that others should also be strong enough to resist temptation – and that if they don't, they are bad people. Indeed, our sense of moral superiority gets the better of us, and we judge others more harshly.

Cognitive dissonance and law enforcement

Consider the situation of a law enforcement official who has played a significant role in the imprisonment of a criminal defendant. Perhaps the alleged crime was a serious one, and the prison sentence a long one. No one is going to feel good about being part of a *wrongful* conviction. The moral dissonance may be overwhelming if evidence later arises indicating that the prisoner is innocent. The officer may even try to resolve his or her dissonance by discounting the evidence in some way.

In a frightening book, *Blind Injustice*,[423] former prosecutor Mark Godsey shows example after example of how prosecutors and police officers have rejected the most compelling scientific evidence of innocence (and argued for the most ridiculous propositions imaginable) in order to resolve such moral dissonance. One example is particularly bone-chilling. In 1968, a grandmother was raped and murdered in the middle of the night in her own living room. Then, in a nearby bedroom, her six-year-old granddaughter was raped, beaten, and left for dead. However, she survived. When asked by the police to describe her attacker, whom she had seen for only a few seconds in the darkness before she was knocked unconscious, the six-year-old said that he *looked like* her uncle Clarence. After a couple of rounds of questioning by the police, they had converted that to it *was* Uncle Clarence and they concluded that he (Clarence Elkins) was the perpetrator. After that point, virtually every piece of evidence that was uncovered pointed away from Clarence Elkins as the perpetrator, but none of it swayed the police and prosecutors who had made up their minds.

Elkins' wife testified that Elkins was with her several miles away in their home. She had been up most of the night with a sick child and would have known if he had left. She certainly had no strong motive to protect the killer of her own mother. Although the murder house was a bloodbath, there was not a single fingerprint or hair traceable to Clarence. Nor could the police find blood on any item belonging to Clarence. They even looked in his shower drains to see if there was any blood from the victims. Nope. Nonetheless, the prosecution convicted Elkins, who had no criminal record, and sent him to prison for life.

When DNA testing advanced, the Ohio Innocence Project (OIP) had new DNA tests performed that found semen from a male in the grandmother's vaginal cavity and skin from the same male on the panties of the six-year-old girl. The DNA did not match Elkins. He clearly was not the perpetrator. Yet, when the OIP asked for Elkins' exoneration, the prosecutors and police fought like wildcats with the most ridiculous arguments that one can imagine. Even when the DNA was matched with a prisoner with a history of violent crimes (who resembled Elkins) and had been living just two doors away from the victims and *admitted* the crime, the prosecutors still argued that Elkins was guilty, which is a typical prosecution reaction to exonerating DNA evidence. Indeed, police officers and prosecutors are so eager to believe that they did not send an innocent person to jail that cognitive dissonance causes their minds to accept the most outlandish theories and to reject the most compelling evidence. And, in fact, their actions caused Elkins to remain in jail much longer than he should have given the overwhelming evidence of his obvious innocence.

Mark Godsey also explores the Central Park jogger case in *Blind Injustice*. In 1989, five teenagers confessed to raping and beating a jogger in Central Park. Although the teenagers quickly retracted their confessions, blaming them on police coercion, and no physical evidence linked them to the crime, the police and prosecution made up their minds. They charged and convicted all five teenagers, even though semen in the victim came from only one person. Donald Trump called for their swift execution in a full-page newspaper ad. Thirteen years later, another man, who had been convicted of several other rapes in the area, confessed to the crime. His DNA matched the semen recovered from the victim, and that should have led to the Central Park Five's immediate release.

Unfortunately, the lead prosecutor continued to maintain that the five teens were guilty, and that the man with the only physical link to the crime must have been the sixth rapist. The head detective was outraged that anyone would believe this man's confession, saying: "This lunatic concocts this wild story and these people fell for it." This is how hard the prosecution and police wished to believe that they were *not* the reason five innocent young men went to jail for 13 years for something that they didn't do.[424]

Corporate cognitive dissonance

Moral dissonance is a phenomenon that affects each of us individually, of course. But when several people inside an organization all suffer from moral dissonance, it can be viewed as a case of *corporate cognitive dissonance*. In his book on the Volkswagen "Dieselgate" scandal, author Jack Ewing characterized "[t]he deployment of defeat devices at the same time that Volkswagen trumpeted its commitment to the environment" as an "extreme case of corporate cognitive dissonance."[425]

Mitigating moral dissonance

The psychological pain of moral dissonance can, of course, be mitigated by doing the right thing, and in that way ensuring that our actions match our self-concept. Boom! End of problem.

Unfortunately, there are also numerous psychological mechanisms we can use to mitigate moral dissonance without doing the right thing. One such mechanism is *ethical amnesia*, where our memories of our wrongful actions often become less clear and vivid than other memories.[426] Psychologist Julie Irwin and colleagues found, for example, that many people believe strongly in being ethical consumers, but sometimes really want to purchase something that might not conform to their values. Their study showed that people's memories can conveniently fail in order to enable the "unethical" purchase: "No one enjoys feeling torn. The easiest way for conscientious shoppers to avoid this inner conflict is to yield to their consumerist whims by forgetting details that might trigger ethical concerns."[427]

Self-deception is another promising mechanism for alleviating moral dissonance. For example, workers in dangerous jobs who don't want to quit either have to live with fear or resolve the dissonance by convincing themselves that their jobs are not so dangerous. They often do the latter.[428] Similarly, people in jobs that ask them to engage in questionable practices either must live with the moral dissonance "or convince themselves that their choices are ethically neutral."[429]

We often recruit *rationalizations* to dilute or defeat moral dissonance, too. We'll discuss rationalizations at length in Chapter 21, but here's a brief introduction to two categories of rationalization – denial of victim and denial of injury.

Denial of victim is a classic rationalization[430] where we say to ourselves: "I know I shouldn't have done that, but they deserved it." Russell Wasendorf, who went to prison for stealing $215 million from his clients, also overstated his brokerage's revenues by $200 million in order to pretend to have satisfied capital requirements established by regulators. He minimized the moral dissonance his fraud created by concluding that the regulators had treated him in a mean-spirited fashion, and had therefore "asked for it." "I have to say I don't feel bad having deceived the Regulators," Wasendorf said.[431] Wasendorf is not alone. Psychologists who study moral dissonance are quite familiar with self-justification based on blaming the victim.[432]

Denial of injury is another classic rationalization where we say: "I know I shouldn't have done that, but no one was *really* hurt." Organizational psychologists Debra Comer and Gina Vega point out that we "convince ourselves that behaving at odds with our values does not matter much because what we do has only a trivial impact on others."[433] In other words, we see our bad actions as only having a small impact on others, or we make it appear less than it actually is.

Willful blindness is yet another mechanism for coping with moral dissonance. We can minimize the dissonance by ensuring that we remain as ignorant as possible about the consequences of our actions.[434] For example, if we drive a Hummer and suspect that there might be something to this climate change thing, we may purposely avoid any news stories about the climate. In short – what we don't know, we can't feel bad about.

Moral compensation (which we studied in Chapter 12) can also dilute moral dissonance. In this case, we know we've done something that didn't match our moral standards, but by doing something good, we can compensate for it. Behavioral ethics researchers Max Bazerman and Ann Tenbrunsel point out that when we do something we know we shouldn't do,

> so strong is the need to [reduce moral dissonance] that researchers found in one study that offering people an opportunity to wash their hands after behaving immorally reduced their need to compensate for an immoral action (for example, by volunteering to help someone). In this study, the opportunity to cleanse oneself of an immoral action – in this case, physically – was sufficient to restore one's self-image; no other action was needed.[435]

Whether by washing our hands, or temporarily "forgetting," or minimizing our knowledge, or one of the many other ways in which we create *moral disengagement*, the bottom-line result is the same: ethical blindness and moral wrongdoing. We'll talk more about the various mechanisms of moral disengagement in Chapter 21. The best way to avoid moral dissonance, of course, is to do the right thing.

ETHICS UNWRAPPED RESOURCES

Videos

Cognitive Dissonance
Series: Concepts Unwrapped

Related Videos

Rationalizations
Series: Ethics Defined

Jack & Rationalizations
Series: In It To Win

Case Studies

The Central Park 5

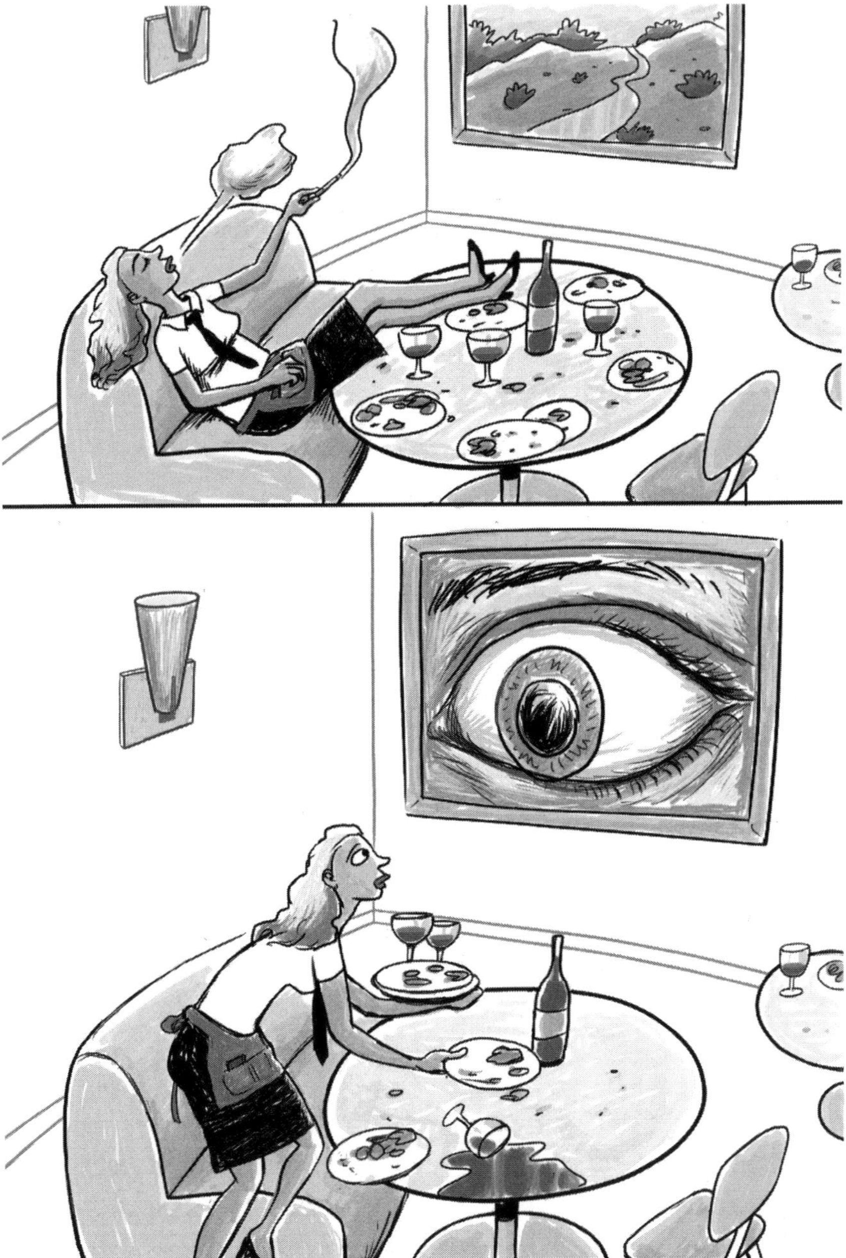

17
GENERAL SITUATIONAL FACTORS

> *"The experimental record suggests that situational factors are often better predictors of behavior than personal factors. . . . To put things crudely, people lack character."*[136]
>
> – John Doris

Introduction

Character counts – a lot. But it probably doesn't count as much as we tend to think it does. It seems to us that because we *want* to be good people and because we were raised right (or read the right books, or took the right classes, etc.) we will do the right thing today, tomorrow, and always. But of course, it turns out that it's not that easy.

First, character can be derailed by all the social and organizational pressures and cognitive heuristics and biases discussed in previous chapters. In addition, a surprising number of situational factors – forces that often go unnoticed – can affect our decision making in all sorts of ways. These factors can even affect our moral judgments and moral action decisions, sometimes overriding our good character.

A fascinating experiment undertaken decades ago began to articulate some of these situational forces. Let's go back to a time before the prevalence of cell phones when the landscape was dotted with pay phone booths (for those of you too young to have seen a phone booth, think of Dr. Who's TARDIS). In the experiment, psychologists had an accomplice walk by a phone booth and drop a bunch of papers right after the person making a phone call had hung up. Sometimes, the psychologists put a dime (free money!) in the phone's change slot, which would make any caller happy because this was back in the day when you could actually buy something with a dime. Of the callers who had just found a dime (and were likely in a good mood) 88 percent helped the person who dropped the papers. But only 4 percent of callers who did not find a dime helped at all. The study indicated that simply being in a good mood made it 22 times more likely that people would engage in prosocial conduct.[437] Another experiment found that people were much more likely to do a favor for a stranger (in this case, give change for a dollar) if they were near a good-smelling bakery than if they were near a neutral-smelling dry goods store.[438]

While many experts believe that character is the dominant factor in determining whether someone will act in a moral fashion in a given situation,[439] other experts – called *situationalists* or *situationists* – believe that situational factors often dominate character.[440] Your authors see merit to both positions, but this chapter emphasizes various situational factors ("Hey, I just found a whole dime!") that impact our moral decision making in ways that are often unnoticed. As economist Daniel Houser and colleagues note:

> When humans are given the chance to behave dishonestly (e.g., they have the opportunity to cheat to their own advantage), [economist Gary] Becker predicted their behavior would be determined by the costs and benefits of their actions. In fact, the decision to act dishonestly seems to be influenced by a much broader set of variables than these.[441]

Philosopher Christian Miller surveyed the psychological studies on moral character and action and concluded:

> Lesson 1: There are many situations in life where most people will demonstrate the finest forms of moral behavior. . . . Lesson 2: There are many other situations where most people will exhibit the worst forms of ethical behavior. . . . Lessons 1 and 2 apply to the *very same people*. In other words, it isn't just that there are a bunch of "good people" who usually act well, and then a different bunch of "bad people" who usually act poorly. Rather, the upshot is this: Lesson 3: For most of us, we will behave admirably in some situations and then turn around and behave deplorably in other situations. . . . Lesson 4: Our changing moral behavior is extremely sensitive to features of our environment, and often we do not even realize what those features are.[442]

In this chapter, we'll survey some of the most important of these environmental features. Your authors stress, however, that the scientific studies discussed here are often controversial, more than with any other chapter in this book. Not every psychologist is convinced that these findings are solidly established.

Time pressure

In one study, seminary students were asked to record a talk on either the parable of the Good Samaritan or on what jobs seminary students subsequently enjoy the most. The experimenters set up three conditions – one in which the students were not in much of a hurry, one in which they were in a hurry, and one in which they were *really* in a hurry. On the way to record the talk, all the participants walked past an accomplice of the experimenters who was lying in an alley apparently in distress. This decoy needed a Good Samaritan. But the study showed that the topic the students were about to speak on had no impact on their actions. Their degree of haste did. Sixty-three percent of the participants in the "low hurry" group stopped to help, 45 percent of those in the "medium hurry" group also stopped, but only 10 percent in the "high hurry" group made time for the person in distress. In other words, subjects who were really in a hurry were only one-sixth as likely to stop to help as those who were not in a hurry. It's unlikely that any of the people realized how time pressure affected their actions.[443] In fact, when other people are told of this experiment, they often

> remain insistent that someone who scuttled past the groaning man must be particularly black of heart, rather than merely a pawn of his pressing affairs. . . . They were no more sensitive to how we are all influenced by our current situation than were other students who knew little about the original experiment.[444]

Several other studies have also indicated the adverse impact that time pressure can have on our moral decision making. For example, auditors engage in more unethical behavior when faced with time pressure.[445] And time pressure has been cited as a contributor to ethical lapses ranging from Enron to Abu Ghraib by organizational behaviorists Joshua Margolis and Andrew Molinsky, who note that "moral leadership can easily be compromised when time is scarce."[446]

Lack of transparency

In the *Republic*, Plato's character Glaucon tells the tale of Gyges, a shepherd who found a gold ring that rendered him invisible. Gyges exploited his invisibility by seducing the queen, killing the king, and seizing control of the kingdom. Glaucon suggested:

> No man would keep his hands off what was not his own when he could safely take what he liked out of the market, or go into houses and lie with any one at his pleasure, or kill or release from prison whom he would, and in all respects be like a God among men. Then the actions of the just would be as the actions of the unjust.[447]

One of your authors (Biasucci) agrees with Glaucon, and the other (Prentice) is not quite as down on humanity. But Glaucon is correct that (in general) an ability to hide our actions tends to not move them in the right (ethical) direction. Supreme Court Justice Louis Brandeis famously argued that sunlight is the best disinfectant and electric light the best policeman.[448] He had a point – transparency (or lack thereof) significantly affects human moral decision making.

As we've discussed in other chapters, many experts believe that social norms – including moral ones – evolved to enable people to live together cooperatively. Philosopher Jeremy Bentham realized (a couple of centuries ago) that "it is sufficient for people to know that they are *seeable*, that there is the potential for them to be judged, evaluated, and punished. Being seeable is enough to trigger us to restrain our unsocialized impulses through self-control."[449] Psychologist Jonathan Haidt further suggests that:

> Moral psychology is the operating system of human social life. To the extent that we're able to interact with strangers it's because we create these dense webs of moral norms and then we judge each other relentlessly on them and know that we'll be judged, and that's what makes it all work."[450]

This web of moral norms does tend to work pretty darn well. The effect of this constant monitoring is that "simply being watched keeps people mostly in line most of the time."[451] The moral emotions (such as shame, embarrassment, etc.) kick in and constrain our impulses to do wrong, as we discussed in Chapter 2.

We shouldn't be surprised, therefore, that increased use of security cameras induces better behavior. It led to a 65 percent drop in soccer hooliganism in one experiment.[452] Other studies have found that increased monitoring reduced cheating by students[453] and diminished corruption in a public hospital.[454] Indeed, dozens of studies indicate that we will commit fewer wrongs and act more pro-socially if we are prompted to feel, even subconsciously, that we are being monitored. One study showed that we will act worse if we are alone than we will in the presence of a child, or even of a dog.[455] In another study, a psychologist "accidentally" dropped a big stack of papers in front of a person. That person was 30 percent more likely to help pick the papers up in the presence of a security camera.[456]

Astonishingly enough, just being in the presence of a *drawing* of eyes has such a psychological impact on people that it seems to cause them to:

- Be more diligent about bussing their own tables in a self-service cafeteria.[457]
- Contribute three times as much to an honesty box used to pay for drinks in a university coffee room.[458]
- Be more generous in playing "public goods games" where they are asked to decide how much of a windfall to keep and how much to contribute to a shared resource.[459]
- Be more generous in a "dictator game" where they are asked to decide how much of a windfall to keep and how much to share with another person.[460]
- Litter less.[461]
- Recycle more.[462]
- Donate more to a charity bucket.[463]

Studies also show that people will feel more like they are being watched when prompted to think of God (the "eye in the sky") and will therefore interact more prosocially, at least if they're believers.[464] Interestingly, being in the presence of a mirror also subtly cues people to feel that they are being monitored. Studies demonstrate that a mirror will:

- Cause people to make less selfish decisions regarding fairness.[465]
- Reduce cheating (by ten times as much in one study).[466]
- Make children less likely to violate a social norm (by five times as much in one study).[467]

Why does a mirror have such an impact? Philosopher Christian Miller suggests that it has to do with our ability to deceive ourselves:

> If a person can (subconsciously) deceive himself into not comparing this act of cheating with his moral norms, then the threat to his self-concept is diminished. That is why a seemingly trivial variable like the placement of a mirror can have such a dramatic effect on behavior. The mirror gives the person much less room to hide. With increased self-awareness, the difference between what the person's moral beliefs require and his temptation to cheat is made especially salient, so that it becomes that much more difficult for participants to deceive themselves into thinking they are still honest.[468]

Along those same lines, studies reveal that brighter lighting will make people subconsciously feel more exposed to observation and lead them to cheat less.[469] On the other hand, wearing a Halloween costume will make children feel less observed, dramatically increasing stealing (of candy) behavior.[470] Likewise, wearing sunglasses will make adults feel less scrutinized, thereby reducing their prosocial behavior.[471]

Primatologist Frans de Waal says simply: "Watched people are nice people."[472]

Self-control exhaustion

Self-control is important for morality. It takes self-control to resist the various temptations that come our way. In fact, psychologist Paul Bloom suggests that lack of self-control may be the biggest reason psychopaths act as they do (rather than having a lack of empathy, as other experts have suggested).[473]

There is evidence that self-control wanes over time, even for us non-psychopaths.[474] This is called *ego depletion*. Stress and tiredness also make it more difficult for people to act morally, at least in part because those forces adversely impact self-control.[475] Indeed, we can exhaust our "moral muscle." For example, nurses who were sleep-deprived due to long shifts at the hospital showed depleted self-control and increased workplace deviance.[476]

One study found that judges were more likely to grant paroles at the beginning of the day, and right after scheduled food breaks, than they were at other times when they were more tired or hungry.[477] Similarly, studies show that fatigue can make people more likely to cheat or be dishonest.[478] Numerous studies have demonstrated that people, given the opportunity to cheat in order to "earn" a reward, are much more likely to do so if they have engaged in a previous activity that depleted their self-control.[479] Studies also show self-control depletion causes people to be less prosocial.[480] We can use up our self-control, for instance, when we diet, train for marathons, or just work really long hours.

Clearly, self-control is important and, in part, defines our character, but it has limits. As psychologist Walter Mischel noted:

> President Clinton had the self-control and delay [of gratification] ability to win a Rhodes Scholarship, attain a Yale law degree, and be elected to the presidency, apparently combined with little desire – perhaps no ability, and certainly no willingness – to exert self-control for particular temptations like junk food and attractive White House interns. . . . [L]ike all skills, self-control is exercised only when we are motivated to use it. The skill is stable, but if the motivation changes, so does the behavior.[481]

In other words, if we dismiss what people say and observe what they actually do, studies show that people aren't consistent in their social behavior. While not all scientists are convinced that self-control depletion has a significant impact on moral decision making and behavior, it seems to us that it's worthwhile to keep our eyes on this human vulnerability.

Money changes everything

Cindy Lauper sang that "Money Changes Everything," and she was right. In fact, thinking about money often seems to change our preferences in an antisocial way. In one study, two groups of people were given a choice between an activity that was more social and one that was more solitary. The members of the group who were prompted to think about money were much more likely to choose the solitary activity than members of the other group, who were not prompted to think about money.[482]

In another study, people in a group primed to think about money:

- Were less helpful when others asked for assistance.
- Were more reluctant to ask for assistance themselves.
- Donated less to charity.
- Maintained greater social distance when meeting someone new.
- Chose more often to work alone rather than with a peer.[483]

In yet another study, participants primed to think about money chose to work more (and socialize less) than similar participants not so primed.[484] And in one recent longitudinal study, the researchers found that lottery winners tended to vote more conservatively and value equality for all classes *less* after hitting the jackpot.[485] All of these studies point to the fact that being influenced (even subconsciously) by money tends to lead people to separate themselves from others, be more isolated, less social, and less caring.

But, does money influence people to *act* less ethically? At least one study indicates yes. Participants in one group were primed to think about money, while those in the other group were not. Then everyone was asked how likely it was that they would do something unethical like take a ream of paper from work when they'd run out at home. A significantly higher percentage of money-primed subjects indicated that they would do the unethical acts. Other money-primed subjects in the study also:

- Lied more often to other subjects in a deception game where they could profit by lying.
- Lied more often to the experimenters to gain monetary rewards.
- Were more likely to say that they would hire a job candidate who promised to bring a competitor's confidential information (if hired).

The authors concluded that priming people to think of money caused them to evaluate their decision in a business frame, which freed them to ignore the consequences of their decisions for others.[486]

Although some of these studies are controversial, one expert did a meta-study and concluded:

> Money priming experiments (totaling 165 to date, from 18 countries) point to at least 2 major effects. First, compared to neutral primes, people reminded of money are less interpersonally attuned. They are not pro-social, caring, or warm. They eschew interdependence. Second, people reminded of money shift into professional, business, and work mentality. They exert effort on challenging tasks, demonstrate good performance, and feel efficacious.[487]

All of us but the most money-hungry have other values – aside from those associated with work success – that we would like to embody. We all need to be aware that when we work in an environment where the goals, incentives, and metrics are money-oriented, it will certainly be more difficult to advance nonmonetary values such as honesty, transparency, integrity, and ethics. As business ethics scholar John Hendry wrote:

> In the limited, abstract world of finance, . . . money *is* the measure of everything.
>
> One danger of working in such an abstract world is that when moral issues do arise, they aren't recognized, partly because people aren't looking for them and partly because the language – in this case the language

of monetary calculations – has no way of expressing them. Just as money can't buy love, or goodness, or right or wrong, it also can't easily measure or represent them in a net present value calculation.[488]

Minimizing situational influences

Simply knowing that we may be influenced by these various situational factors is the first step to minimizing their adverse impact. As with all the pressures and biases discussed so far, we can't guard against something that we don't know exists: "[K]nowledge is power. Once people recognize ways in which they are prone to situational influences, they may be better at resisting them."[489]

Time

Time pressure can warp our perspective, and interfere with good judgment. When making important decisions that we know will have moral implications, we should take our time, if it's at all possible to do so. It is also beneficial to take the time to get *other* people's points of view, and to take advantage of their wisdom. Research shows that the act of slowing the process down means that we ourselves will likely make better decisions.

Money

As with time pressure, money can also be a corrupting influence. An acquaintance of ours owned a check-cashing business and told us that most employees she hired saw the cash they handed to customers as just the "inventory" of the business. Those who couldn't see money in that light (but saw it as M-O-N-E-Y!) usually didn't last very long. Along the same lines, financial journalist Michael Lewis comments:

> The question I've always had about this army of young people with seemingly endless career options who wind up in finance is: What happens next to them? People like to think they have "character," and that this character of theirs will endure, no matter the situation. It's not really so. People are vulnerable to the incentives of their environment, and often the best a person can do, if he wants to behave in a certain manner, is to choose carefully the environment that will go to work on his character.[490]

Transparency

Clearly, a lack of transparency can prevent us from being our best selves, too. Feeling insulated from scrutiny can lead us to lower our moral guard. We can help ourselves by using "the newspaper test" – and using it often. If we can truly envision our planned action being covered on the front page of the newspaper or on social media, we will probably choose not to do it if it's truly unethical. Business scholar Eugene Soltes interviewed Sam Waksal, who went to jail for insider trading. As Soltes reports:

> Sam Waksal remembers one of the first conversations he had with his lawyer, Lewis Liman, after being indicted for committing securities fraud in conjunction with his insider trading. "I kept saying to him that I didn't really do anything wrong," Waksal recalls. "Lewis said to me, 'Sam, would you have done the same thing if you were being filmed?'" Waksal remembers pausing to think about the question and soon responded: "Probably not."[491]

Ultimately – newspaper test or no – it's up to us to think carefully (and continuously) about how our actions would look in the harsh light of day. If we can do that, it will help us stay on the straight and narrow.

Self-control

Of course, exhausting our reservoir of self-control is definitely problematic and can interfere with our best intentions. Getting enough sleep, and carefully monitoring ourselves when we face temptations are good ideas. Psychologists Daniel Wegner and Kurt Gray suggest:

> Self-control is one domain where psychology actually does offer some pretty good tips on how to increase agency. The general tip is to *never rely on self-control*. . . . The best way to assert self-control is never put yourself in situations where you have to exert it, and instead focus on structuring your environment such that succumbing to temptation is impossible.[492]

Conclusion

Philosopher David Edmonds notes:

> The [situationist] research is a blow to the idea that character traits are stable and consistent, that the brave person will always be brave, the stingy person stingy, and the compassionate person compassionate. This has implications for government and education policy. Perhaps we should be focusing more on shaping conditions than character.[493]

So, given that situational factors significantly influence our moral decisions and actions (and conditions may be beyond our control), it's critical that we keep *working on our character!* Some studies indicate, for example, that people with strong moral identities – who sincerely and seriously wish to be good people – are less likely to act in a self-centered way than are other people.[494] And, additional studies have found that some people just don't cheat, even when the temptation is high. Their character serves them well.[495]

As we've discussed previously, some research indicates that people with an acute sense of guilt tend to be among the most moral folk around, while people with low moral character commit more than their share of harmful behaviors. Psychologists Taya Cohen and Lily Morse study moral character, and they conclude: "The impact of moral character on ethical and unethical behavior is significant and consequential."[496]

At the end of the day, don't forget what philosopher Jonathan Glover says:

> There are two truths. One is that people with different characters respond very differently to moral crises. There is a difference between those who go along with murder and those who do not. . . . However, the sense of moral identity does not always hold people back from doing terrible things. It may fail in several ways.[497]

This chapter has highlighted some of those ways.

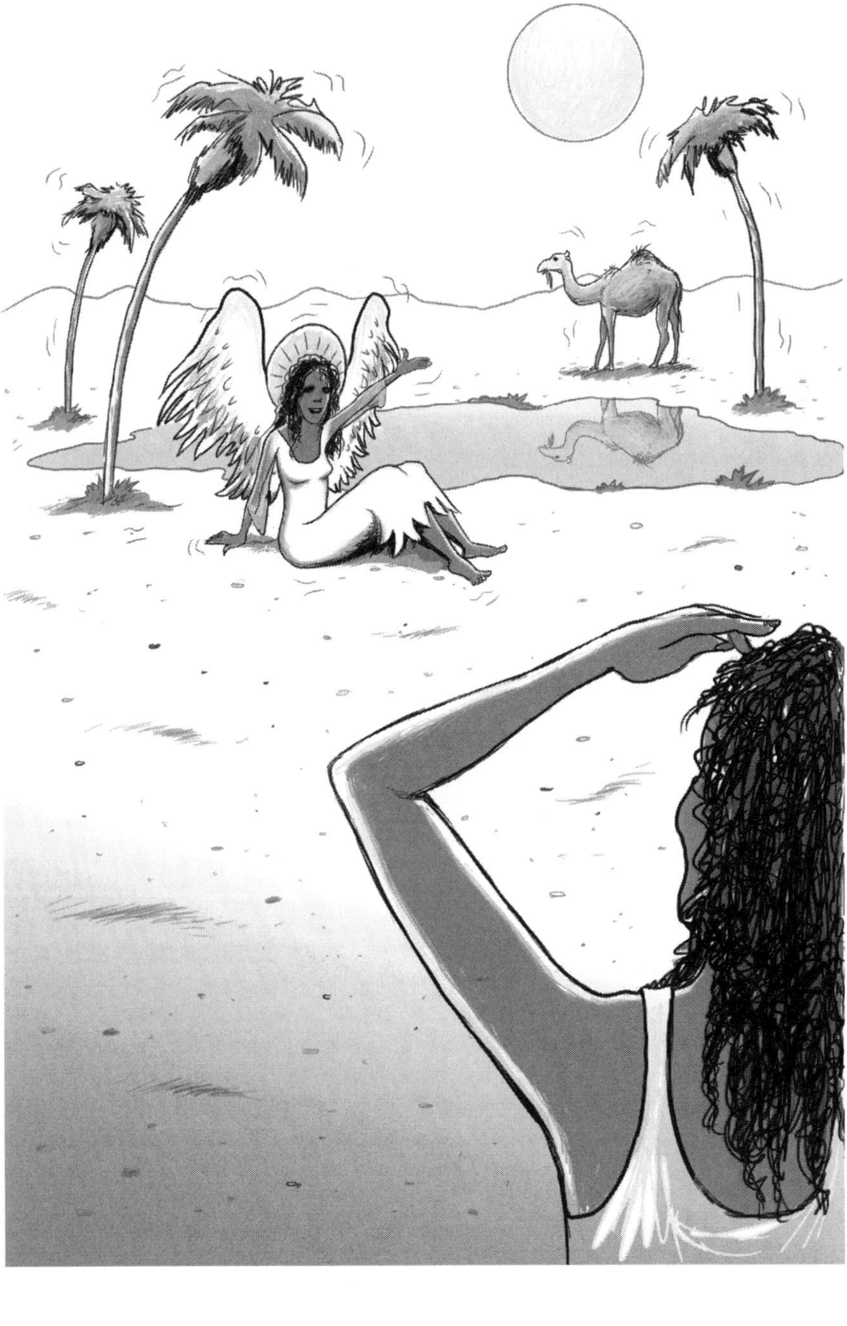

18
TEMPORAL FACTORS

"[W]omen's preferences for anesthesia in childbirth changed with the time horizon. Perhaps not surprisingly, women preferred to avoid anesthesia prior to active childbirth, preferred anesthesia during childbirth, and once again turned against anesthesia one month after childbirth."[498]

– John Payne, John Bettman & Eric Johnson

Introduction

Although this book has already given you many reasons to be concerned about pressures, biases, and other factors that might sabotage your moral decision making, your authors know (from the research) that it's difficult for you to fully believe that you, too, will be affected. After all, you want to be a good person, you were raised the right way, you read the right books, you took the appropriate philosophy class, and so on. We will make another attempt to convince you that it's really hard to be the kind of person your dog thinks you are every day . . . no matter how you were raised or what you've learned or done since. If you don't fully appreciate this fact, you leave yourself open to unintended moral error and its many consequences. You've been warned!

In this chapter, we draw primarily from an article entitled "The Ethical Mirage: A Temporal Explanation as to Why We Aren't as Ethical as We Think We Are," by psychologists and business ethics scholars Ann Tenbrunsel, Kristina Diekmann, Kimberly Wade-Benzoni, and Max Bazerman.[499] This article provides a very useful lens through which to view the many ways in which good people can err. It focuses on the situational factor of time. This is not just *time pressure*, which we've discussed in previous chapters, but the factor of *time passing*.

About time

Psychologists and other scientists have long known that time is a factor that influences our decision making,[500] including our moral decision making.[501] Time affects our preferences, for example. As we discussed in Part I, economists used to model human decision making as perfectly rational, assuming that a) if you prefer a chocolate bar next Tuesday to an apple next Wednesday, that b) you'd also prefer the chocolate to the apple on a Tuesday and a Wednesday a month from now, a year from now, and a decade from now. In other words, these models assume peoples' preferences stay stable, and are the same over time. However, studies have shown that over time, our preferences often reverse. For example, Tonya might prefer a chocolate bar on Tuesday of this week to an apple on Wednesday, but thinking about her preferences four weeks from now may prefer the apple on Tuesday, not the chocolate bar.[502]

Studies also show that when we think about movies we might watch in the future, we tend to give more weight to movies that we think we *should* watch, like documentaries. But when we're choosing movies to watch *right now*, we may well find ourselves watching something much more frivolous. At some level, we know we should watch enlightening documentaries, but when push comes to shove, we choose to watch the mindless rom-com.[503]

Time pressure affects our moral frameworks, too. If we must decide a moral question quickly, for example, we will tend to act intuitively and emotionally (as we've seen in earlier chapters). We also are more likely to apply a deontological, rule-based framework if we are rushed. However, if we are urged to take our time in deciding and be thoughtful, we're more likely to invoke our reasoning (Kahneman's Systems 2 faculties) and ultimately apply a utilitarian framework.[504]

As we have also already seen, the passage of time impacts our moral judgments and moral action decisions. If there is a change in our environment over time, we slowly adjust. The change becomes the "new normal," and this lays the groundwork for the potentially insidious impact of incrementalism.[505]

Time delays may also impact our ethical (and legal) decision making in part because of the notion (or burden) of delayed gratification. Megan, for example, may want a new Porsche and be willing to work for four years to save enough money for a down payment. Pat may want the same Porsche, but not have Megan's self-control, so she decides to embezzle the money at her job now for an immediate down payment.[506] Unsurprisingly, studies show that heroin addicts tend to have greater difficulty delaying rewards than other people.[507] Indeed, when under the influence of drugs and alcohol, our brain's executive function – the higher order part of the brain that makes decisions – is suppressed, and we tend to act impulsively and without deliberation.

Of two minds

So, let's get back to the "Ethical Mirage" paper by Dr. Tenbrunsel and colleagues. We tend to be of two minds: the *"should" self* and the *"want" self*.

On the one hand, we want to be good people and do the right thing. This is our "should" self in action – the metaphorical angel sitting on one shoulder telling us to be good and to do good. On the other hand, we also want stuff. We want food, and drink, and sex, and power. We want to please the boss, to get along with other people, to get raises and promotions, to be seen as successful, and so on. Like Oscar Wilde, we can resist anything except temptation![508] This is our "want" self in action – the devil sitting on the other shoulder, telling us not to worry so much about right and wrong.

In other words, we want to tell the truth to our customers about the product we're selling, but we also want to close the sale and earn the promised commission. We want to be honest and transparent with our family, but we also want to avoid conflict at family gatherings so we defer and dissemble when discussing politics (or religion or whatever the "touchy" topic is) in those settings. So, as human beings, we are in constant tension between our "should" and "want" selves.

Poor predictors

Not only are we torn between two minds, often we are also very poor predictors of what will happen. For example, we are relatively bad at predicting what will make us happy in the future.[509] We think that a new car or a new house will make us happy, but studies show that a month later we're often much poorer than before but no happier.[510] We buy gym memberships but vastly overpredict how often we'll actually go exercise. Of course, gyms know this and often sell 20 times more memberships than they have capacity for.[511] And, studies show that young people who predict their sexual activity (e.g., Will I wear a condom? Will I engage in unusual sex acts?) are often incorrect because they fail to consider how being sexually aroused will impact their future decision making.[512]

We often err in predicting how ethically we will act in the future, and the research tends to show three things:

- We tend to be overly optimistic regarding how ethically we will act in the future.
- We tend to remember being more ethical than we actually were.
- When we act, we often fail to act as ethically as we had predicted that we would or (for that matter) as ethically as some day we will remember that we did.

Why this mismatch?

Why do we mispredict our future ethical actions? Well, when we sit around thinking about how morally we'll act in the future, we are focusing totally on ethics as our frame of reference. As we've learned, framing always heavily influences our decisions.

We often seem to assume that ethical issues will be obvious – the issues will announce themselves and capture our attention, "Hey! Good person! Do the right thing here!" However, like fog, ethical issues often sneak in on little cat feet. Our vision is obscured. We don't even notice the moral challenge because we're fully occupied thinking about some other aspect of the situation.

Remember the overconfidence bias from Chapter 6? In addition to being distracted by our frame of reference, we tend to be utterly confident in our own moral character. We think we're more ethical than our friends, our competitors, our peers (than Mother Teresa, for Pete's sake!), so naturally we believe that we'll do the right thing when an ethical challenge arises. This is another reason we err in predicting our future ethical actions.

Unfortunately, in these ways and others, we're often not taking into account our bounded ethicality (discussed in Part I). We are ignoring the human tendency to be obedient to authority and to conform to the behavior of those around us. We're ignoring the overconfidence bias, the self-serving bias, implicit bias, and other psychological biases. We're ignoring the impact of situational factors like money or a lack of transparency. Or, if we're not ignoring these influences altogether, we are likely underestimating their impact on our moral decisions and actions. Indeed, we bet that even though you're almost done with Part I, you're still probably underestimating the impact of these factors and forces on your *own* moral judgments and decision making. Put simply, it's very difficult to get these lessons through to our own minds, and to truly believe that we're more susceptible to ethical failings than it might seem.

Why do we remember our ethical actions incorrectly?

Although it seems to us that our brains are a repository of movies about all the moments of our lives,[513] in truth our minds reconstruct our memories. When our mind is performing that reconstruction, it's inevitably impacted by the self-serving bias and other influences that affect the accuracy of our memories:

> When we recall our own memories, we are not extracting a perfect record of our experiences and playing it back verbatim. Most people believe that memory works this way, but it doesn't. Instead, we are effectively whispering a message from our past to our present, reconstructing it on the fly each time.[514]

Our "should" self tends to reconstruct our memories in such a way as to preserve our moral self-esteem. Social psychologist Albert Bandura notes that "in the mix of doing good and bad things, people remember the good things they have done but recall less of the harmful ones. When people are socially influenced to behave punitively, their recollection is that the harm done was less severe than was actually the case."[515] In other words, we will tend to remember our actions as less harmful than they actually were.

Studies highlight the phenomenon of *ethical amnesia* (also known as *motivated forgetting*), which is the tendency for memories of our bad behavior to gradually become less clear than other memories, in order to preserve our self-image.[516] Some studies, for example, show that soon after cheating at a task, participants tend to misremember the rules they were told and how they acted.[517] This ethical amnesia can mitigate the moral dissonance created by the clash between our positive self-image and our wrongful actions.[518]

In fact, when we reconstruct our ethical lives, we tend to think of bad stuff that we did a long time ago, but good things that we did more recently. This way, as we look at our lives, we can tell ourselves a story of constant improvement (in the arc of our moral lives) building toward perfection.[519] Ultimately, though, as researchers Ann Tenbrunsel and colleagues found, "[w]hile convenient for our self-esteem (and even our happiness), the selective memory mechanism represents a barrier to an accurate understanding of our ethical selves and thus impedes our ability to strive for higher levels of ethics in our everyday lives."[520]

So the bottom line here is this – our self-serving memories make it easier to feel like we're being ethical, but harder to accurately assess our actions and thus to act ethically.

We act less ethically than we predict we will (but remember a different story)

When we're thinking about our future ethical lives (or remembering our past ethical lives), we're focusing on the ethical aspects of the decisions we will face (or did face) and likely minimizing the other factors and influences present in the situation. However, when it's actually time to act in real life, the ethical issues often fade away and we don't notice them. The "should" self may hibernate, or at least take a catnap. More tangible factors – such as the desire to succeed, to get along with others, to please the boss, to gain the wealth (or recognition or fame) that most of us desire, and so on – may come to the fore instead. In other words, the "want" self may dominate.

Consider the following studies, all of which describe our tendency to believe that we're more ethical than we actually are, and to predict that we'll act more ethically than we actually do.

In one experiment, a number of young women were asked how they would react if a male job interviewer asked them sexually harassing questions, such as: "Do you have a boyfriend?" and "Do men think you're 'hot'?" Almost every one of the women predicted that they would refuse to answer the question, or would get up and walk out, or would complain to the interviewer's supervisor as soon as the interview was over. Then, the experimenters placed a group of similar women in what they thought were real job interviews. The male interviewer asked them similarly harassing questions. Not one of the women walked out or protested in any way. Because these women were now focused on the job (that they thought they were interviewing for) their "want" selves dominated their "should" selves. Their physical response to the improper questions (such as crossing arms and legs) indicated that they knew the questions were inappropriate, but their desire for the job prevented them from objecting in the moment, or afterwards.[521]

In a different experiment, nurses were asked what they would do if a doctor (who was not on staff) called and asked them to inject a patient with a drug that was not on the hospital's approved list. Thirty-one of thirty-three nurses answered that they would not give the injection. Then the experimenters staged just such a phone call to nurses actually on duty at a hospital. Twenty-one of twenty-two nurses were preparing to give the injection when they were stopped by the experimenters! Again, the nurses predicted how they would act from their "should" self, focusing on their professional ethical standards. But the action decisions were made by the nurses' "want" self, concentrating on their desire to please the doctor and be obedient to those in a position of authority.[522]

Another study tested college students. An accounting professor asked his students how they would act if their employer accidentally put too much money in their paycheck one week. Some students predicted that they would tell the employer of the mistake. Others predicted that they would keep the money. Later in the semester, the professor handed back an exam with obvious grading errors that granted students too many points. Some students called the professor's attention to the error. Some did not, and quietly kept the undeserved points. What was especially significant – there was *no correlation* between the students who had predicted they would report the erroneous paycheck and those who did report the erroneous grade.[523]

Yet another study on college students asked a group of students to provide the names of fellow students who might serve as subjects for an experiment. Then the students were told something along the lines of:

> We will be testing the impact of sensory deprivation on brain function. When we did this before at another university, the results were traumatic. The subjects panicked and found it a frightening experience. But we want to continue the study, so I need you to write a testimonial to the students whose names you have provided telling them that you have agreed to participate and that it will be "exciting" and "incredible." Do not mention the negative effects in the previous experiment. This will mean money for you.

The students were left alone twice during this exercise, and could have left. Additionally, they were given a clear opportunity to anonymously blow the whistle on the experiment if they thought it violated ethical norms. When the experiment was described to 138 students, only 3.6 percent predicted that they would write the letter, 44 percent predicted they would refuse, and 37 percent predicted they would refuse and blow the whistle. But when the experiment was run on 149 other students, 77 percent complied, only 14 percent refused, and just 9.4 percent blew the whistle.[524]

In another experiment, 50 percent of college students (when surveyed) predicted that they would speak up if they were in the presence of someone who said racist things to a minority student. But when experimenters set up a scenario where exactly that happened, only 16 percent of students said anything.[525] According to psychologists Nicholas Epley and David Dunning (who conducted similar experiments with college students), participants "consistently, and grossly, overestimated the likelihood that they themselves would act in a selfless and altruistic manner, whereas the predictions made about others tended to converge more closely with reality."[526]

Conclusion

There are more studies, but you get the idea. As human beings, we tend to predict that we will act more ethically than we actually do when the time comes. We often overestimate the influence of the angel on one shoulder and underestimate the influence of the devil on the other.

Research by scholars Kristina Diekmann, Ann Tenbrunsel, and Adam Galinsky found that if we think about the motivations we'll be feeling at the time we have to make a decision and take action, we can better align our behavioral forecasts with our actual behavior.[527] We can try to balance the needs of the "should" self and the "want" self.

Tenbrunsel and colleagues suggest in "Ethical Mirage" that the most important thing we can do is to increase the "should" self's influence when we take action. When we keep ethics in our frame of reference at all times, we don't lose focus and become a victim of ethical fading. However, when ethics fade from view we are often putting our attention elsewhere. Perhaps we're focusing on pleasing our boss or meeting a deadline. That is when we are most likely to ignore our "should" self. Tenbrunsel and colleagues also suggest (quite sensibly) that, in order to better align our predictions of our behavior with what we actually do, we must tamp down the influence of our "want" self when we take action as well. In Chapter 21, we'll explore some avenues to help bolster our "should" self and muffle our "want" self.

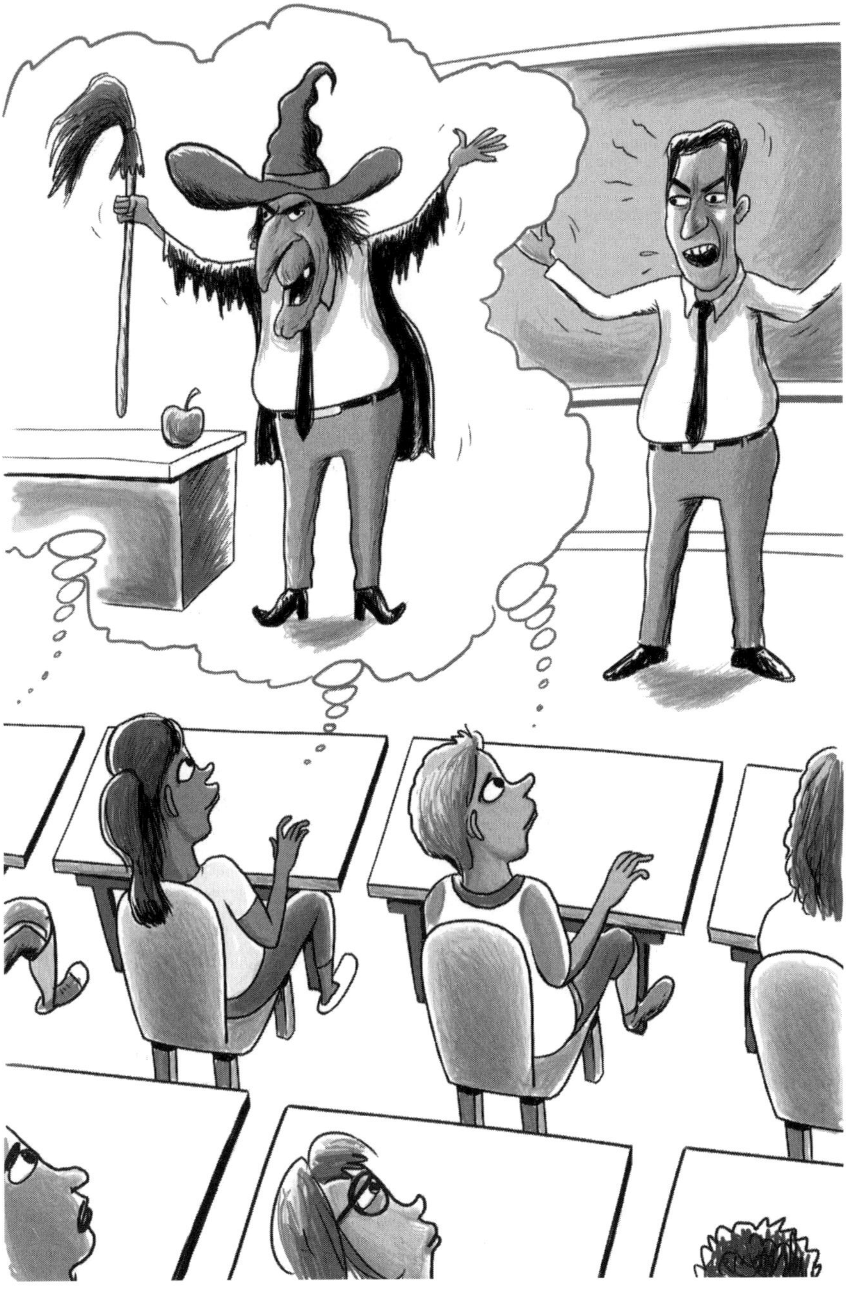

19
FUNDAMENTAL ATTRIBUTION ERROR

> *The fundamental attribution error . . . is one of the main reasons why we grossly underestimate our capacity to behave unethically. We fail to properly appreciate the power of the situations, and its ability to shape how we respond.*[528]
>
> —Dennis Gentilin

Introduction

We know from the previous two chapters that our ethical decisions are often significantly impacted by various situational factors. The *fundamental attribution error* (FAE) is the tendency we have to overemphasize personal characteristics and ignore these situational factors in judging *other people's* behavior.[529] This tendency is also known as the *correspondence bias*,[530] the *dispositional bias*, and *lay dispositionism*.[531]

As psychologists John Sabini, Michael Siepmann, and Julia Stein write in their seminal article on FAE:

> What are the important findings of social psychology since World War II? Were one to survey social psychologists with that question, we believe that many would give something like the following answer: Social psychologists have discovered that, to a far greater degree than laypeople realize, and that social psychologists had previously realized, people's behavior is caused externally (by situations) rather than internally (by disposition). The tendency to underestimate the degree to which behavior is externally caused has been called the Fundamental Attribution Error (FAE).[532]

Because of the fundamental attribution error, "[p]eople have a tendency to think others are how they act,"[533] even if they've viewed only one instance of behavior.

We may see someone fighting and conclude that he has a violent temper when, in actuality, he may be fending off an attacker.[534] The FAE effect is generally stronger when the behavior is negative rather than positive.[535]

As psychologists Dan Gilbert and Patrick Malone put it:

> When people observe behavior, they often conclude that the person who performed the behavior was predisposed to do so – that the person's behavior corresponds to the person's unique dispositions – and they draw such conclusions even when a logical analysis suggests they should not.[536]

Of course character counts. A fundamentally honest person is likely to tell the truth most of the time. A pathological liar is not. A generally decent person will treat people well most of the time. A complete jerk will not. But as noted previously, people's behavior is also often significantly influenced by external factors. The psychological evidence is overwhelming that under the right conditions, "[g]ood people can be induced, seduced, and initiated into behaving in evil ways."[537]

Indeed, we may act differently than we typically would if:

- We are exhausted because we just got off a long shift at work.
- We are hurried because we just got a call that our spouse is ill and can't pick up the kids at day care.
- We are sad because we just received news that a close friend has been diagnosed with cancer.
- We are anxious because our company is going to announce its latest round of layoffs later in the week.

And so on.

FAE studies

Academics have had a lot of fun studying the fundamental attribution error over the years:

- In one experiment, students were paired up. One student was encouraged to ask difficult, esoteric questions to the other in a "quiz game." Although the questioners had an obvious advantage in that they could create questions that matched their own preexisting base of knowledge, observers tended to conclude that the students who were asking the questions were more knowledgeable than the students who were given the role of answering the questions.[538]
- In another study, psychologists asked subjects to assess people's true attitudes toward former Cuban dictator Fidel Castro based on essays that those people had written. Although the subjects knew that people were assigned to write

either pro- or anti-Castro essays, they still inferred that those who wrote pro-Castro essays were more pro-Castro and those who wrote anti-Castro essays were more anti-Castro. Somehow, they managed to largely ignore that the essayists had no choice in which view they took.[539]
- In yet another study, participants tended to attribute a teacher's exhibition of anger to the teacher's natural disposition, even if the subjects were aware that the anger was in response to student misbehavior.[540] Students might say: "Mr. Helmer really lost it when we had that spitball fight in class today. He is such a jerk!"

FAE causes

One psychological factor that reinforces the FAE is the bias of the tangible and the abstract (discussed in Chapter 13), where our minds are more heavily influenced by immediate factors than by remote or abstract factors. When we observe another person, the actions we see are tangible. Psychologists have long concluded that "[b]ehavior . . . has such salient properties that it tends to engulf the field. . . ."[541] In other words, the behavior of another person is all engrossing to us, and we often miss everything else. The situational factors that may have influenced that person's actions are probably unknown to us, and so will likely be underweighted or discounted by us. This phenomenon has been called *the invisibility problem*.[542]

FAE and ethics

Why do we talk about the FAE in an ethics book? First and foremost, it often causes us to make judgments about other people's actions, intentions, and character that are both erroneous and unfair. We've all done things that we shouldn't have (and probably now regret). But doing one bad thing doesn't necessarily make us a bad person. However, the FAE may cause other people to draw that conclusion anyway. For example, if we see Jamila act more honestly in a situation than Sofia did, we tend to not only conclude that Jamila is a more honest person than Sofia, but also to predict that in similar situations in the future, Jamila will consistently act more honestly.[543]

However, probably because of situational factors, the correlation between how honestly we act in separate incidents over time is low. In other words, our tendency to lie (or otherwise misbehave) varies greatly depending upon the situation.[544] And, according to one study, the impact of the FAE helps to explain why human beings are such poor lie detectors.[545]

The actor-observer bias

The second reason that the FAE is very important to ethics is its inverse – the *actor-observer bias* (also called the *situational attribution bias*). This bias causes us to underestimate our own unethical behavior by *overestimating* the impact of situational factors.[546]

In the throes of the actor-observer bias, for example, we might say: "The other guy cheated on his test because he is a bad person. I cheated on my test because I was too sick to study." Or, "She manipulated earnings because she is a crook. I manipulated earnings because my boss made me." Or, "He cut in line in front me because he's an inconsiderate oaf. I cut in line because I was running late to pick up my kids."

When judging other people's actions, we typically know little of their situations. But, we are well aware of our own. And because of the self-serving bias and the overconfidence bias, we just know that we are good people who will do good things. So if we make an ethical error, we reason that our screw-up must be because of outside factors. It couldn't possibly be *our* fault! In fact, because of this actor-observer bias, we often "grossly underestimate our [own] capacity to behave unethically."[547]

The third base effect

Historian Michael Shermer suggests that yet another phenomenon caused by the FAE is what we might call the *third base effect*. People who are born on third base often erroneously conclude that they have hit a triple. Because good things have happened to them, they conclude that they must deserve those good things, and that other people (who haven't been born to such fortunate circumstances) must not be as deserving.

Shermer points to research by social psychologist Paul Piff and colleagues, which shows that randomly giving certain players more money or more properties in a Monopoly game caused those players to act more privileged and entitled.[548] When these privileged players won the game, they felt proud (as if they deserved to win) even though their own skill and judgment had little to do with the game's outcome.[549]

Piff's studies also show that rich people often feel entitled. They think that their success must be due to their innate qualities (such as intelligence and hard work). They discount the situational – the good luck, or introductions to the "right people" that they may have had, for example. Even children of rich people tend to feel entitled, even though they may have done nothing to deserve their bounty, and simply had the good fortune of being born to wealthy parents.[550]

As with all psychological biases, the fundamental attribution error is not universal. It doesn't apply to all people in all circumstances. But FAE has been found across cultures,[551] genders, ages, incomes, and levels of education.[552] In various studies, the percentage of people influenced by the FAE ran from slightly more than 50 percent to 86 percent.[553] Indeed, the impact of the FAE, of the actor-observer bias, and of (what we've called) the third base effect, are influential enough that we should all guard against their potentially deleterious effects on our moral judgments and actions.

ETHICS UNWRAPPED RESOURCES

Videos

Fundamental Attribution Error
Series: Ethics Defined

Fundamental Attribution Error
Series: Concepts Unwrapped

Case Studies

Limbaugh on Drug Addiction

Michael Flynn: Under Investigation
Scandals Illustrated

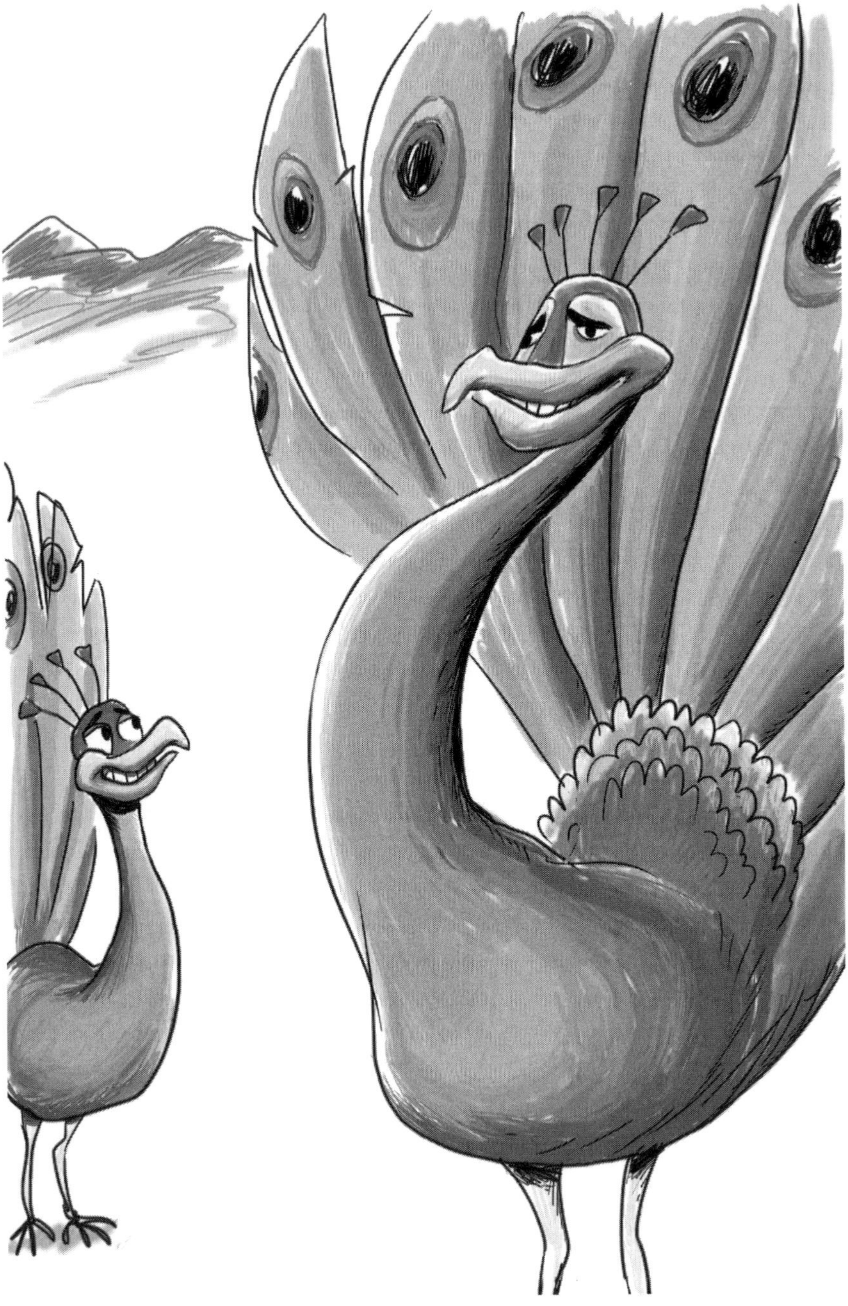

PART II

How to improve your chances of living a life you can be proud of

Part I of this book focuses on explaining why good people sometimes do bad things. The four chapters in Part II, on the other hand, take a broader look at ways to mitigate the problems caused by bounded ethicality. Think of it as tips on how to be your best self.

James Rest has noted that there are four key steps to doing the right thing,[554] and we have adjusted those slightly here to argue that being your best self requires:

- Moral awareness
- Moral decision making
- Moral intent
- Moral action[555]

First, *moral awareness* is critical. To be a good person, you must be able to recognize ethical challenges when they appear. As we've seen in Part I, factors such as the self-serving bias, obedience to authority, the conformity bias (and the rest of the biases, pressures, and circumstances we've discussed) often blind people to the ethical dimensions of the choices they face. *Ethical fading* and *moral myopia* – which is a distortion of moral vision that keeps ethical issues from coming clearly into focus[556] – are real problems. Chapter 20 will discuss moral awareness as part of a big-picture approach to mitigating the various roadblocks you face in living an ethical life.

Second, once you recognize a moral choice, then *moral decision making* requires you to be able to come to a defensible resolution of the issue. This may mean reading a little philosophy, but not often. Usually a little deliberation, and perhaps some consultation with trusted friends or advisors, can lead us to justifiable, good-faith conclusions. But often we will reach our decisions intuitively and nearly automatically, with no true reasoning involved. The first three chapters in

Part I explained how emotions (and other factors) can adversely affect our moral decision making, and this topic will receive attention in the next chapter as well.

Third, if you realize that you face an ethical challenge and formulate a defensible moral choice, you still must have *moral intent* – a desire to do the right thing. Most people generally want to do the right thing. However, sometimes self-interest, or the desire to protect a family member, or to help a friend, or to be loyal to our company or our group can cause us to choose to do the wrong thing. Chapter 21 focuses on *rationalizations* and other mechanisms of *moral disengagement*, which provide the primary avenues by which we sometimes decide that we don't really want to do the right thing. We give ourselves permission (just this once, of course!) not to live up to our own ethical standards.

Fourth and finally, even if we're aware of an ethical challenge, know what the right thing to do is, and wish to do the right thing, we may still fall short if we can't engage in *moral action*. Moral action can require courage. Moral action may also be ineffective if we don't know how to articulate our values persuasively to others. Borrowing liberally from Mary Gentile's book *Giving Voice to Values: How to Speak Your Mind When You Know What's Right*, Chapter 22 will teach you how to effectively stand up for the right thing.

In the last chapter of this book, we address organizations (and organizational behavior) rather than people (and individual behavior). Using the teachings of behavioral psychology, behavioral economics, and related academic fields, people have recently been *nudged* to engage in certain behaviors (such as saving money) and to avoid other behaviors (such as littering) by governments, corporations, and other organizations. In Chapter 23, we use that same literature to show you how to make it easier to do the right thing, and harder to do the wrong thing, for people in your organization.

Living a life you can be proud of   **171**

ETHICS UNWRAPPED RESOURCES

Videos

BYBS, Pt. 1: Moral Awareness
Series: Concepts Unwrapped

BYBS, Pt. 2: Moral Decision Making
Series: Concepts Unwrapped

BYBS, Pt. 3: Moral Intent
Series: Concepts Unwrapped

BYBS, Pt. 4: Moral Action
Series: Concepts Unwrapped

Related Videos

Bounded Ethicality
Series: Ethics Defined

Ethical Fading
Series: Ethics Defined

Moral Myopia
Series: Ethics Defined

Rationalizations
Series: Ethics Defined

ETHICS UNWRAPPED RESOURCES

Case Studies

*Teaching Blackface:
A Lesson on Stereotypes*

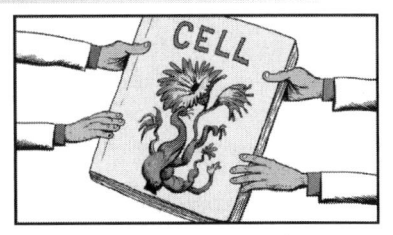

*Retracting Research:
The Case of Chandok v. Klessig*

*Christina Fallin:
"Appropriate Culturation?"*

High Stakes Testing

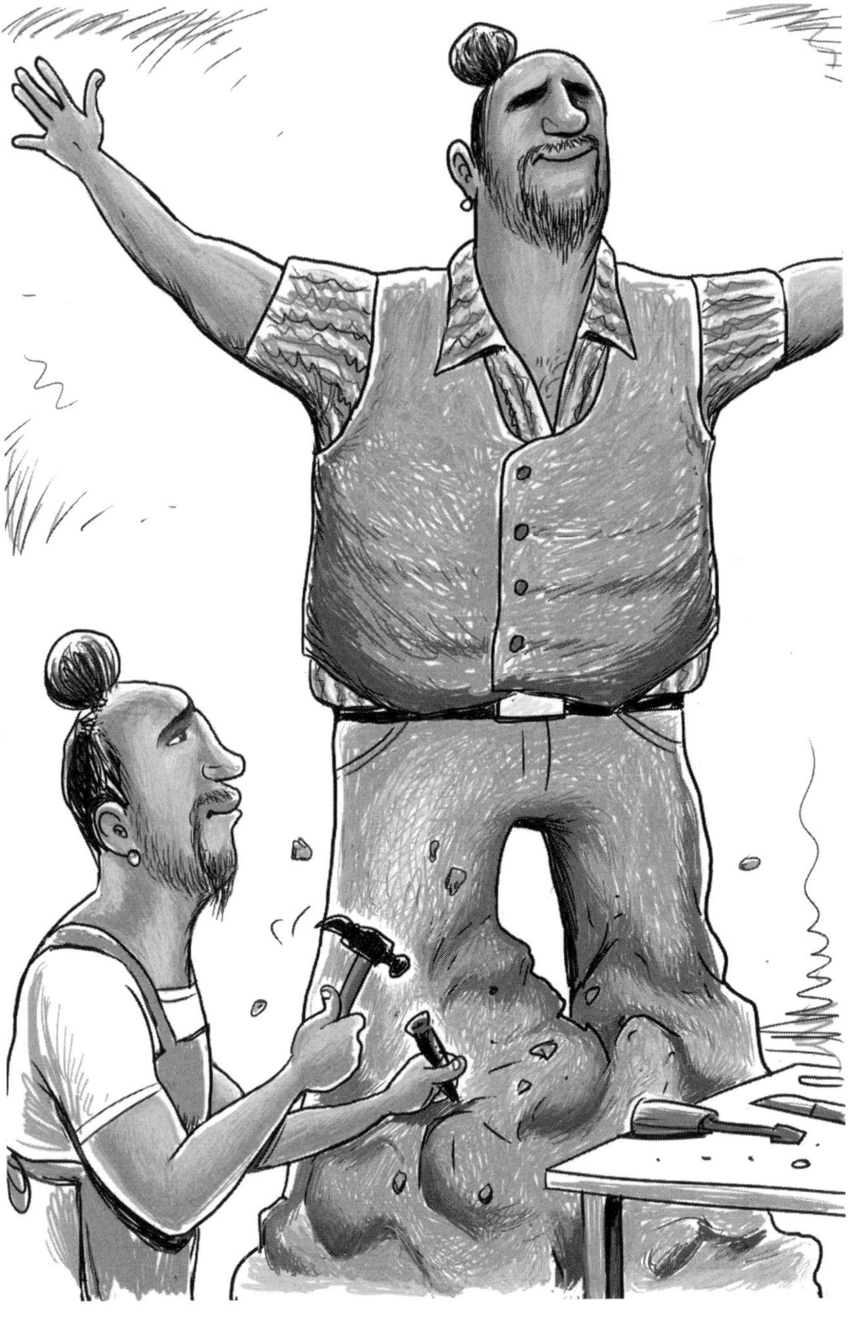

20
BEING YOUR BEST SELF

> *"'The individual defendants [in a famous criminal case] were almost universally described by their attorneys as upstanding citizens, community leaders, church vestrymen, Little League Organizers.'"*[557]
>
> – John G. Fuller

Introduction

The first two chapters of this book tell a cautionary tale: the moral judgments you make are not as straightforward as they seem. It appears to you that you use your big human brain to reason through your moral dilemmas to fair resolutions, but it's very clear that much more is going on. Primatologist Richard Wrangham writes: "[p]eople do not follow any general moral principle. Instead moral decisions are influenced by a series of unconscious and unexplained biases."[558]

Making moral judgments

Some experts believe that we make most of our moral judgments intuitively and nearly automatically, using lots of emotion but very little cognitive brain power. Wrangham, for example, asserts that "in making moral choices, we tend to act first and think later."[559] Other experts believe that quite a bit of reasoning does go into our moral judgments.[560] In either event, "[t]here is no bright line dividing reason from emotion"[561] and our moral judgments are plagued by biases and other forms of errors. In Chapter 3, we discussed this suite of harmful influences on our moral reasoning:

- The Omission Bias
- Moral Luck

- Knobe Effect
- Just World Hypothesis
- Indelible Victim Effect

There are other moral reasoning failures as well, including:

- *The Side Effect Bias.* If Nation A and Nation B are at war, and Nation A deliberately bombs a civilian neighborhood in Nation B, people tend to judge Nation A more harshly than if it bombed a military base next to a civilian neighborhood in Nation B, even if the same number of civilians *foreseeably* died in each raid.[562]
- *The Noncontact Bias.* Other things being equal, if Sam and Mike injure Carl in equal amounts, but Sam did so without touching Carl, and Mike did touch Carl, people will tend to judge Mike more harshly.[563]
- *The Attractiveness Bias.* As in so many areas of life, attractive people get a break when people judge the ethicality of their actions. The less aesthetically appealing among us are judged more harshly.[564]

Biases such as these lead to *moral dumbfounding* – the fact that we often intuitively reach moral judgments that we cannot rationally defend. Philosopher Garrett Cullity suggests it might be for the best that we cannot rationally explain our moral judgments and action choices:

> An impressive feature of the interviews with [people who rescued Jews from the Holocaust] is how little they have to say about their motives for acting: "I don't know. I don't think so much because I don't have that much to think with. . . . It's pretty near impossible not to help." . . . [T]here seems to be a particularly pure form of goodness in the inarticulately altruistic rescuers. Their inarticulacy stands as a guarantee of the directness of their concern for the people they helped. They did not have to talk themselves into what they did; they saw the situation as demanding action, not as inviting reflection; they did not think of their action as standing in *need* of justification. Their attention was directed outward, towards the needs of those they helped: those needs provided them with the reasons to which they responded, but the idea of needing to identify reasons – of seeing this as an occasion for *deliberation* – does not seem to have occurred to them.[565]

Indeed, Cullity notes that moral theorizing carries twin dangers:

> One is that it will deaden our responsiveness to reasons we have not succeeded in capturing in our theory, because the theory is too crude. The other is that it will actually make us worse, as agents, at the [part of morality] that tells us to connect ourselves to others, directly, motivating ourselves out of a concern for them, and not out of a concern to exemplify our own theory.[566]

In other words, limiting ourselves to acting only on reasoned ethical decisions may blunt the immediacy of our internal drive to help those in need. While we appreciate Cullity's point, your authors don't draw the same ultimate lesson. We don't wish to discourage you from reading Aristotle or St. Thomas Aquinas or Jeremy Bentham, and molding your own theory of morality. But the lesson we draw from Cullity is to be humble. It's difficult for even the best of us to be unbiased in our judgments and free from influences that we scarcely even notice (often to ill effect).

That's not to say that the impact of some of these biases cannot be overcome, or at least moderated. Researchers, for example, have found that by nudging people who subscribe to the Just World Hypothesis (the assumption that the world is a fair place) to focus on the perpetrators of a crime rather than the victims, it lessens the amount of blame that those people place on the victims.

More generally, we might carefully consider philosopher Hanno Sauer's *"triple-process account moral psychology."*[567] Following on Daniel Kahneman's dual-processing System 1 and System 2 description of how our brain works (see Chapter 1), Sauer takes it up a level and names a "System 3." System 3 prompts System 2 to reexamine the judgments reached by System 1. According to Sauer:

> Triple-process moral psychology is first and foremost a theory of *intuition override* – how it works and when it is called for. . . . Competent moral judgment, especially under modern conditions, critically depends on subjects' ability to *detect* the need for such override, properly *initiate* it, *monitor* its execution, and *check* its results for accuracy.[568]

Most importantly, when making moral judgments, we can be open to the views, reflections, and criticisms of others. The more the better. It's not that your authors believe in *moral relativism* – the notion that all moral views are equally valid. Instead, we believe that with the proper factual investigation and philosophical deliberation, it's possible to identify the most defensible ethical view. And we simply ask you to remember that out of the hundreds of thousands of possible viewpoints throughout the world, it is unlikely that the sources of your moral beliefs (e.g., your parents, teachers, religion, culture) are the ones who happened to get it 100 percent right on everything.

Moral action decisions

There are psychopaths who just don't care whether or not they are doing the right thing. And there are people who, due to what they perceive to be inescapable circumstances (e.g. poverty, addiction, incarceration) believe they have no choice but to do harmful things. But the rest of us probably figure that we're in good shape. We were given proper moral guidance by our parents who dragged us to the right church or synagogue or mosque. We had teachers who were good role models. We hung out with the good kids. We took the right philosophy classes. And so on.

And yet, as we learned in the first 19 chapters of this book, it's actually not that easy. Human beings are boundedly ethical creatures. If we don't realize that a choice we're about to make has a moral dimension to it, the odds go way, way down that we will make the right choice. Our (over)confidence in our good character is usually based on a vision we have of ourselves as facing an ethical challenge, summoning our good character, and acting heroically (or at least properly).

Unfortunately, when ethical dilemmas come, they often sneak up on us; we may make the wrong decision before we even realize that a choice has a moral dimension. The most common thing that white-collar criminals tend to say when asked to explain why they committed their offense is: "What was I thinking?" For example, we may be so focused on pleasing our boss (obedience to authority), getting along with co-employees (conformity bias), meeting a production target (framing), unconsciously advancing our own interests (self-serving bias), playing the role of loyal employee (role morality), working on a deadline (time pressure), or looking at immediate impacts rather than more remote but perhaps more significant impacts (tangible and abstract), that we don't even notice an ethical issue until we have already screwed up.

Legal scholar and behavioral ethics researcher Yuval Feldman made this point:

> Behavioral ethics research suggests that this type of misconduct occurs not because people are unethical or deliberately choose to act unethically, but because they fail to understand that their behavior is indeed unethical and can have harmful consequences. Studies show that employees have a "blind spot" that prevents them from seeing the ethical and legal meaning of their own behavior.
>
> Research also suggests that much banal, unethical behavior isn't due to deliberate decisions or unethical employees; rather it's triggered by particular situations. For example, unethical behavior is more likely to occur when norms about how people should behave are ambiguous (e.g., their behavior may seem to be reasonable or in the best interest of the firm); when the conflict of interest is subtle (e.g., when it is based on friendship and familiarity, rather than money); when the victim is not identified (as is the case of securities fraud where the effect is on public shareholders); when performance goals are unrealistic; or when the decision is being made not by individuals, but by groups (such as in corporate board decision making).
>
> In such situations, behavioral ethics research suggests that an especially large proportion of the population (in some studies more than 50 percent) may behave unethically, because their ability to objectively interpret the ethicality of their own behavior is highly limited.[569]

Keep your ethical antennae up

So, if we want to be ethical all the time, we'd best keep our ethical antennae extended all the time. Only then do we have the best chance of seeing those ethical traps before we fall into them. Those around us may be more concerned with other factors, so it's up to us to keep ethics in our own frame of reference.

More than simple moral awareness, we must strive for *moral attentiveness*, which is an active searching for moral content in situations we encounter.[570] Think of the iron ring that many Canadian-trained engineers wear to remind themselves constantly of their profession's ethical obligations.[571] Unless we are always looking for the ethical aspects of a decision, change blindness (explained in Chapter 9) can cause us to overlook an ethical issue.

Guard against biases and influences

We know from the first 19 chapters that many influences and pressures can cause a good person to do a wrong thing, often unintentionally. And, of course, we must be aware of such forces if we are to take steps to mitigate their dangerous influence.

Here are steps you can take to avoid errors now, and be your best self:

- You can remember that your brain is wired to be *obedient to authority*. Yet, you should not abandon your own moral compass for anyone, including your boss. Remember Stanley Milgram's observation that some of his subjects, having become aware of their susceptibility to the influence of authority, were "better able to resist authority when it conflict[ed] with [their] conscience."[572]
- You can predict that because of your (and everyone else's) tendency to take your cues for how to act from those around you (the *conformity bias*), you should not hang with the mean girls or the bad boys! If you surround yourself with friends and coworkers who try to do the right thing, it will be so much easier for you to do the right thing as well.[573] In fact, the most important thing a well-meaning employee can do is to go to work for an honest employer.
- You can, as a check on your own natural tendency to be victimized by the *overconfidence bias* regarding your moral character, utilize Nobel Prize-winner Daniel Kahneman's idea of a "pre-mortem."[574] Mentally look a year into the future and imagine that the important decision you are about to make went tragically wrong. By seriously and thoughtfully analyzing the possible consequences, you have a better chance that your decision will not take you off an ethical cliff.
- You can remember the impact of *framing* and place ethics in your frame of reference every time you make an important decision. Any time a decision that you make will impact others (or any *subject of moral worth*), your decision likely carries moral consequences. You can keep ethics in your frame of reference by constantly reminding yourself of your values, and of the negative forces that can undermine them.[575]

- You can guard against cutting that first small ethical corner, knowing that *incrementalism* can blind you to bigger changes and trends. Studies show that people can come to think of extreme climate change as the new normal in as little as two years.[576] As we noted earlier, just being educated as to incrementalism and its dangers enables us to "pay more attention to early cases of transgression and help[s] us apply the brakes before it is too late."[577]

We could go on through each of the causes of bounded ethicality introduced in Part I, but you get the general idea. There are constructive ways you can guard against the social and organizational pressures, psychological biases and cognitive heuristics, and situational factors that can derail your moral action choices.

Enlist allies

Other points of view can help us find the right answer and resist the self-serving bias, in-group bias, and implicit bias. Objective third parties or friends (willing to speak truth to your power) can be invaluable in helping us to see our decision through objective eyes. Often that other point of view will lead us to say: "Wow, what was I thinking?!"

Enlisting allies can also bolster our moral courage when we have decided upon the proper course of action. Enrolling allies can often help us advocate for our views more effectively, too, as we emphasize in Chapter 22.

Use moral imagination

Many scholars, including business ethicists Mark Johnson[578] and Patricia Werhane,[579] have used the term *moral imagination*, often in different ways. Borrowing from these scholars and others, we believe the legitimate ways of thinking about moral imagination are:

- Giving serious and sustained thought to what your values are and the kind of person you wish to be.
- Being realistic about the limitations and blind spots in your moral decision making that are created by the various factors surveyed in Part I.
- Being sensitive to how even seemingly routine decisions and actions may affect other people and subjects of moral worth, and thereby carry moral implications.
- Evaluating (creatively) the potential impact that your important action decisions may have on other people and subjects of moral worth who may be far away (either geographically or temporally) and therefore seem abstract rather than concrete.
- Developing your sense of empathy.
- Using your imagination to consider how you might produce creative, "out-of-the-box" solutions to difficult moral challenges.

- Contemplating thoughtfully how you might make the world a better place through your decisions and actions.

So, it is ACTIVITY TIME! Here are two exercises you can do (and should do now!) to improve the chances that you'll be able to harness moral imagination and stand up for the right thing when the time comes to do so.

First, let us steal an exercise from Professor Marianne Jennings who taught business law and ethics at Arizona State University for many years (and may have borrowed it from someone else herself). Please ask yourself these questions: If you could guarantee that you would *not* be caught or punished by others, would you do any of the following in order to significantly advance your career:

- Set off an atomic bomb in downtown Chicago?
- Murder a single person?
- Seriously pollute the Mississippi River?

Would you? We didn't think so. But would you:

- Lie to a customer?
- Take credit for a coworker's idea?
- Fudge the numbers if your boss insisted upon it?

Again, we hope you wouldn't, but certainly other people have.

Professor Jennings' point is that we're all going to face incentives to do things we know we shouldn't. We should start setting boundaries now, and imagine how we will deal with these inevitable temptations. She had her students write down things that they would *never* do (kill, cheat, lie, etc.) to get ahead in their careers on a card. She urged them to always carry those cards with them. Students have come back and told her that remembering the promises they'd made to themselves in her class later helped them resist the temptation to advance their careers in a wrongful manner. The exercise didn't save everybody. It probably didn't even save most of her students, but it helped some of her students. And it's a way that you can improve your chances of living a moral life because it is darned hard to be ethical on the fly.

Second, let's borrow another little exercise, this time from Mary Gentile, author of the wonderful *Giving Voice to Values* book that we'll study in detail in Chapter 22. Let's pre-script!

Psychologists wanted to know why some people act heroically while others don't. Why does one person rush into the burning building to save the baby while everyone else is milling around out on the sidewalk? They interviewed as many people who had acted heroically as they could find, and a common explanation they received was that these heroes had thought about the situation *in advance.* Again, it's hard to be ethical on the fly. While other bystanders' minds were racing (but not getting much of anywhere), those who acted heroically already had a plan of action. Consider this story, for example, about famed pilot Sully Sullenberger who heroically landed an airplane in the Hudson River, saving the lives of 155 people aboard:

> Sullenberger had been a middle-school student in Denison, Texas, in 1964, when he first heard about [the death of Kitty Genovese who had been stabbed to death while scores of bystanders did nothing to help her]. He asked himself how New Yorkers could be so cold. "I made a pledge to myself right then and there, at age thirteen, that *if I was ever in a situation where someone such as Kitty Genovese needed my help, I would choose to act.* No one in danger would be abandoned," he recalled. In the hour after his "Miracle on the Hudson," as Sullenberger and his passengers stood shivering on the plane's wing while boaters rushed to help, he felt as if New York was "reaching out to warm us."[580]

Or consider this description from New Orleans in the heart of Hurricane Katrina when a doctor was ordered to abandon a storm-ravaged hospital:

> Riopelle, a past president of the state humane society coalition, had quietly decided earlier in the day to disobey the authorities and stay. There was no way he was leaving behind the sixty or seventy pets at the hospital, including his own, just because some twenty-year-old fireman from Shreveport had ordered him to go. *He'd made a pledge to himself years earlier,* after touring the Holocaust concentration camp at Dachau, to refuse to comply with misdirection.[581]

Character

We have also learned in Part I that having good character is far from a guarantee that we will always act ethically. In fact, some experts believe that character is overrated, and that even people of sterling character are easily buffeted by the winds of social and organizational pressures, biases, situational factors, and all the rest. Other scholars believe that character is very important in determining whether we will act morally or not. Almost no one believes that character is completely unimportant. All that said, having good character can't hurt, and it may help.[582] The optimistic view is:

> [M]oral fiber matters. Joseph Stalin was cruel, heartless, insensitive, brutal, and ruthless. These character traits were part of his moral fiber, and led him to behave in ways that were horrendous as the leader of the Soviet Union. By some estimates, he was responsible for twenty million or more deaths.

Mother Teresa, on the other hand, served thousands of the desperately poor, sick, and orphaned in India for forty-five years. She was loving, compassionate, kind, selfless, and forgiving. Those character traits were part of her moral fiber and led her to behave in ways that were saintly.[583]

Social-cognitive theory suggests that moral functioning is interactive. It involves both the types of influences we emphasized in Part I *and* personal influences, such as your *moral identity* – which is the extent to which we anchor our self-concept in moral characteristics.[584] According to *virtue ethics* – as developed by Aristotle and the ancient Greeks – good character is the basis for ethical action. So we would do well to keep plugging away at developing and perfecting our character. Practice all the Boy Scout virtues – "a scout is trustworthy, loyal, helpful, friendly, courteous, kind, obedient, cheerful, thrifty, brave, clean, and reverent" – and throw in honesty, integrity, reliability, empathy, and other virtues. In fact, placing ethics at the center of our being – *really* wanting to be a good person – is correlated (some studies indicate) with doing good things,[585] with not doing bad things,[586] and with avoiding the harmful mechanisms of moral disengagement discussed in the next chapter.[587]

We should keep our eyes peeled, too, looking for moral issues. Research shows that a person who is morally attentive is more likely to be morally aware, and more likely to do the right thing when the time comes.[588] We should exercise our moral muscles, too. When it comes to being virtuous (as with any skill) practice makes perfect. Make being a good person a routine:

> [P]eople focused on moral progress, growth, and development may be more likely to look for ways to establish patterns and routines aimed at moral improvement. For example, a religious person might regularly read sacred texts, attend worship services, and participate in daily prayer. An environmentalist might make it a habit to recycle everything and commute to work on a bike. Others might make it a habit to write in a gratitude journal every night, donate a specified amount to charity each year, or perform a random act of kindness each week – often with the goal of becoming a better person.[589]

Behavioral science indicates that we can help ourselves to be our best self by taking inspiration from the kind (or perhaps even heroic) actions of others. Read books that carry inspiring stories of moral action such as William Damon and Anne Colby's *The Power of Ideals*,[590] Colby and Damon's *Some Do Care*,[591] and Philip Paul Hallie's *Lest Innocent Blood Be Shed*.[592] In these (and other) stories, we will find motivation and some role models worth emulating.

ETHICS UNWRAPPED RESOURCES

Videos

Moral Reasoning
Series: Ethics Defined

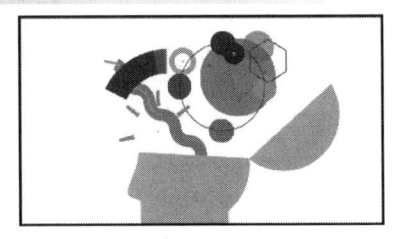

Moral Imagination
Series: Ethics Defined

Moral Imagination
Series: Concepts Unwrapped

Virtue Ethics
Series: Ethics Defined

Related Videos

Integrity
Series: Ethics Defined

Altruism
Series: Ethics Defined

Case Studies

*In-FUR-mercials:
Advertising & Adoption*

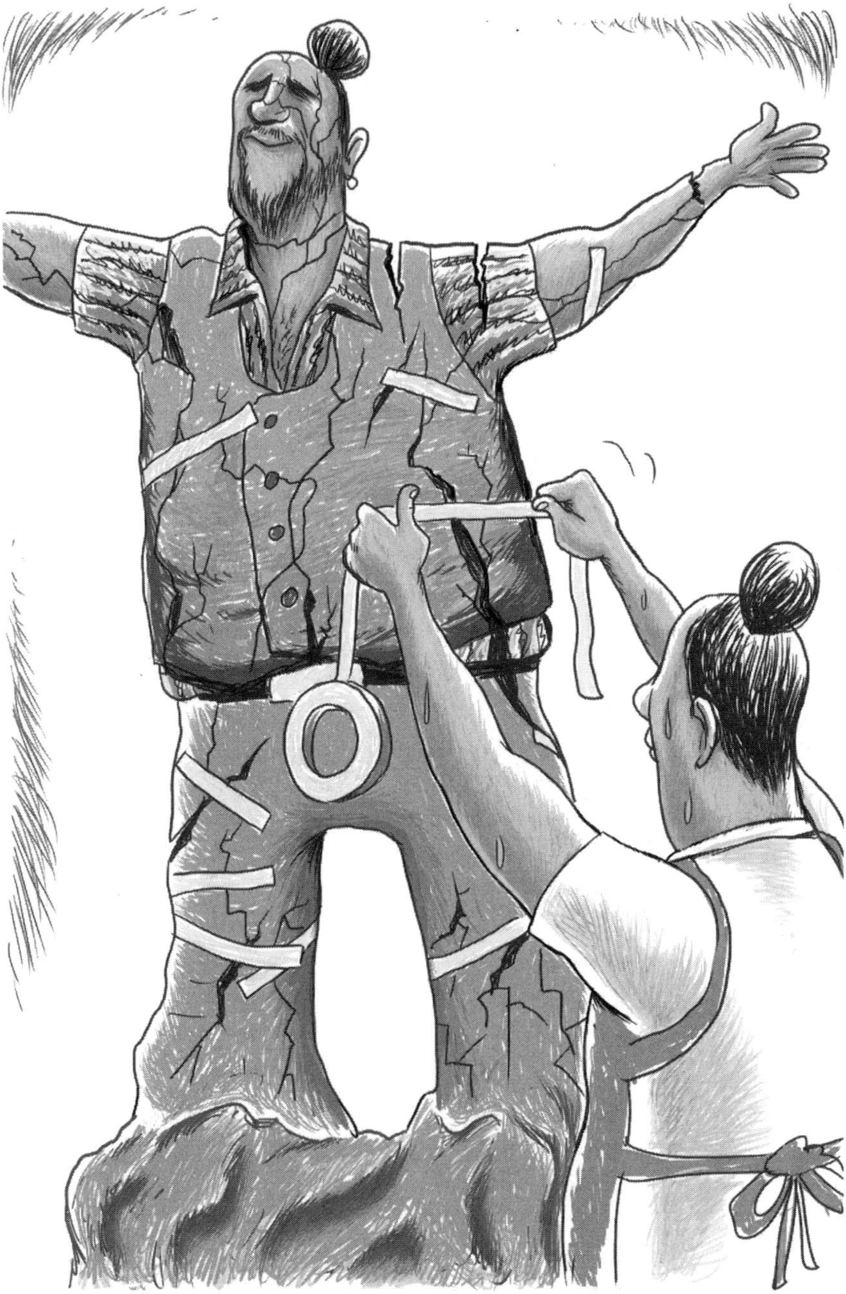

21

RATIONALIZATIONS AND OTHER MECHANISMS OF MORAL DISENGAGEMENT

> "Much as the road to hell is paved with good intentions, the road to bad behavior is paved with rationalization."[593]
>
> — Joshua May

Introduction

As we've said more than once, to be a good person, you must want to be a good person. To live a moral life, you must want to do the right thing every time you face a moral issue. In this chapter we're going to talk in detail about *rationalizations* and (borrowing from psychologist Albert Bandura) other mechanisms of *moral disengagement*. These are the excuses we give ourselves for choosing not to live up to our own moral standards on particular occasions. They are hazardous and we must guard against them in order to be our best selves.

Rationalizations

Dictionary.com defines the verb *rationalize* to mean "to invent plausible explanations for acts, opinions, etc., that are actually based on other causes."[594] Rationalizations are surely forms of moral disengagement in that we use them to distance ourselves from our wrongful actions. According to one analysis, rationalizations:

- Are self-serving explanations.
- Assist in making behavior appear more acceptable to both self and others.
- Involve a degree of self-deception.
- Often occur outside the realm of the conscious mind.

- Can reduce feelings of responsibility and/or anxiety for the negative aspects of behavior.
- Can neutralize the impact of legal or ethical issues involved in a decision.[595]

To preserve our self-image as "good people" even as we do things that we wouldn't want to appear on our social media feed, we often invoke rationalizations:

> In the process of creating a self-narrative, the role of rationalization is crucial. It is at the heart of how we consciously and unconsciously create consistency between our version of events and reality. Because life often provides information and experiences that contradict our self-narrative, rationalizing these contradictions helps us to "patch up" the holes in our story and maintain a sense of self. It also allows us to reinterpret our view of events, particularly when events challenge our notion of ourselves as "good people."[596]

There are many ways to classify rationalizations. Your authors are partial to the "Common Categories of Rationalizations" applied by business ethics scholars Vikas Anand, Blake Ashforth, and Mehendra Joshi, and we'll discuss each category in turn. Here are their Common Categories of Rationalizations:[597]

- Denial of Responsibility
- Denial of Injury
- Denial of Victim
- Social Weighting
- Appeal to Higher Loyalties
- Metaphor of the Ledger

Denial of responsibility

Anand and colleagues describe this type of rationalization as one where "[t]he actors engaged in corrupt behaviors perceive that they have no other choice than to participate in such activities." The basic idea is that we find ourselves doing something wrongful, but convince ourselves that it is actually someone's else's responsibility (not our own). So we feel that we are free and clear! But of course we aren't. We are still the agent of our actions.

Adolf Eichmann, one of Hitler's major organizers of the Holocaust, relied upon this category of rationalization to excuse his participation in the murder of millions:

> What I said to myself was this: The head of State has ordered it, and those exercising judicial authority over me are now transmitting it. I escaped into other areas and looked for a cover for myself which gave me some

peace of mind at least, and so in this way I was able to shift – no, that is not the right term – to attach this whole thing one hundred percent to those in judicial authority who happened to be my superiors, to the head of State – since they gave the orders. So, deep down, I did not consider myself responsible and I felt free of guilt. I was greatly relieved that I had nothing to do with the actual physical extermination.[598]

So, if we find ourselves saying: "I know I shouldn't do this, but my boss is making me" or "I know this is wrong, but it's what my friend (or client, customer, etc.) wants" then a little alarm bell should go off in our head. We're about to give ourselves a pass for doing something wrong by placing the blame elsewhere. Don't.

Denial of injury

Another common rationalization is denial of injury, which Anand and colleagues describe as a situation where "[t]he actors are convinced that no one is harmed by their actions; hence the actions are not really corrupt." In other words, we know that what we're doing is wrong, but it's a "no harm, no foul" sort of situation – "I tried to shoot the guy but, hey, I missed! How can it be wrong if no one was hurt?"

Michael Lewis, the author of such popular books as *Moneyball*, *The Blind Side*, and *The Big Short*, also wrote *Liar's Poker* about his tragicomic experience in the finance industry. Lewis tells the tale of being a newbie in the finance business when some of his coworkers at Salomon Brothers tricked him into "blowing up" a client by selling it crappy bonds that Salomon was trying to get off its own books. When he realized what he had done, Lewis resorted to a classic denial of injury rationalization:

> There was a convenient way of looking at this situation. . . . Anyway, who was hurt besides my German? . . . The German's bank had lost sixty thousand dollars. The bank's shareholders, the Austrian Government, were therefore the losers. But compared with the assets of the nation as a whole, sixty thousand dollars was a ridiculously small sum.[599]

Of course, the alarm in our head should go off if we find ourselves saying, "I know I shouldn't do this, but they've got lots of money and won't even notice" or "I know this is wrong, but the impact isn't that bad – it sure could be worse!" Indeed, the denial of injury rationalization enables all too many good people to conclude that it's okay to lie to insurance companies (or the IRS) because "they've got lots of money anyway."

Denial of victim

Anand and colleagues describe this rationalization as a situation where "[t]he actors counter any blame for their actions by arguing that the violated party deserved whatever happened."

In *Liar's Poker*, after invoking denial of injury, Michael Lewis doubled down with denial of victim, concluding that his client "was partly responsible." At Salomon Brothers, the employees invented a phrase, "born to be a customer," which really meant "born to be a sucker." As Lewis says, if your customers are born to be suckers, then there is nothing wrong with taking advantage of them – they deserve it.

Similarly, notorious lobbyist and convicted felon Jack Abramoff often referred to his Native American clients as "monkeys," "morons," and "troglodytes." In so doing, he was paving the way to feel just fine about himself even though he was ripping off these clients for millions of dollars.[600]

So, if we find ourselves thinking, "I know I shouldn't do this, but this person is an idiot and deserves to be screwed" or "I know this is wrong, but if she's playing the stock market, she should know that she's going to have to take some losses from time to time," then be aware! We are probably about to give ourselves permission to do the wrong thing.

Social weighting

According to Anand and coauthors, there are two forms of the social weighting rationalization: condemn the condemner, and selective social comparison.

Condemn the condemner is the first form of social weighting where "[t]he actors deflect blame by criticizing those who criticize them." One of your authors (Prentice) was once a research attorney in a federal district that contained the U.S. Penitentiary in Leavenworth, Kansas, the U.S. Disciplinary Barracks (military prison) in Leavenworth, and the Kansas State Penitentiary in Lansing, Kansas. In that position, he met many of the sorts of people you tell your children not to date. Some admitted their crimes. Some did not. Regardless, many inmates fervently believed that the prosecutors were worse people than they were, and therefore weren't entitled to criticize the convicted criminals.

So, if we find ourselves saying something along the lines of "I probably shouldn't have done that, but who is he to criticize me anyway?" we are condemning the condemner – which really doesn't absolve us of responsibility.

Selective social comparison is the second type of social weighting rationalization where we deflect guilt by comparing our wrongs (favorably) to the wrongs of other people. For example, during the LIBOR scandal, which involved banks blatantly manipulating an important international interest rate, one banker wrote to other bankers: "Don't worry mate – there's bigger crooks in the market than us guys."[601]

So, if our inner voice is telling us, "I know I shouldn't do this, but the other students cheat even more" or "I know this is wrong, but you should see what my competitor does" then we are rationalizing, and about to go down the wrong moral fork in the road.

Appeal to higher loyalties

According to Anand and colleagues, with the appeal to higher loyalties, we explain away our violations by blaming them on a higher order value. That higher order value, for example, might well be loyalty – to employer or family – or some other "positive" value.

To illustrate: Once upon a time the B.F. Goodrich Company wanted to sell fighter plane brakes to the U.S. Air Force. Unfortunately, the brakes kept flunking performance tests. Nonetheless, Goodrich superiors ordered Kermit Vandivier to begin preparing information for a qualification report, as if the brakes were just fine. Vandivier complained to his supervisor, Ralph Gretzinger, who became very angry about the situation and went to confront *his* bosses. According to Vandivier:

> In about an hour, [Gretzinger] returned and called me to his desk. . . . "You know, I've been an engineer for a long time, and I've always believed that ethics and integrity were every bit as important as theorems and formulas, and never once has anything happened to change my beliefs. Now this. . . . *Hell, I've got two sons I've got to put through school. . . .*"[602]

After swearing that no false reports would ever come out of his lab, Gretzinger knuckled under to his superiors' wrongful instructions (obedience to authority) and participated in writing a report that said the brakes were fine when, in fact, they were defective and endangered pilots' lives. While it seems unlikely that his sons would have wanted their father to act as he did, at the crucial moment Gretzinger felt his higher loyalty was to his family.

So, if we find ourselves saying, "I know I shouldn't lie about this, but my company is struggling and really needs me to close this deal" or "I know this is wrong, but I have bills to pay and I need this job to feed my family," we are treading on dangerous moral territory.

Metaphor of the ledger

According to Anand, Ashforth, and Joshi, this rationalization involves telling ourselves that we are "entitled to indulge in deviant behaviors because of [our] accrued credits (time and effort) in [our] job." For example, part of lobbyist Jack Abramoff's web of rationalizations involved reminding himself that he gave a large percentage of his income to charity.[603] If you give a lot of money to charity, then maybe you're justified in the scandalous things you do to gain that money in the first place. Or not!

In other words, we might say to ourselves: "I know I shouldn't pad my expense account, but I'm the best employee in my section, and yet I'm never recognized for it" or "I know I shouldn't take office supplies home for personal use, but I am the lowest paid employee in my division." If we ever hear ourselves mentally invoking this sort of rationalization, it's time to stop and think carefully – likely it's not our best self about to take action.

The Common Categories of Rationalizations is certainly not an exhaustive list of all the rationalizations that we use to convince ourselves that it's permissible (just this once!) to do something immoral and unethical. But it is a good start, and provides a solid mental checklist.

Moral disengagement

The remainder of this chapter will focus on the work of prominent psychologist Albert Bandura and his concept of *moral disengagement*.[604] Some of Bandura's ideas will plow ground we've already covered, but they will give us a new lens through which to contemplate some of the important points. His theories will also present many new ideas to consider.

Bandura's insights offer us valuable ways to guard against common moral mistakes. Often we still manage to think (at some level) that all this behavioral ethics research applies only to "the other person." It's the reason that 100 percent of the MBA students in a Harvard class thought that they'd be less susceptible to the pressure to be obedient to authority than the average student in the class.[605]

Bandura's four categories

People generally do the right thing for a number of reasons. We might fear punishment by our legal system if our unethical act violated the law. Religious people might be worried about divine punishment. We might dread the other-condemning emotions of others – such as anger, contempt, and disgust – if we're discovered to have acted immorally. Perhaps the most important reason is that we would feel guilty if we acted immorally (and might suffer shame and embarrassment, if we are discovered). As Chapter 2 pointed out, moral emotions play a huge role in our moral action decisions.

Bandura believes that various mechanisms of moral disengagement can sever the link between people's actions and their moral emotions:

> A humane and self-governing society is rooted in moral self-sanctions. People continuously preside over their behavior and must live with the self-evaluative consequences of what they do. Moral self-sanctions keep behavior in line with moral standards. However, even the power of moral self-sanctions can be neutralized. Social cognitive theory specifies the psychosocial mechanisms by which this neutralization is achieved. *Disengagement of moral self-sanctions from detrimental behavior enables people to behave harmfully and still live in peace with themselves.*[606]

Bandura places these psychosocial mechanisms of disengagement into four broad categories:

- First, mechanisms with a *behavioral locus*. There are three mechanisms – moral, social, and economic – that focus on our behavior, which we manage to excuse even if it's improper.
- Second, mechanisms with an *agency locus*. Two mechanisms cut the connection between our actions and our "agency" – that is, our free will. If the actions we took weren't truly our own, then we're not at fault, are we?
- Third, mechanisms with an *effects locus*. For example, if I tried to cheat you but wasn't successful, then I didn't really harm you. If no one was harmed, then how could it have been a bad thing to do?
- Finally, two mechanisms with a *victim locus*. For example, if A harms B, A's action can't be immoral if B deserved to be hurt, can it?

The behavioral locus

Lying, cheating, stealing, robbing, killing, and other such actions that harm other people seem to be immoral. How can such behaviors not be wrong? And yet our brains can often convince us that we're not bad people even if we do something that is normally bad. Bandura focuses upon three primary mechanisms in this broader category of moral disengagement that help our minds sever the connection between our bad behaviors and our sense of wrongdoing.

Criminologist Donald Cressey argued that embezzlers don't begin their schemes until they can verbalize (in their own minds) the language that rationalizes their behavior as acceptable, so they can continue to think of themselves as good people.[607] Bandura agrees, writing that "[p]eople do not usually engage in harmful conduct until they have justified to themselves the morality of their actions."[608] Such justifications often come in moral, social, or economic forms.

Moral, social, and economic justification

In an example of a moral and social justification, Bandura relates the story of Sergeant Alvin York, an American hero from World War I. York was a fundamentalist Christian who sought a conscientious objector exemption to escape from serving in the war. However, his battalion commander used selected passages from the Bible to convince York that it was his Christian duty to not ignore the alleged German war crimes in Belgium. As York (supposedly) explained to his fellow congregants: "If some feller was to come along and bust into your house and mistreat your wife and murder your children, you'd just stand for it? You wouldn't fight?"[609] And so Alvin York went from "Thou shalt not kill" to

"Thou shalt kill" – quickly and very effectively, his war record shows – when he became convinced (through Bible-reading and earnest prayer) that morality required him to fight against Germany.

The appeal to higher loyalties category of rationalization put forth by Anand and coauthors provides an example of moral justification, too. Didn't B.F. Goodrich's employee Ralph Gretzinger justify his decision to help with the brake fraud by focusing on the moral duty he owed (as a father) to his sons?

Of course, winners write the history books, so your two American authors might accept Alvin York's excuse to kill German soldiers. But we might not be quite so accepting of Germans, whose reading of *Mein Kampf* convinced them that they owed a patriotic duty to the Fatherland to help exterminate Jews. Nor of Anders Behring Breivik, who killed 77 people (mostly on Norway's Otoya Island), for the supposed purpose of preserving Norway's culture from Islamic immigrants and feminists. It appears that religious, moral, social, cultural, familial, and similar influences can be wielded by each of us to convince ourselves that our harmful actions are justified.

Bandura is also concerned with economic justifications as means of moral disengagement:

> The customary justification in the finance industry – and indeed, industry as a whole – takes the following form: Unfettered by intrusive regulations, commercial innovations flourish, and productive industries fuel economic growth. . . . By vigorously pursuing their own self-interests, financiers are advancing the common good.[610]

Thus, those in business can use the theory of unfettered capitalism to evade regulation, and to justify the costs and other externalities that they impose on people, while still feeling good about themselves and the large paychecks that they deposit regularly into their bank accounts.

The agency locus

Displacement of responsibility and diffusion of responsibility are the two main mechanisms by which we disengage morally using the agency locus, according to Bandura.

Displacement of responsibility overlaps significantly with the denial of responsibility rationalization discussed earlier in this chapter. If we feel we had little or no choice but to do something (that our boss demanded or our customer requested) then we won't feel personally responsible for the action.[611] In the B.F. Goodrich case described earlier, for example, a lower-level employee tried to convince one of the bosses to do something about the fraud. The boss refused to help, reasoning that the bigger bosses probably knew about it already, and he refused to worry about things he had no control over. When asked if his conscience would bother him if a pilot died during the test flights, the boss responded: "Look. I just told you I have no control over this. Why should my conscience bother me?"[612]

Just as we can decide that we are not to blame for wrongdoing because the real responsibility lies with another person (such as our boss or client), we can also avoid feeling meaningful responsibility if we aren't the sole actor in a situation. This diffusion of responsibility may happen, Bandura says,[613] in at least three situations:

- Group-decision making. Clearly, we feel less responsible if we're merely contributing to a group decision than if we make the decision all by ourselves. Absent that greater sense of responsibility, the restraining emotions of guilt, shame, etc. will exert much less influence.
- Division of labor. Naturally, we feel less responsibility if we contribute only to one part of an action than if we perform every part of that action ourselves.
- Collective action. Acting as a group creates a sense of anonymity, which is why crowds can be particularly violent and mean. Inside a crowd, we will often act more cruelly than we ever would when acting alone.

The effects locus

As discussed earlier regarding the denial of injury rationalization, we are able to think of ourselves as moral if the immoral thing we did had no harmful consequences. Indeed, our actions are often viewed as immoral primarily because they injure subjects of moral worth. But Bandura explodes this "no harm, no foul" rationalization by pointing out that often, indeed, there is harm, but by (a) ignoring it, (b) distorting it beyond recognition, or (c) simply engaging in denial, we can protect our positive moral self-image.[614]

There's a lot of the tangible and abstract bias (see Chapter 13) going on here as well. If we cannot see the harm, or if we only vaguely feel the harm that we do, then it is easier to do harm. The effects locus – whereby we disregard, distort, or deny harmful effects – is exacerbated by evidence that:

- If we want to do something we suspect will cause harm, we may intentionally attempt to remain as ignorant as possible regarding that harm. For example, if we don't wish to pay more taxes, we may choose to ignore articles and videos about economic and social inequality in our society.
- If we're doing something that arguably causes harm, the self-serving bias may distort our views. For example, if we work for a tobacco company, we may find the evidence that tobacco causes cancer much less persuasive than other people do.
- We often remember the harm we caused as less severe than it truly was.[615] Indeed, our brains may reconstruct our memories in ways that protect our self-image.

The victim locus

The first mechanism of moral disengagement with a victim locus is dehumanization. We can't be acting immorally if the people we harm are not subjects of moral worth, or so our thinking goes. People who wish to harm other people naturally convince themselves that their victims are not, in fact, human, and are therefore not deserving of moral treatment: "To the extent that the victims are dehumanized, principles of morality no longer apply to them and moral restraints against killing are more readily overcome."[616]

Dehumanization is obviously the most extreme version of the denial-of-victim rationalization. It seems absurd to propose that other human beings are *not*, indeed, human. Nonetheless, "[t]ragically, history has shown how possible it is for people to dehumanize others."[617] Thus Nazis dehumanized Jews. Settlers in America's old west dehumanized Native Americans. American soldiers dehumanized Vietnamese civilians. Hutus dehumanized Tutsis. ISIS fighters dehumanized Christians.

Attribution of blame is the second mechanism of moral disengagement with a victim locus. This mechanism tracks nearly perfectly the denial of victim rationalization described by Anand and colleagues, and so needs no further discussion. However, Bandura provides a discouraging number of examples that exemplify this mechanism, including tobacco industry representatives who argue that "because not every smoker develops cancer, the causes lie in smokers' faulty biological makeup and unhealthful lifestyle habits."[618]

Euphemistic language

According to Bandura, language matters. We think he is right, too, as we noted in Chapter 8 when discussing the concept of framing. About language, Bandura said:

> Language shapes the perception of events and the thought patterns on which people base many of their actions. The personal and social acceptability of given activities, therefore, can differ markedly depending on what those activities are called. Euphemistic machinations are used widely to detach and depersonalize doers from harmful activities. Cloaking detrimental activities in euphemisms can be a powerful weapon.[619]

Bandura notes that philosopher Richard Gambino identified three kinds of euphemisms.[620] The first kind is "sanitizing and convoluted language." Thus, people can refer to their fraudulent financial activities as "creative accounting," "financial engineering," or "tax optimization."[621] Mass firings become "right-sizing," dead civilians become "collateral damage," lies become "alternative facts," and stealing becomes "borrowing." Mass murder becomes the "final solution." This is not just theory. Empirical studies demonstrate that "euphemistic labels can psychologically sanitize unethical practices, facilitating our participation in them."[622]

Gambino's second category of euphemisms is use of "the agentless passive form." To put things in a passive voice removes our agency, diminishes our responsibility, and makes us appear (certainly in our own minds and hopefully to others) to be merely victims of unfortunate circumstances. This sort of language is captured in the title of social psychologists Carol Tavris and Elliot Aronson's classic book: *Mistakes Were Made (But Not By Me)*.[623]

Gambino's third kind of euphemism is "borrowing specialized jargon from a respectable enterprise." Bandura gives this example from the infamous Watergate scandal:

> To add cover to their criminal activities, the Watergate burglars cloaked them in metaphors of admirable teamwork and sportsmanship. In Watergate jargon, criminal conspiracy became a "game plan," and the conspirators were "team players" with qualities befitting the best sportsmen. Their domestic spying operation was called a "new intelligence unit" in the likeness of a legitimate information-gathering agency. Like dutiful seamen, the burglars were "deep-sixing" incriminating documents, not destroying them illegally. Seeing oneself as a team player faithfully executing a game plan against a political foe will rouse weaker self-restraint of transgressive conduct than seeing oneself as a common burglar committing criminal acts.[624]

Advantageous comparison

Euphemisms, and other kinds of linguistic illusions, can help to support advantageous comparisons. Bandura's notion of advantageous comparison is similar to (and encompasses) Anand and colleagues' rationalization of selective social comparison that we discussed as part of social weighting.

As Bandura explains, by using advantageous comparison, not only can we compare our bad acts to others' worse acts to make ourselves feel better ("Don't worry mate – there's bigger crooks in the market than us"), we can also engage in uplifting comparisons that are inaccurate yet feel good ("As Rosa Parks fought for the rights of black Americans to sit at the front of the bus, we continue to fight for the freedom of pharmaceutical companies to charge what they choose for the drugs that they own!").

Moral disengagement by observers

The explanation for why we disengage morally when we *observe* harmful actions largely follows the same reasoning for why we disengage morally when we *act* wrongfully. As such, this part of Bandura's discussion needs little extra attention.

Bandura illustrates how people who observe immoral acts can disengage morally with a lengthy discussion of officials inside the Catholic Church who didn't blow the whistle on the sexual abuse of children.[625] Church officials invoked most of the rationalizations we discussed earlier, including:

- Denial of Responsibility ("I was just a note taker. . . . I don't think it was my role to follow through").
- Denial of Victim (in a "lot of cases, the . . . youngster is the seducer").
- Selective Social Comparison (criticism of the Catholic Church is like persecution of the Jews).

Conclusion

To meet our own moral goals, we must not only guard against the social and organizational pressures, psychological biases and mental shortcuts, and situational factors that can make it hard to do the right thing. We must also guard against the human tendency to rationalize and adopt other mechanisms of moral disengagement. This chapter alerts you, dear reader, to many of the most dangerous of these mechanisms and rationalizations. Now it's up to you to watch out!

ETHICS UNWRAPPED RESOURCES

Videos

Rationalizations
Series: Ethics Defined

BYBS, Pt. 3: Moral Intent
Series: Concepts Unwrapped

In It To Win: The Jack Abramoff Story
Series: In It To Win

Jack & Rationalizations
Series: In It To Win

Related Videos

Diffusion of Responsibility
Series: Ethics Defined

Subject of Moral Worth
Series: Ethics Defined

Tangible and Abstract
Series: Ethics Defined

Framing
Series: Ethics Defined

ETHICS UNWRAPPED RESOURCES

Case Studies

Abramoff: Lobbying Congress

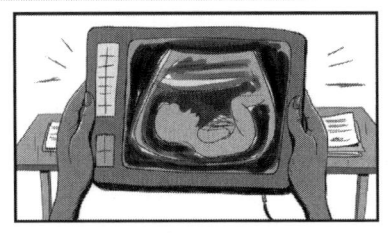

Prenatal Diagnosis & Parental Choice

Daraprim Price Hike
Scandals Illustrated

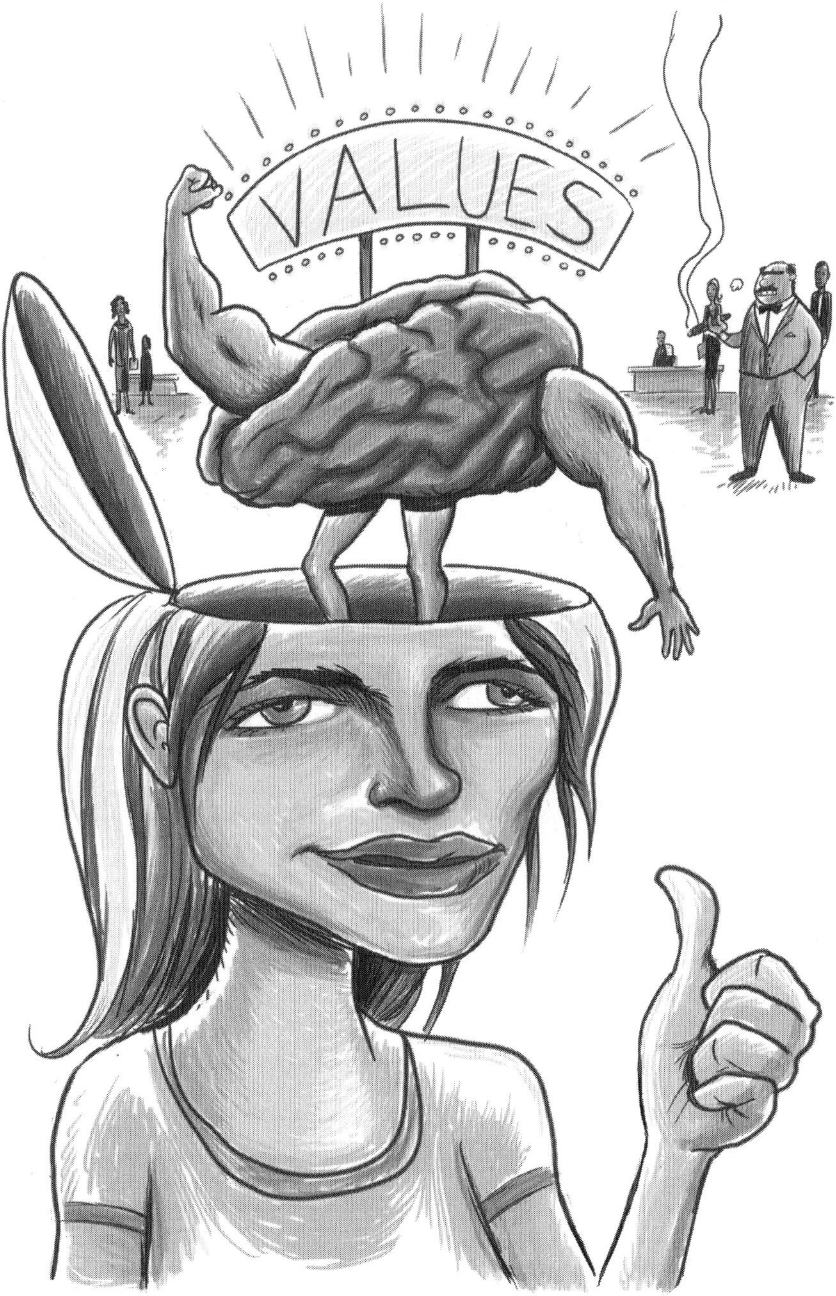
VALUES

22
GIVING VOICE TO YOUR VALUES

"An all-embracing morality includes doing good things, not just refraining from bad ones."[626]
– *Albert Bandura*

Introduction

If you ever get the chance, listen to Helen Sharkey Gebhard tell her story.[627] As an employee working for the CFO of energy trading firm Dynegy (a competitor of Enron), she found herself in a room full of bankers and lawyers who wanted to do a deal that Helen knew would violate accounting conventions and securities laws. To be competitive with Enron, Dynegy was seeking to pull the same type of financial shenanigans that Enron was using to hide debt on its books. Helen knew what was wrong with the proposed deal, and she knew why it was wrong. But she didn't know how to speak up for her values. She was the youngest person in the room, and had less corporate authority than anyone else present. Helen said that "[f]or the first time in my life, I gave up on myself and stopped fighting for what I knew to be right." She told herself that if she just kept quiet, didn't sign any documents, and then transferred out of the CFO's office as soon as possible, she would probably be okay. She wasn't. Helen later pled guilty to federal securities fraud (a felony) and did time in federal prison.

Like Helen, most of us have probably seen something wrong (whether in the business world or in our personal lives) yet not spoken up to call attention to it or stop it. Most of us were probably luckier than her regarding the consequences of our silence. But most of us are like Helen – we find it easier to avoid doing wrong ourselves, than to speak up against wrongdoing by others. Yet, as the introductory quotation to this chapter indicates, to be a good person we must sometimes step up and take action. "Ethics can't be a side hustle."[628]

So how do we engage in moral action, and do so effectively? Dr. Mary Gentile, a leadership educator and management consultant, has created a program called "Giving Voice to Values" (GVV) that is aimed at helping people speak up for, and act on, their values. She has written a very accessible book[629] as well as written (and narrated) an eight-part video series on GVV which is available on the Ethics Unwrapped website.[630] In this chapter, we summarize Mary Gentile's immensely helpful GVV program.[631]

Giving voice to values

Traditional, philosophy-based ethics courses tend to silently assume that if people facing an ethical challenge know the right thing to do, they will do it. Why wouldn't they?

Behavioral ethics research teaches that there is often a huge gap between knowing the right thing to do and actually doing it. As illustrated earlier in this book, biases and pressures, and even seemingly innocent situational factors, can cause us to fail to do the right thing even if we know what it is. Often times, of course, we are subject to ethical fading or similar phenomena that distort our ethical vision.

As noted in the Introduction to Part II, there are four key steps to doing the right thing:

- Moral awareness
- Moral decision making
- Moral intent
- Moral action

The first three steps are crucial, of course. But even assuming that we clearly see a moral issue, make a defensible moral judgment as to what the right thing to do is, *and* want to do the right thing, there is still one more step – *moral action*. We often want to do the right thing, but don't. Why? How can we increase the chances that we, unlike Helen Sharkey Gebhard, will *act* on our desire to do the right thing? That is where Giving Voice to Values comes into play.

Gentile's GVV program assumes that most of us have good values, and wish to stand up for them. Some of us stand up for the right thing often. Some of us do it from time to time. Gentile's primary thesis is "that if enough of us felt empowered – and were skillful and practiced enough – to voice and act on our values effectively on those occasions when our best selves are in the driver's seat, business would be in a different place."[632] So how can we maximize the likelihood that we'll stand up for our values when the time comes, and that we will do so effectively?

Assume, for example, that you work for an automobile manufacturer. Its new autonomous car is scheduled to hit the market in a couple of months, but it has flunked multiple safety tests. Management plans to begin selling the new car anyway, and your coworkers seem willing to go along with the decision. What do you do?

Or perhaps, you're a software engineer on a team that has been tasked with developing software to fool government equipment used to test the safety of your company's product. Your team members have thrown themselves into the task with enthusiasm – it seems like an intriguing challenge to them. But you have deep misgivings. What do you do?

Dr. Gentile builds GVV on seven pillars, or principles, that cumulatively aim to help us speak up for our values successfully in such situations. The overall emphasis is on rehearsal, pre-scripting, and action planning.[633] Here are the seven pillars of GVV:

- Pillar #1: Values
- Pillar #2: Choice
- Pillar #3: Normalization
- Pillar #4: Purpose
- Pillar #5: Self-knowledge and Alignment
- Pillar #6: Voice
- Pillar #7: Reasons and Rationalizations

Pillar #1: values

We all have values, and we should think carefully about what they are. This is initially important because if we know what our values are, then we can answer with confidence when we ask ourselves, "Is this a hill I wish to die on?" Also, we'll naturally be more committed and more persuasive if we're speaking to advance our own true values than if we're defending values that don't truly resonate with us.

A second reason to consider values is that (in any kind of persuasion) it's extremely helpful to appeal to the values we share with those we are attempting to persuade.[634] Research shows that "if a communicator can effectively frame an issue as especially relevant to a particular value, he or she might sway the attitudes of those who place high personal priority on that value."[635] Indeed, it's much easier to rally people to our cause if we can persuade them that we're striving to advance values that they themselves believe in.[636]

One list of commonly shared values includes wisdom, courage, humanity, justice, temperance, and transcendence.[637] Another lists honesty, respect, responsibility, fairness, and compassion.[638] Convincing other people that we should all try to advance values such as these should not be too heavy a lift. Therefore, it's important to frame our argument in terms of these or similar values, if possible. If we can convince others that our view will advance shared values, and encourage others to consider those who will be affected by the actions (e.g. customers, employees, the community, future generations, the planet), then we're more likely to be successful in advocating for our position.

Pillar #2: choice

Mary Gentile bases the choice pillar of GVV on the simple assumption that most of us have probably given voice to our values at some time in our lives. And, similarly, we have probably failed to give voice to our values at other times. So she suggests that we take part in a simple exercise.

First, we should think about a time that we *did* speak up for, and act on, our values. Then, we should ask ourselves four questions:

- What did we do, and what was the impact?
- What motivated us to speak up and act?
- How satisfied are we? How would we like to have responded?
- What would have made it easier for us to speak and act?

Second, we should think about a time that we *failed* to speak up for and act on our values. Again, we should ask ourselves four questions:

- What happened?
- Why didn't we speak up and act? What would have motivated us to do so?
- How satisfied are we? How would we like to have responded?
- What would have made it easier for us to speak and act?[639]

These exercises allow us to identify a list of "enablers" and "disablers" that either make it easier or harder for us to speak up for our values and act on them. If we recognize the existence and impact of these different factors, then perhaps we can reinforce the enablers and neutralize the disablers.

Allies

Because of the conformity bias, it is easier to do the right thing when we have allies to help us advance our moral objectives. Having our own posse, even if it consists of only one other person, is usually enough to enable us to:

- Resist authority. In his famous shock experiment (see Chapter 4), Stanley Milgram found that if the person who was being asked to administer shocks was placed with two peers (who were Milgram's accomplices) and one of those peers refused to administer a shock, then 90 percent of the experiment's subjects would also refuse.[640]
- Resist conformity. If one of Solomon Asch's accomplices in the line experiment (see Chapter 5) gave the right answer, study subjects found it easy to do so as well.[641]
- Help others. In one study, two people were working in a room when someone in the next room called out in distress. If one of the people (an accomplice of the experimenter) ignored the cries for help, the other person usually

did so too, in a manifestation of the conformity bias. But if the accomplice said, "That sounds bad – you go in and I'll find the person in charge," then the subject went to help every single time.[642]

Gentile goes further. She urges us, when we face an ethical challenge, *to talk out loud about it to another person*. More than almost any other action we can take, this action will make it more likely that we'll speak up for, and act on, our values. According to Gentile, those people who were able to take action in support of their values "had said something, at some point, out loud and to someone outside their own heads. This single act makes the decision feel more real, less hypothetical, less easily avoided. We have brought it into the light."[643]

Selection and sequencing of audiences

If you're a sophomore in high school, and a senior that your parents don't know has asked you to the high school prom, you may quickly decide which parent you wish to approach first to ask for permission to go. Past experience as to which parent is more easily persuaded in such settings will likely guide your strategic choice.

In the same manner, consider a workplace situation where your boss has suggested a course of action that you believe would be unethical. You might confront your boss directly and immediately. However, you might consider whether it would be wiser to first recruit some allies – other employees who might support you if you push back against the boss. Indeed, they might actively join you, or even take the lead in pushing back.

In addition, you should consider who among the available options has the most influence with the boss, and start your recruiting efforts with them. In doing this recruiting, you should also consider whether you're likely to have more luck talking to people alone or in groups. Sometimes, members of a group can bolster one another's courage when facing a difficult task. Sometimes, it's better to address people one at a time. Also, if someone you wish to recruit to your side has already publicly supported the wrongful course of action, you should probably talk to him or her privately. Most people have an easier time changing their minds in private. Gentile also reminds us that it's never too late to persuade. People have been known to change their minds late in the game, so give it a try.

The critical importance of information

This is a no-brainer. If we go off half-cocked and ill-informed, we might decide to challenge an action that is perfectly fine in all respects. Or, even if the planned action is immoral, without proper preparation (such as data gathering, fact-finding, enrolling allies, etc.) it is unlikely that we'll be able to challenge the unethical action in a persuasive manner.

Framing

We know from earlier chapters how important framing can be in our decision making. Of course, the ability to frame an argument appropriately and strategically can improve its persuasive impact. As Gentile writes:

> One of the most powerful enablers we have identified has been the ability to reframe a position: an opportunity with less than ethical attributes is reframed as a risk we all want to avoid; a disagreement that appears to throw the ethics of our audience into doubt is reframed as a "learning dialogue" wherein we are trying to uncover the true parameters of a possible decision; a win-lose choice is reframed through the use of argument and research as a win-win situation; seemingly self-evident assumptions or "truisms" are reframed as debatable or even patently false.[644]

Pillar #3: normalization

As a college professor, author Prentice gets a terrible feeling in the pit of his stomach when he catches students cheating. There is a feeling of betrayal, but also a painful realization that he must now go to the (not insubstantial) trouble of filing charges with the student integrity office and pursuing the case through to its conclusion. Similarly, in the workplace when you find out that your boss or a coworker desires to embark on an unethical course of action, you may well ask yourself: "Why has this landed in *my* lap? Why me?"

Given human nature, and the demands of the modern workplace, we shouldn't be surprised when an ethical challenge knocks on our door. This is the norm. Stuff happens! In today's world, all of us must view standing up for (and acting to advance) our values as an integral part of our job, not some sort of one-off situation that we can safely ignore. Gentile quotes a manager who said:

> In retrospect, this problem really wasn't that overwhelming once I figured out what I wanted to do. But before I had done that, I lied – I instinctively lied – hoping that it just wouldn't happen again. Now I realize such choices are an inevitable part of our business journey and it doesn't seem so huge.[645]

In fact, values conflicts and moral dilemmas are an inevitable part of the business world, and of life in general. We must become accustomed to the idea that it's normal to have these conflicts, and normal to resolve them from time to time. Developing the skills to do so is as important as learning a little French if your job takes you to Paris or keeping up with new IRS pronouncements if you're a tax accountant. Among the GVV tips for handling such situations:

- Take the emotion out of the scenario.
- Realize that the people challenging your values by proposing or doing wrongful acts probably don't think of themselves as bad people.

- Consider what all parties to the conflict have at stake.
- View the situation within a broader organizational context to facilitate finding a solution that all sides can benefit from without violating the law or relevant moral values.

Pillar #4: purpose

Right now, before an ethical dilemma lands in your lap, it's time for you to think carefully about why you do what you do. If you're a student, do you learn only so that you can get a good job, make a lot of money, and become rich? If you're a college instructor, do you teach only so that you'll earn a paycheck? Or, have you chosen a career in teaching so that you can improve young peoples' lives (and the world in general) by being an effective and inspiring educator? Is your goal the narrow one of grubbing for a paycheck, or the grander one of living a life of worth and thereby leaving a positive legacy? Research shows the latter approach is certain to lead to a more meaningful and happier life.[646]

Likewise, Dr. Gentile suggests that by taking a higher and broader view – such as setting a goal of helping to build a company that is a respected corporate citizen – we can establish a "set of positive principles and goals we can refer to and use to guide our behavior."[647] This is an important part of voicing our values, and it involves mustering the moral imagination we discussed in Chapter 20. To see ourselves as part of an endeavor to accomplish something admirable, Gentile writes,

> gives us more arguments for presenting our point of view.
> It also dignifies the values conflicts themselves. These are not seamy little dilemmas that we squirm over quietly and try to forget, rationalizing that they are simply the unfortunate "price we must pay" to survive in a particular firm or industry. Instead, they become opportunities to take a step toward building or preserving an organization that we can be proud of. Instead of normalizing the loss of our values, we can normalize the fact that we will be called upon to preserve them in the face of predictable challenge.[648]

In making decisions where values clashes are on the horizon, it's imperative to keep our own integrity in our frame of reference. And it's critical to keep an ambitious view of what we, and our organization, can contribute to society. We would do well to remember that winning a moral victory for ourselves (and saving our company and our coworkers from an ethical disaster) can become one of our life's most important and satisfying moments.

Pillar #5: self-knowledge and alignment

Stepping up and being a hero may seem like a daunting challenge, but novelist Mary McCarthy wrote that we are all the heroes of our own story.[649] So perhaps all we need to do is write our own "self-story" in a way that enables us to be heroes in our own minds. Gentile suggests that we can be more effective in voicing our values if we generate a personal narrative about our decision that is consistent with our values and builds on our strengths.[650] Many of us might be intimidated, for example, by the notion that we have to stand up and be heroic. But if all we have to do is stand up and be ourselves, taking action might seem more manageable.

Gentile quotes social entrepreneurship scholar Gregory Dees and economist Peter Cramton, who (in writing about negotiation) say that people tend to view themselves as either idealists, pragmatists, or opportunists.[651] Gentile believes that most business people fall into the pragmatist category most of the time. Unlike idealists (who tend to act on their moral values no matter what) or opportunists (who are always looking to advantage themselves), pragmatists seek a balance. Pragmatists want to do the right thing, and may be willing to pay some price for acting on their values, but they don't wish to disadvantage themselves systematically. On the other hand, if pragmatists have a chance to be effective in standing up for their values, they may well be willing to take the chance.

In fact, perceived efficacy is a big factor in people's decision to stand up – people are obviously more likely to take on a difficult challenge if they believe they have a legitimate chance to succeed.[652] To minimize the chance that we will crack under pressure and take the easy way out (slinking away without standing up for our values) Gentile suggests:

> By actively considering our personal-professional profile in advance of conflicts and crafting a self-story that aligns our values, behaviors, and self-image with the kind of person who can make the hard choices and act on their values, we are anticipating those choices and pre-scripting our interpretation *before* we have the chance to be influenced or to rewrite our story under pressure. We make a kind of anticipatory commitment, to head off that tendency to self-justify after the fact. But unlike the typical effort to establish precommitments to values-based action, the commitment here is to being more of who we are, rather than someone different.[653]

If Helen Sharkey Gebhard had been familiar with the GVV pillars, and had crafted her self-story before landing in that room full of lawyers and bankers, there is every chance that she would *not* have given up on herself, and instead would have fought for what she believed in.

Pillar #6: voice

Just as we can learn a foreign language, or master the most recent professional standards, or study the newest features of our favorite app, we can learn the skill of voicing our values.[654] To do so doesn't require us to be a hero or a saint. We simply need to be an effective version of ourselves. We must be able to clarify the ethical issue, bring it to the attention of the relevant people, persuade them as to the proper path, and motivate them to take it.

Being "preachy" is seldom the most effective approach to persuasion.[655] Don't play the saint. Don't be a martyr. Being humble is almost always a good persuasive strategy.[656] *Dialoguing* with our target audience is usually more impactful than *sermonizing* at our target audience.[657] In addition, try to provide workable solutions and compromises.

In general, face-to-face meetings are more successful than sending an e-mail.[658] But Gentile recommends that we consider our own strengths. If talking with someone would likely be better, would you be most comfortable in a one-on-one meeting with your target? Would you be more effective if you brought along a "wingman"? Would a group meeting provide a better opportunity to make your case? Knowing your own strengths and weaknesses will help you determine what setting will be best for you to express yourself and feel supported.

The first time we stand up for our values may be difficult. But with practice, we should feel more comfortable. Over time, we will learn lessons as to what works and what doesn't. We will likely learn that enlisting mentors and others to help us is generally a better idea than playing the Lone Ranger. Most of us find it more difficult to voice our values alone.

It's also difficult to be ethical on the spot or in the spur of the moment. Speaking up in those circumstances can be particularly tough, which is why a key message of this GVV pillar is: practice, practice, practice. It's how you get to Carnegie Hall, and it's how you give yourself the best chance to voice your values effectively. As Gentile writes, "[y]ou are most likely to say those words that you have pre-scripted and already heard yourself express, at earlier times in your career or in practice sessions."[659]

Because author Prentice knows how hard it can be to be ethical spontaneously, he requires his business school students to write a pre-scripting essay describing (a) an ethical challenge they will likely face in their careers, and (b) how they hope they will respond. Over the years, he's received feedback from many students who have later faced exactly the scenario that they'd described in this prescripting exercise. These former students found that the class essay had helped them find their voice and effectively speak their values, just as Gentile predicted.

In another example, in 2019 there was a depressingly common school shooting at Highlands Ranch High School in Colorado. Teenager Kendrick Castillo heroically lunged at one of the gunmen, losing his own life while saving others. Before the shooting, Kendrick had told his father emphatically that he would act if confronted by a gunman in school.[660] His pre-scripting saved lives.

Neither your authors nor Dr. Gentile expect you to risk your life. However, we do hope that you'll pre-script so that you can more readily live up to your moral standards when the time comes to act.

Pillar #7: reasons and rationalizations

It's important not only to be prepared to make a positive case for our values, but also to be aware that the supervisors, co-employees, and others whom we are trying to persuade have their own reasons and rationalizations for the course of action they're taking, and we'll probably have to overcome those reasons and rationalizations as well. So, we might as well give them some thought up front. One of the reasons it's hard to be ethical on the fly is that it's also hard to be a persuasive advocate on the fly, unless you have substantial experience as a debater or speechwriter.

In Chapter 21, we examined the most common rationalizations in detail ("Everybody does it"; "No one is really hurt"; "Our competitors do even worse things") that we are likely to hear from people who are preparing to flout our values (and their own). With some planning, we should be able to prepare responses in advance so that when these excuses are rolled out, we may rebut them effectively.

Gentile recommends, among other things, that in standing up for our values we:

- Frame issues using a long-term lens. Sometimes, others in our organization will be looking to take an unethical shortcut to solve an immediate problem. For example, it may seem attractive to fudge the numbers to make earnings projections this quarter. But we can emphasize the long-term negative impact to the company's reputation that will occur when that fraud ends up splashed across the internet. The long-term damage will swamp any short-term benefits. Remind everyone of the "newspaper test" – would they want to see their misdeeds in the headlines or on social media?
- Consider the situation in terms of the group's, and the company's, wider purpose. Sometimes, employees get caught up in "subgoal pursuit"[661] and will consider doing something unethical to advance their immediate work unit's goals in a way that will likely damage the overall company. For example, perhaps your software team is supposed to solve "Priority One" problems within 24 hours, but is given 48 hours to solve "Priority Two" problems. Your team is having difficulty solving a certain class of Priority One problems within 24 hours, so your manager plans to simply relabel them as Priority Two problems. You can point out that while this improves the appearance of your team's performance record, it hurts the company overall by slowing down the solution time for truly important tasks.
- Watch out for false dichotomies. Often, employees will consider acting unethically to solve a particular problem while not realizing that there are other means of solving it. For example, a sales representative may say: "I'm going to lose this sale unless I lie to the customer about our widget's performance." Perhaps you can suggest a legitimate "sweetener" that the sales rep can throw into the negotiations, such as an extended guarantee or a service contract that will make the overall package your company is offering preferable to the competitor's, even though your widget is inferior in a head-to-head match-up.
- Position ourselves as an agent of "continuous improvement" rather than a source of complaint. As noted earlier, it's typically not an effective approach

to frame ourselves as the saint whose job it is to harass other employees into living up to our own very high standards.
- Always look for suggestions that align the ethical path with a practical, forward-looking path of improvement. People don't want to hear only about the problems; they want to hear about solutions, too. If we can encourage others to do the right thing and remind them how good they will feel if they help create an ethical result, we'll be more persuasive than if we just try to make others feel guilty about not living up to our standards.[662]
- Be attuned to the fact that the pressures, biases, and situational factors discussed in detail elsewhere in this book may be the motivating factors for the people who are suggesting the course of action that we believe to be unethical. We can use our knowledge of these insidious influences and forces (and the suggestions this book makes for combatting them) to "unpack and respond to the reasons and rationalizations proffered by *others* for taking an action that violate our own values."[663]

Conclusion

There is more to the Giving Voice to Values program than is summarized here, so your authors strongly recommend that you buy and read Mary Gentile's book or, at a minimum, watch the eight GVV videos on the Ethics Unwrapped website. You really *can* make a difference. You can learn to effectively speak up for your values. You can fight the good fight and improve the chances of leading a life you can be proud of, even if you don't win every battle.

One of the more encouraging bits of information in Gentile's book is her summary of the reports of students applying for an MBA program. Many of the applicants had been asked in their careers to do things that conflicted with their values – things like padding billable hours, fudging earnings reports, and adjusting economic forecasts. In fact, almost all the applicants had such a story to tell. According to Gentile:

> Despite the similar stories they told, these students' responses were sometimes quite different. Many reported their discomfort with such conflicts but a quiet acceptance of the impossibility of resisting the organizational demands. Others, while reporting seemingly identical conflicts and pressures, decided to voice their objections and found ways – sometimes very creative ways – to resolve the conflicts. These students did not appear to be more articulate or more intelligent. Their essays did not express a greater sense of discomfort than the essays of those who did not voice or act on their values. *They did, however, make the decision to say something.* Sometimes they spoke persuasively; sometimes they appeared to be a bit naïve or clumsy. Some succeeded in changing the practice they addressed; others did not. But they spoke up, and that put them on a different path.[664]

As Mary Gentile notes, what makes it most likely that we will voice our values and stand up for the good is the fact that we have prepared. We've thought in advance about how we will handle such a challenge and we have said aloud to someone else that we would, in fact, speak up for our values if need be. Indeed, you can do those things right here, right now, before you turn the page.

ETHICS UNWRAPPED RESOURCES

Videos

Intro to GVV
Series: Giving Voice to Values

Pillar 1: Values
Series: Giving Voice to Values

Pillar 2: Choice
Series: Giving Voice to Values

Pillar 3: Normalization
Series: Giving Voice to Values

Pillar 4: Purpose
Series: Giving Voice to Values

Pillar 5: Self-Knowledge & Alignment
Series: Giving Voice to Values

Pillar 6: Voice
Series: Giving Voice to Values

Pillar 7: Reasons & Rationalizations
Series: Giving Voice to Values

ETHICS UNWRAPPED RESOURCES

Related Videos

Values
Series: Ethics Defined

Justice
Series: Ethics Defined

Framing
Series: Ethics Defined

Rationalizations
Series: Ethics Defined

Case Studies

Pao & Gender Bias

Freedom of Speech on Campus

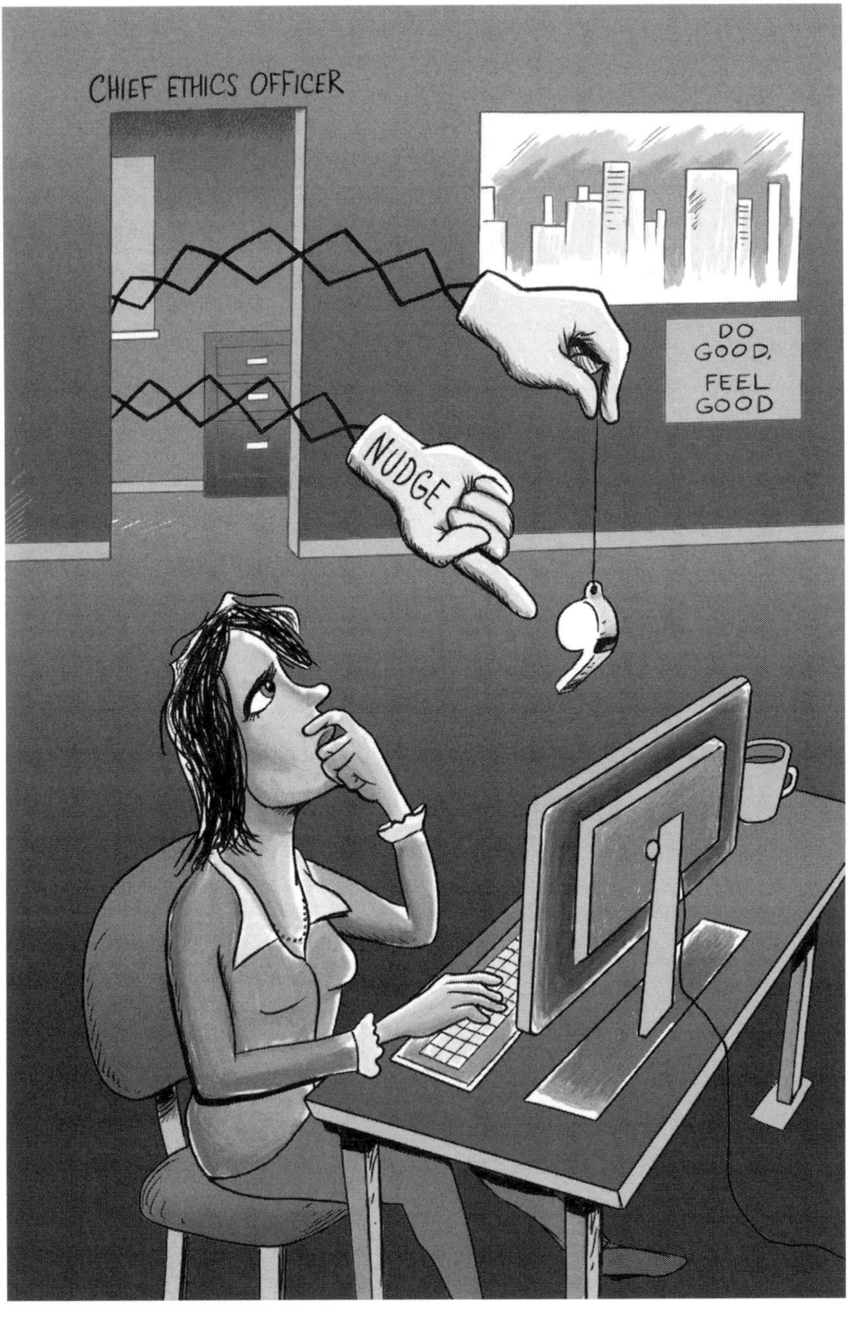
CHIEF ETHICS OFFICER
NUDGE
DO
GOOD.
FEEL
GOOD

23

CREATING A CULTURE THAT MAKES IT EASIER TO DO THE RIGHT THING

> *"It is comforting to assume that one bad apple or renegade faction within an organization is somehow responsible for the corruption we too often observe."*[665]
>
> – Ashworth, Gioia, Robinson & Trevino

Introduction

Business ethics scholar Lamar Pierce has often made the point that the easiest way to run an honest business is to hire honest employees. Companies agree, which is why some organizations administer "integrity tests" to job applicants to reveal how guilt-prone those potential employees are.[666] Research indicates that the more guilt-prone people are, the more likely they are to be attentive toward moral issues, and the more honest they will be overall. This is very important because most corporate wrongdoing is committed by just a few employees.[667]

But we also know from the behavioral ethics research already discussed in this book that even the most honest people in the world will struggle to do the right thing if they find themselves inside a morally toxic corporate culture. Much of our ethical decision making is influenced more by where we are than by who we are.

For instance, Wells Fargo's employees created millions of fake accounts for customers who had not authorized them, and didn't need or want the accounts. When the scandal was uncovered, the bank began by firing some 5,300 employees. However, this wrongdoing was not caused by 5,300 "rogue employees" that the bank had accidentally hired. It was caused by a corporate culture that emphasized performance at all costs and shoved ethical considerations to the side, thereby causing normal people to commit fraud.[668]

Nudging in the right direction

In Part I of this book, we learned about factors and forces that can make it difficult for even good people to do the right thing. So far in Part II, we've focused on the lessons behavioral ethics research has for individuals struggling to live more ethical lives. In this final chapter, we focus at the organizational level. Behavioral ethics research has lessons that organizations can apply to make it easier for their employees and others to do the right thing, and harder to do the wrong thing. As psychologists Nick Epley and Amit Kumar note:

> Interventions to encourage ethical behavior are often based on misperceptions of how transgressions occur, and thus are not as effective as they could be. Compliance programs increasingly take a legalistic approach to ethics that focuses on individual accountability. They're designed to educate employees and then punish wrongdoing among the "bad apples" who misbehave. Yet a large body of behavioral science research suggests that even well-meaning and well-informed people are more ethically malleable than one might guess.[669]

Nobel Prize-winning economist Richard Thaler and legal scholar Cass Sunstein wrote a famous book about how behavioral science can help organizations "nudge" people to make better decisions to improve their health, wealth, and happiness.[670] By using behavioral research to change the *choice architecture* – the conditions under which people make decisions – governments, companies, and other organizations can dramatically affect people's decisions. Sunstein notes:

> In the United States, a number of initiatives have been informed by relevant empirical findings and behavioral economics has played an unmistakable role in numerous domains. These initiatives enlist such tools as disclosure, warnings, and default rules, and they can be found in multiple areas, including fuel economy, energy efficiency, environmental protection, health care, and obesity. As a result, behavioral findings have become an important reference point for regulatory and other policymaking in the United States.
> In the United Kingdom, Prime Minister Cameron has created a Behavioural Insights Team with the specific goal of incorporating an understanding of human behavior into policy initiatives. The official website states that its "work draws on insights from the growing body of academic research in the fields of behavioural economics and psychology which show how often subtle changes to the way in which decisions are framed can have big impacts on how people respond to them." The team has used these insights to promote initiatives in numerous areas, including smoking cessation, energy efficiency, organ donation, consumer protection, and compliance strategies in general. Other nations have expressed interest in the work of the team, and its operations are expanding.[671]

Private organizations have also used these behavioral nudges. For example, because of the *status quo bias* – which is the tendency we have to prefer things the way they are to other alternatives – companies have been able to significantly increase the amount of money that their employees save for retirement simply by changing employee forms to raise the amount of money that will be withheld from paychecks if employees don't check a different box.[672]

This behavioral research can be used to improve our *moral* decision making as well as our decisions about health and wealth. EthicalSystems.org, founded by psychologist Jonathan Haidt, is an organization aimed at improving business integrity through behavioral science research focusing largely on organizations.[673] Some organizations are already moving in this direction. The Dutch National Bank has used behavioral research to improve its employees' ethical decision making.[674] The Royal Bank of Scotland formed "behavioral risk teams" for the same purpose.[675] Goldman Sachs has created a behavioral unit that monitors data regarding its employees' behavior, so that the bank can learn "what it needs to do to enhance the ethics and values of its employees."[676]

Things to try

Our expectations for the impact of the measures that we talk about in this chapter (and in the entire book) must be tempered by the statement of Azish Filabi, former Executive Director of Ethical Systems: "We are really at the infancy of behavioral science, particularly with respect to ethics." Nonetheless, organizations wishing to improve their people's ethical decision making and behavior should (among other things) keep the following lessons in mind, all of which are derived from behavioral ethics research.

Because we can feel "'elevated' by witnessing good deeds and moral exemplars,"[677] organizations should recognize their employees who do good deeds. They can also develop origin stories, or other foundational tales, of employees who have done the right thing.[678] A classic example: The accountant Arthur Andersen supposedly told a client (early in his company's history) that there was "not enough money in the city of Chicago" to make him sign off on inaccurate accounting because his mother had taught him a simple mantra – "Think straight, talk straight."[679] Inspiration from this tale helped Arthur Andersen become one of the world's most successful accounting firms, until its top managers forgot this lesson in the 1980s and 1990s.

Because of phenomena like obedience to authority and the conformity bias, it's critically important that leaders walk the walk, as Arthur Andersen apparently did while he was alive. Studies show that just as employees who see unethical conduct above and around them in a company are more likely to act unethically, employees are more likely to act ethically if surrounded by people, particularly leaders, who do the right thing.[680] When leaders exhibit moral humility by respecting and validating their employees' moral character, the impact on employees' moral behavior can be especially beneficial.[681]

Research shows that reminding students not to cheat reduces cheating by keeping moral norms salient in the students' minds.[682] Studies demonstrate that when people are reminded of their values, they are more likely to act consistently with them.[683] So, organizations should frequently remind their employees of the organization's values and commitment to honesty.

Ethics training is another method of keeping morality foremost in employees' minds. Studies indicate that "businesspersons employed in organizations with formalized ethics training have more positive perceptions of organizational ethics than do those working for firms without such training"[684] and that "individuals exposed to ethics programs were more likely to have refused to take an unethical action when confronted with their most serious ethical dilemma than were other respondents."[685] Feel free to use this book in your organization's ethics training!

We know from earlier chapters how significantly framing affects moral decision making. In an organization where ethics are frequently discussed and emphasized, moral principles are more likely to be included in employees' frame of reference when they face an ethical challenge. Best Buy is a company that has successfully followed this path.[686] According to behavioral economist Francesca Gino:

> Another way to make our standards shine is to discuss them more often. Increasingly, organizations are doing this by design. For instance, Kathleen Edmond, the Chief Ethics Officer at Best Buy, created a website where company employees can read about the company's policy regarding ethically questionable behaviors and learn tips on how to best defend themselves from crossing ethical boundaries. The website highlights the extent to which the organization cares about morality and honesty, and Best Buy reports that it has positively influenced employee behavior.[687]

A good way to remind employees and others of an organization's values is to have a code of ethics. Research indicates that adopting an honor code can improve ethical behavior in an organization.[688] Behavioral research indicates that "best practices" for a code of ethics include:

- Simpler is better.
- Engage employees in drafting and revising the code rather than relying exclusively on outside "experts."
- Top brass must buy in.
- The code should be communicated persistently throughout the organization.
- Managers should actually use the code in resolving ethical issues.
- Strengthening and updating the code should be a continual priority.

Incrementalism is dangerous, as we know. For managers of organizations, research into what is called *regulatory focus theory* finds that people tend to have one of two self-regulatory focuses – either a "promotion (of being ethical) focus" that concentrates on progress by making changes to the status quo, or a "prevention (of being unethical) focus" that is concerned with maintaining the status quo against a worse state. Studies show that people with a natural prevention focus, or a focus induced by nudges, are more likely to avoid the slippery slope.[689] In other words, when organizations concentrate their employees' attention on avoiding the losses that might be caused by unethical behavior, employees are less likely to slide down the slippery slope.[690] Therefore, business ethics scholar David Welsh and colleagues recommend that managers ward off the slippery slope by:

- Ensuring that their organization possesses a strong ethical culture that quickly addresses even small deviations from proper conduct.
- Setting clear standards and openly spelling out ethical pitfalls that must be avoided.
- Encouraging a prevention focus by (for example) encouraging "employees to be vigilant in identifying financial mistakes rather than creative in attempting to find new financial loopholes."[691]

Of course, in-group biases can foster an "us-against-them" mentality where companies not only battle their industry competitors, but may also go to war against regulators, communities, and even customers. Research shows that companies may reduce employee misconduct by de-emphasizing the duties that employees owe to their employer, and instead emphasizing the duties that employees owe to the larger community.[692] Studies indicate that employees who perceive that their employer promotes responsibility to customers and the community are less likely to misbehave.[693]

As discussed in Part I, we know time pressure can cause problems for ethical decision making. Organizations should take this into account as well. Our automatic responses (Kahneman's System 1 thinking)[694] tend to be more dishonest than our responses rendered after being given more time to think about the issue.[695] Therefore, providing people with more time to make an ethical choice can improve the quality of their ethical decision making.[696] Research suggests that adopting structures and systems to deliberately slow down decision making can help eliminate the errors caused by time pressure. Organizations should establish procedures to ensure that decisions with moral implications are not made before other people can be consulted, a team of deciders can be assembled, a review process is constituted, and other safeguards are established. This can minimize errors brought on by time pressure.[697]

Studies also show that surgeons can dramatically improve patient safety by using checklists to help them navigate all the key steps of complex surgery.[698] In fact, a company called Broadcat uses behavioral insights to create ethical checklists for employees engaged in various activities, such as traveling abroad.[699] Of course, companies can easily create such checklists themselves to improve compliance with, for example, the Foreign Corrupt Practices Act. Many companies (e.g., Google, Facebook, Bank of America) have hired in-house behavioral scientists to nudge employees in the right direction using a variety of influences, including checklists.[700]

The metaphor of the ledger that we discussed in Chapter 21 is a classic rationalization by which employees give themselves permission to fail to follow their own (or their company's) ethical standards. When we feel that we've been treated unfairly, we are much more likely to cheat our employer or otherwise misbehave. Therefore, any organization that wishes to encourage its employees to act ethically should do its best to treat those employees fairly. It's a simple solution, and it's the right thing to do, too.

Other studies show that people lie and cheat less when working in a clean room rather than in a dirty one,[701] and in a well-lit environment rather than a dark one.[702] These are easy fixes.

Problem areas

Four particular areas present very difficult challenges for companies and other organizations that wish to do the right thing. In these four areas, research has taught us a lot, but probably not yet enough.

Implicit bias in hiring and related matters

The Varsity Blues college admissions scandal of 2019 confirmed what we already knew – life is not always fair. It's not fair for those who are denied a rightful place in a university's freshman class, and are thereby prevented from showing what they can do. It's also not fair for those of us who are not hired because of the implicit bias of a company's hiring committee. Explicit bias is bad as well, of course, but implicit bias is especially difficult to detect.

Structural changes to minimize the impact of implicit biases seem to provide the most promising avenue for improvement. The most famous example deals with orchestras. For years, women made up but a small portion of the musicians in symphony orchestras. Nature, so it seemed, favored men with whatever magic it takes to be a musical virtuoso. But some suspected that men benefited from implicit bias when orchestra tryouts occurred, not from natural selection. When orchestras began holding blind auditions (the applicants played behind a curtain) and the genders of those auditioning were unknown to the judges, the percentage of women chosen to play in symphony orchestras rose by 500 percent.[703] Many professors set up a system, for instance, where they grade papers and exams without knowing the identity of the student until they have finished, which should eliminate any implicit bias.

However, in many settings, it's impossible to maintain anonymity. So what other structural changes can organizations make? When medical professionals realized that most physicians seemed to suffer from an inaccurate "female = low cardiac risk" stereotype, the National Heart, Lung, and Blood Institute issued recommendations that *everyone* over the age of 20 have their cholesterol checked at least every five years. Thus, doctors who follow these guidelines don't need to make any independent judgment about who is or isn't a cardiac risk. Indeed, following these guidelines circumvents implicit bias.[704]

Consider implicit bias in the hiring process. For most jobs in an organization, we will have to meet the candidates before hiring them. And we won't wish to speak to the candidates only through a curtain or a scrambler that disguises their voice and therefore their gender. So here are some structural steps that any organization can take to mitigate implicit bias while hiring:

- Before you start, consciously commit to a process that will be as inclusive and bias-free as possible.
- Establish, broadcast, and reinforce a policy of nondiscriminatory hiring.
- Create and extensively advertise nondiscriminatory hiring criteria.
- Cast a wide recruiting net – one that will provide new sources of diverse candidates.
- Provide all members of the hiring committee with training to minimize implicit bias.
- Ensure that all candidates are treated equally as their resumes are evaluated.
- Ensure that all candidates who are interviewed are treated equally in all respects (e.g., all candidates should be asked the same questions).
- Collect and monitor hiring data so you can measure success.[705]

Structuring and managing incentives

This is another challenging area. We tend to respond to incentives (no big surprise there!). But if incentives are too extreme – either rewards are too great or punishments too strong – this can inevitably lead to gaming the system, especially if specified goals are unrealistic. Wells Fargo didn't hire 5,300 bad people who created and sold unauthorized accounts to customers. Rather, Wells Fargo created insanely high sales targets, and the only way employees could meet those targets was to fabricate accounts.

Similarly, when Sears changed employees' compensation at its auto repair shops from hourly wages to a commission structure, it shouldn't have been surprised that there was a dramatic uptick in sales of unnecessary parts and services to customers, which ultimately led to Sears paying substantial monetary fines and settlements.[706]

So how can organizations create a Goldilocks incentive system that is "just right" – incentivizing employees to work hard and be productive, but not over-incentivizing them so that they lie, cheat, and steal? It's not easy hitting that sweet spot. But being aware of the behavioral science and its consequences can help. Overall, one important rule is to punish ethical errors, which seems to reduce unethical behavior.[707] Just as importantly, organizations should explicitly reward ethical behavior. Studies show this also seems to move employee ethicality in the right direction.[708] Lockheed-Martin, for example, has instituted a "Chairman's Award" to visibly and emphatically reward employees who exemplify the company's aspirational ethical standards.[709]

Importantly, reward and control systems within organizations may not only have a short-term impact on employees' behavior, but may also have a long-term beneficial effect by enhancing employees' moral ownership: "These systems can signal what is valued in organizations, and research has shown that although individuals may initially comply with norms for strategic self-presentation, over time, such norms can cause identity changes that can impact the individual's sense of responsibility to take moral action."[710]

Also, remember one thing that significantly complicates an incentive system is loss aversion. As we learned in Chapter 10, we dislike losses approximately twice as much as we like gains. This has implications for an incentive system, of course. When trying to incentivize employees to do the right thing, companies might try a loss frame. For example, they might model their incentives after government programs where consumers have been more effectively persuaded to buy new energy efficient appliances when their attention was focused on how much money they would lose (if they didn't buy the energy efficient appliance) rather than on how much money they would save if they did.[711] A company might reward employees with stock shares, for example, as compensation for future good behavior, with the condition that the shares will be returned to the company should the employee become the subject of a regulatory action or significant customer complaint.

Transparency

We know from Chapter 17 that a lack of transparency can prevent us from being our best selves. In fact, one study showed that even children cheat less when they feel they're being seen as opposed to when they're wearing a Halloween costume with a mask.[712] Similarly, feeling insulated from scrutiny can lead employees to lower their moral guard. So how can organizations use this knowledge?

Obviously, organizations can install surveillance systems, which seem to reduce misbehavior.[713] Employers can also increase employees' subconscious feelings that their conduct is observable by installing cameras, brightening the lights,[714] adding windows or mirrors,[715] or even putting up drawings of eyes.[716] But the key is to subtly let employees know that appropriate scrutiny is being exercised without going so far as to make them feel so spied upon that they rebel. "Heavy surveillance is a signal of distrust, which may produce less trustworthy behaviors in response to expectations."[717] Clearly, this can be a difficult balance to strike. More research will point the way.

Whistle-blowing

Volkswagen had no whistle-blowing system in place. Employees who knew about its software to cheat environmental testing machines had nowhere to go to try to stop the fraud.[718] Wells Fargo supposedly had a whistle-blower system in place yet somehow it managed to repeatedly punish whistle-blowers who tried to stop the fake account scandal.

Smart organizations would do well to encourage a speak-up culture: "If you see something, say something." The importance of leaders' conduct cannot be overemphasized, as noted earlier. But even followers can have a significant impact on their leaders' behavior when they "speak truth to power."[719] Of course, almost everyone finds it easier to do the right thing themselves than to call others out for their wrongful behavior. Choosing to blow the whistle is hard, but organizations benefit when their employees feel comfortable in speaking out in this way. However, because we tend to be obedient to authority and to conform to the conduct of those around us, "it takes a village" to create an organizational culture that supports internal whistle-blowers.[720]

External whistle-blowing is somehow never as appealing to organizations as internal whistle-blowing (which may not be welcome either!). But if that is the only way that illegal and/or unethical behavior will be stopped, then it will probably save the company money if employees blow the whistle sooner rather than later. Fortunately, in the U.S. there are many laws (e.g. False Claims Act, Sarbanes-Oxley Act, Dodd-Frank Act) that reward and/or protect external whistle-blowers, under at least some circumstances. Some other countries have similar laws.

Some experts have argued that organizations should go further, claiming that at least some industries might be better off under a regime that *punishes* employees who know about corrupt practices yet *fail to report them*.[721] Companies could implement such sanctions themselves to encourage internal whistle-blowing.

While there seems to be no clear consensus on the best way to establish a speak-up culture or a broader moral culture inside an organization, business ethics scholar David Hess suggests:

> A firm using compliance-based programs focuses its efforts on deterrence through threat of detection and punishment for violations of the law or code of conduct. A firm using an integrity-based approach, on the other hand, focuses its efforts on establishing legitimacy with employees through internally developed organizational values and self-governance. . . .
>
> Subsequent research has confirmed that an integrity-based program is more effective than a compliance-based program in reaching positive outcomes for the firm.[722]

Conclusion

Behavioral ethics research provides many lessons on how we can best structure our organizations to encourage moral actions and discourage immoral actions. Many of these lessons will be refined over the coming years by additional research, but it is clear that this information can be productively applied now by organizations that truly wish to improve their employees' moral performance.

Prosocial behavior is a trainable skill.[723] If organizations can nudge employees to act ethically, it can lead employees to begin to think of themselves as ethical people, which then leads those employees to act more ethically in a virtuous circle. In fact, economist Uri Gneezy and colleagues believe that the evidence from economics and psychology suggests that "prosocial behavior may lead [people] to update their views of themselves. If I behaved prosocially, I must be a prosocial kind of person – someone for whom prosocial behavior provides greater utility – and therefore I will behave more prosocially in the future."[724] And that is a win-win for all of us.

Making it easier to do the right thing **229**

ETHICS UNWRAPPED RESOURCES

Videos

Ethical Leadership 1: Perilous at the Top
Series: Concepts Unwrapped

Ethical Leadership 2: Best Practices
Series: Concepts Unwrapped

Related Videos

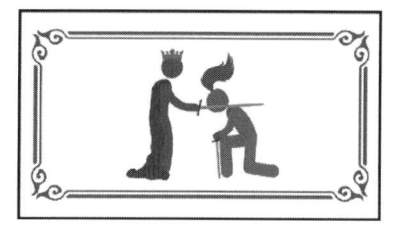

Integrity
Series: Ethics Defined

Corporate Social Responsibility
Series: Ethics Defined

Veil of Ignorance
Series: Ethics Defined

Prosocial Behavior
Series: Ethics Defined

Implicit Bias
Series: Concepts Unwrapped

Incentive Gaming
Series: Concepts Unwrapped

ETHICS UNWRAPPED RESOURCES

Related Videos (Continued)

#MeToo
Series: Ethics in Focus

Case Studies

The Costco Model

The Astros' Sign-Stealing Scandal

Apple Suppliers & Labor Practices

NOTES

Introduction

1 Roosevelt, T. 1906. *Sixth Annual Message to Congress, December 3, 1906.* Dickinson State University.
2 This is our definition of "behavioral ethics." *See also* O'Brien, K., Wittmer, D. and Ebrahimi, G.P. 2017. "Behavioral Ethics in Practice: Integrating Service Learning into a Graduate Business Ethics Course." *Journal of Management Education* 41(4): 599–616 (defining behavioral ethics as "the discipline or study of the factors that influence individuals to act ethically or unethically").
3 Tomlin, K.A., Metzger, M.L., Bradley-Geist, J. and Gonzalez-Padron, T. 2017. "Are Students Blind to Their Ethical Blind Spots? An Exploration of Why Ethics Education Should Focus on Self-Perception Biases." *Journal of Management Education* 41(4): 539–574.
4 Offstein, E., Dufresne, R.L. and Childers, Jr., J.S. 2017. "Novel Lessons on Behavioral Ethics from the U.S. Military Academy at West Point." *Journal of Management Education* 41(4): 480–496.
5 Tomlin, K.A., Metzger, M.L., Bradley-Geist, J. and Gonzalez-Padron, T. (2017).
6 *Id.*
7 Park, J. and Elsass, P. 2017. "Behavioral Ethics and the New Landscape in Ethics Pedagogy in Management Education." *Journal of Management Education* 41(4): 447–454.
8 Schwartz, M.S. 2017. "Teaching Behavioral Ethics: Overcoming the Key Impediments to Ethical Behavior." *Journal of Management Education* 41(4): 497–513.
9 Other websites we recommend for resources in behavioral ethics are www.ethicalsystems.org and https://behaviorallegalethics.wordpress.com/.

Part I

10 Strohminger, N. and Nichols, S. 2015. "Neurodegeneration and Identity." *Psychological Science* 26(9): 1468–1479.
11 Goodwin, G.P., Piazza, J. and Rozin, P. 2014. "Moral Character Predominates in Person Perception and Evaluation." *Journal of Personality and Social Psychology* 106(1): 148–168.
12 Leach, C.W., Ellemers, N. and Barreto, M. 2007. "Group Virtue: The Importance of Morality (vs. Competence and Sociability) in the Positive Evaluation of In-Groups." *Journal of Personality and Social Psychology* 93(2): 234–249.

13 Ariely, D. 2009. *Predictably Irrational: The Hidden Forces That Shape Our Decisions*. Harper Perennial.
14 Smith, I.H. and Kouchaki, M. 2018. "Moral Humility: In Life and at Work." *Research in Organizational Behavior* 38: 77–94.
15 May, J. 2018. *Regard for Reason in the Moral Mind*. Oxford University Press.
16 Yong, E. 2018. "Psychology's Replication Crisis Is Running out of Excuses." *The Atlantic*, Nov. 19. www.theatlantic.com/science/archive/2018/11/psychologys-replication-crisis-real/576223/.

Chapter 1

17 Levy, N. 2007. *Neuroethics: Challenges for the 21st Century*. Cambridge University Press.
18 Kant, I. 2012. *Groundwork for the Metaphysics of Morals*. Cambridge University Press. (Italics added).
19 Park, J. and Elsass, P. 2017. "Behavioral Ethics and the New Landscape in Ethics Pedagogy in Management Education." *Journal of Management Education* 41(4): 447–454.
20 Haidt, J. 2012. *The Righteous Mind: Why Good People Are Divided by Politics and Religion*. Pantheon Books.
21 Hirsh, J.B., Lu, J.G. and Galinsky, A.D. 2018. "Moral Utility Theory: Understanding the Motivation to Behave." *Research in Organizational Behavior* 38: 43–59.
22 Schnall, S., Haidt, J., Clore, G.L. and Jordan, A.H. 2008. "Disgust as Embodied in Moral Judgment." *Personality and Social Psychology Bulletin* 34(8): 1096–1109.
23 Wheatley, T. and Haidt, J. 2005. "Hypnotically Induced Disgust Makes Moral Judgment More Severe." *Psychological Science* 16(10): 780–784.
24 Schnall, S., Benton, J. and Harvey, S. 2008. "With a Clean Conscience: Cleanliness Reduces the Severity of Moral Judgments." *Psychological Science* 19(12): 1219–1222.
25 May, J. 2018. *Regard for Reason in the Moral Mind*. Oxford University Press.
26 Sauer, H. 2017. *Moral Judgments as Educated Intuitions*. MIT Press.
27 *Id*.
28 Brandt, C.A. 2016. "Letter to the Editor." *Napa Valley Register*, Sept. 3. http://napavalleyregister.com/news/opinion/mailbag/wise-up-kaepernick/article_173fa896-f6dd-577f-a781-93a28683950c.html.
29 Poss, S. 2016. "Letter to the Editor." *The Fresno Bee*, Sept. 2. www.fresnobee.com/opinion/letters-to-the-editor/article99349627.html.
30 Sauer, H. 2019. *Moral Thinking, Fast and Slow*. Routledge Focus.
31 Haidt, J. 2012. *The Righteous Mind: Why Good People Are Divided by Politics and Religion*. Pantheon Books.
32 Luhrmann, T.M. 2015. "Faith v. Facts." *New York Times*, Apr. 19. www.nytimes.com/2015/04/19/opinion/sunday/t-m-luhrmann-faith-vs-facts.html.
33 Sloman, S. and Ferbach, P. 2017. *The Knowledge Illusion: Why We Never Think Alone*. Riverhead Books.
34 Gibbs, J.C. 2014. *Moral Development & Reality: Beyond the Theories of Kohlberg, Hoffman, and Haidt*. Oxford University Press.
35 Henrich, J. 2016. *The Secret of Our Success: How Culture is Driving Human Evolution, Domesticating Our Species, and Making Us Smarter*. Princeton University Press.
36 Huemer, M. 2016. "A Liberal Realist Answer to Debunking Skeptics: The Empirical Case for Realism." *Philosophical Studies* 173: 1983–2010.

Chapter 2

37 Shermer, M. 2012. "The Alpinist of Evil." *Scientific American* 307(6): 84.
38 van Schaik, C., Brukart, J.M., Jaeggi, A.V. and von Rohr, C.R. 2014. "Morality as a Biological Adaptation: An Evolutionary Model Based on the Lifestyle of Human Foragers." In *Empirically Informed Ethics: Morality between Facts and Norms*, Christen, M. et al. (eds.), 65–85. Springer.

39 Pinker, S. 2002. *The Blank Slate: The Modern Denial of Human Nature*. Viking.
40 Klass, P. 2017. "Guilt Can Be Good for Your Kid." *New York Times*, Dec. 4. (quoting Malti).
41 Motro, D., Ordóñez, L., Pittarello, A. and Welsh, D. 2018. "Investigating the Effects of Anger and Guilt on Unethical Behavior: A Dual-Process Approach." *Journal of Business Ethics* 152: 133–148.
42 Cohen, T.R. and Morse, L. 2014. "Moral Character: What It Is and What It Does." *Research in Organizational Behavior* 34: 43–61.
43 Prinz, J. 2007. *The Emotional Construction of Morals*. Oxford University Press.
44 Klass, P. (2017).
45 Sapolsky, R.M. 2017. *Behave: The Biology of Humans at Our Best and Worst*. Penguin Press.
46 Ayala, E. 2019. "The College Admissions Scandal is a Morality Play." *San Antonio Express-News*, Mar. 16. www.expressnews.com/news/news_columnists/elaine_ayala/article/The-college-admissions-scandal-is-a-morality-play-13692867.php.
47 Haidt, J. 2012. *The Righteous Mind: Why Good People Are Divided by Politics and Religion*. Pantheon Books.
48 Keltner, D., Kogan, A., Piff, P.K. and Saturn, S.R. 2014. "The Sociocultural Appraisals, Values, and Emotions (SAVE) Framework of Prosociality: Core Processes from Gene to Meme." *Annual Review of Psychology* 65: 425–460.
49 Tomasello, M. 2016. *A Natural History of Human Morality*. Harvard University Press.
50 Singer, T. and Klimecki, O. 2014. "Empathy and Compassion." *Current Biology* 24(18): R875–R878.
51 Bunge, A. and Skulmowski, A. 2014. "Descriptive and Pragmatic Levels of Empirical Ethics: Utilizing the Situated Character of Moral Concepts, Judgment, and Decision-Making." In *Experimental Ethics: Toward an Empirical Moral Philosophy*, Luetge, C., Rusch, H. and Uhl, M. (eds.), 175–190. Springer.
52 Bloom, P. 2018. *Against Empathy: The Case for Rational Compassion*. Ecco.
53 Baumeister, R. 1997. *Evil: Inside Human Violence and Cruelty*. W.H. Freeman & Co.
54 Bloom, P. (2018).
55 Prinz, J. and Nichols, S. 2010. "Moral Emotions." In *The Moral Psychology Handbook*, Doris, J. (ed.), 111–146. Oxford University Press.
56 Shermer, M. 2015. *The Moral Arc: How Science and Reason Lead Humanity Toward Truth, Justice, and Freedom*. Henry Holt.
57 Schwitzgebel, E. 2014. "The Moral Behavior of Ethicists and the Role of the Philosopher." In *Experimental Ethics: Toward an Empirical Moral Philosophy*, Luetge, C., Rusch, H. and Uhl, M. (eds.). Palgrave MacMillan.
58 Shao, R., Aquino, K. and Freeman, D. "Beyond Moral Reasoning: A Review of Moral Identity Research and Its Implications for Business Ethics." *Business Ethics Quarterly* 18(4): 513–540.
59 Strohminger, N. et al. 2014. "Implicit Morality: A Methodological Survey." In *Experimental Ethics: Toward an Empirical Moral Philosophy*, Lutge, C., Rusch, H. and Uhl, M. (eds.), 133–156. Springer.
60 Haidt, J. (2012).
61 Edmonds, D. 2014. *Would You Kill the Fat Man? The Trolley Problem and What Your Answer Tells Us About Right and Wrong*. Princeton University Press.
62 Kelly, D. 2011. *Yuck! The Nature and Moral Significance of Disgust*. MIT Press.
63 *See* Cathcart, T. 2013. *The Trolley Problem*. Workman Publishing Co.; Edmonds, D. (2014); Kamm, F.M. 2015. *The Trolley Problem Mysteries*. The Berkeley Tanner Lectures.
64 Sunstein, C. 2019. *How Change Happens*. MIT Press.
65 Soltes, E. 2017. "Teaching Versus Living: Managerial Decision Making in the Gray." *Journal of Management Education* 41(4): 455–468.
66 Greene, J. 2016. Speaking at a conference on ethics at the Safra Ethics Center, Harvard University, October 21.
67 Remmel, R.J. and Glenn, A.L. 2015. "Immorality in the Adult Brain." In *The Moral Brain: A Multidisciplinary Perspective*, Decety, J. and Wheatley, T. (eds.), 239–251.

68 Edmonds, D. (2014).
69 May, J. 2018. *Regard for Reason in the Moral Mind*. Oxford University Press.
70 Kelly, D. (2011).

Chapter 3

71 Sauer, H. 2017. *Moral Judgments as Educated Intuitions*. MIT Press.
72 Haidt, J. and Bjorklund, F. 2008. "Social Intuitionists Reason, in Conversation." In *Moral Psychology: The Cognitive Science of Morality: Intuition and Diversity*, vol. 2, Sinnott-Armstrong, W. (ed.), 181–217. MIT Press.
73 Spranca, M., Minsk, E. and Baron, J. 1991. "Omission and Commission in Judgment and Choice." *Journal of Experimental Psychology* 27(1): 76–105.
74 Nichols, S., Timmons, M. and Lopez, T. 2014. "Using Experiments in Ethics-Ethical Conservatism and the Psychology of Moral Luck." In *Empirically Informed Ethics: Morality between Facts and Norms*, Christen, M. et al. (eds.), 159–176. Springer.
75 Knobe, J. 2010. "Person as Scientist, Person as Moralist." *Behavioral and Brian Sciences* 33(4): 315–329.
76 Wegner, D.M. and Gray, K. 2016. *The Mind Club: Who Thinks, What Feels, and Why It Matters*. Viking; Gray, K. and Schein, C. 2015. "The Myth of the Harmless Wrong." *New York Times*, Jan. 30. www.nytimes.com/2015/02/01/opinion/sunday/the-myth-of-the-harmless-wrong.html.
77 Dalbert, C. 2009. "Belief in a Just World." In *Handbook of Individual Differences in Social Behavior*, Leary, M.R. and Hoyle, R.H. (eds.), 288–297. Guilford.
78 Niemi, L. and Young, L. 2016. "When and Why We See Victims as Responsible: The Impact of Ideology on Attitudes Toward Victims." *Personality and Social Psychology Bulletin* 94(9): 1227–1242.
79 DeSteno, D. and Valdesolo, P. 2011. *Out of Character: Surprising Truths about the Liar, Cheat, Sinner (and Saint) Lurking in All of Us*. Crown Publishing Group.

Chapter 4

80 Stout, L.A. 2013–2014. "Killing Conscience: The Unintended Behavioral Consequences of 'Pay for Performance." *Journal of Corporate Law* 39(3): 525–561.
81 Milgram, S. 1963. "Behavioral Study of Obedience." *Journal of Abnormal and Social Psychology* 567(4): 371–378.
82 Dolinski, D., Grzyb, T. and Folwarczny, M. 2017. "Would You Deliver an Electric Shock in 2015? Obedience in the Experimental Paradigm Developed by Stanley Milgram in the 50 Years Following the Original Studies." *Social Psychological and Personality Sciences* 8(8): 927–933.
83 Burger, J. 2009. "Replicating Milgram: Would People Still Obey Today?" *American Psychologist* 64(1): 1–11.
84 Zimbardo, P. 2007. *The Lucifer Effect*. Random House.
85 Ajunwa, I. 2014. "'Bad Barrels': An Organizational-Based Analysis of the Human Rights Abuses at Abu Ghraib Prison." *University of Pennsylvania Journal of Law and Social Change* 17(1): 75–105.
86 O'Connor, M.A. 2003. "The Enron Board: The Perils of Groupthink." *University of Cincinnati Law Review* 71(4): 1233–1320.
87 Soble, J. 2015. "Toshiba Inflated Earnings by $12. Billion, a Panel of Experts Says." *New York Times*, July 21.
88 Gentilin, D. 2016. *The Origins of Ethical Failures: Lessons for Leaders*. Routledge.
89 Ewing, J. 2017. *Faster, Higher, Farther: The Volkswagen Scandal*. Basic Books.
90 Lifton, R.J. 1986. *The Nazi Doctors: Medical Killing and the Psychology of Genocide*. Basic Books.
91 Cohan, W.D. 2009. *House of Cards: A Tale of Hubris and Wretched Excess on Wall Street*. Doubleday.

92 Krogh, E. and Krogh, M. 2008. *Integrity: Good People, Bad Choices, and Life Lessons from the White House*. Public Affairs.
93 Tetlock, P.E. 1997. "An Alternative Metaphor in the Study of Judgment and Choice: People as Politicians." In *Research on Judgment and Decision Making: Currents, Connections, and Controversies*, Goldstein, W. and Hogarth, R. (eds.), 657–680. Cambridge University Press.
94 Milgram, S. 1974. *Obedience to Authority*. Harper.
95 Fair, E. 2016. *Consequence: A Memoir*. Picador.
96 Mayhew, B.W. and Murphy, P.R. 2014. "The Impact of Authority on Reporting Behavior, Affect, and Rationalization." *Contemporary Accounting Research* 31(2): 420–443.
97 Feng, W., Ge, W., Luo, S. and Shevlin, T. 2011. "Why Do CFOs Become Involved in Material Accounting Manipulations?" *Journal of Accounting and Economics* 25(1–2): 21–36.
98 Glover, J. 2012. *Humanity: A Moral History of the Twentieth Century* (2nd ed.). Yale University Press.(Italics added).

Chapter 5

99 Oberlechner, T. 2007. *The Psychology of Ethics in the Finance and Investment Industry*. CFA Institute.
100 The conformity bias has also been called "social proof." Cialdini, R.B. 1993. *Influence: The Psychology of Persuasion* (3rd ed.). Quill. It is consistent with social comparison theory which suggests that individuals gauge the appropriateness of their own beliefs and actions by comparing them to the beliefs and actions of others. Festinger, L. 1954. "A Theory of Social Comparison Processes." *Human Relations* 7: 117–140.
101 Frank, R.H. 2009. *The Economic Naturalist's Field Guide Common Sense Principles for Troubled Times*. Basic Books.
102 Haun, D. and Over, H. 2013. "Like Me: A Homophily-Based Account of Human Culture." In *Cultural Evolution: Society, Technology, Language, and Religion*, Richerson, P and Christiansen, M. (eds.), 75–85. MIT Press.
103 de Waal, F. 2019. *Mama's Last Hug: Animal Emotions and What They Tell Us about Ourselves*. Norton.
104 Haun, D. and Tomasello, M. 2011. "Conformity to Peer Pressure in Preschool Children." *Child Development* 82(6): 1759–1767.
105 Asch, S.E. 1951. "Effects of Group Pressure upon the Modification and Distortion of Judgment." In *Groups, Leadership and Men*, Guetzkow, H.S. (ed.), 177–190. Russell & Russell.
106 Berns, G.S. et al. 2005. "Neurobiological Correlates of Social Conformity and Independence during Mental Rotation." *Biological Psychiatry* 58(3): 245–253.
107 As near as we can tell, lemmings generally do not run over cliffs, the urban legend notwithstanding. So says Snopes: www.snopes.com/disney/films/lemmings.asp.
108 Berns, G.S. et al. (2005).
109 Prentice, R. 2003. "Contract-Based Defenses in Securities Fraud Litigation: A Behavioral Analysis." *University of Illinois Law Review* 2003(2): 337–421.
110 Sunstein, C.R. 2011. "Empirically Informed Regulation." *University of Chicago Law Review* 78(4): 1350–1429.
111 Keltner, D., Kogan, A., Piff, P.K. and Saturn, S.R. 2014. "The Sociocultural Appraisals, Values, and Emotions (SAVE) Framework of Prosociality: Core Processes from Gene to Meme." *Annual Review of Psychology* 65: 425–460.
112 Levitt, S.D. and Dubner, S.J. 2006. *Freakonomics: A Rogue Economist Explores the Hidden Side of Everything* (rev. ed.). William Morrow.
113 Bandura, A. 2016. *Moral Disengagement: How People Do Harm and Live with Themselves*. Worth.
114 McCabe, D. and Treviño, L. 1993. "Academic Dishonesty: Honor Codes and Other Contextual Influences." *Journal of Higher Education* 64(5): 522–538.

115 Ariely, D. 2012. *The (Honest) Truth About Dishonesty: How We Lie to Everyone–Especially Ourselves.* Harper.
116 James, C. 2014. *Disconnected: Youth, New Media, and the Ethics Gap.* MIT Press.
117 Ayres, I. 2010. *Carrots and Sticks: Unlock the Power of Incentives to Get Things Done.* Bantam.
118 Mitchell, M.S. and Palmer, N.F. 2010. "The Managerial Relevance of Ethical Efficacy." In *Managerial Ethics: Managing the Psychology of Morality,* Schminke, M. (ed.), 89–108. Routledge.
119 Robinson, S.L. and O'Leary-Kelley, A.M. 1998. "Monkey See, Monkey Do: The Influence of Work Groups on Antisocial Behavior of Employees." *Academy of Management Journal* 41(6): 658–672.
120 Dobson, J. 2003. "Why Ethics Codes Don't' Work." *Financial Analysts Journal* 59 (Nov/Dec): 29–34.
121 Schweigert, F.J. 2016. *Business Ethics Education and the Pragmatic Pursuit of the Good.* Springer International Publishing.
122 It has been told that one former Enron employee put his copy of the code up for sale on e-Bay, describing it thusly: "Brand new. Never been used."
123 Byrne, J.A. 2002. "The Environment was Ripe for Abuse." *Business Week*, Feb. 18. www.bloomberg.com/news/articles/2002-02-24/at-enron-the-environment-was-ripe-for-abuse.
124 Rostain, T. and Regan Jr., M.C. 2014. *Confidence Games: Lawyers, Accountants, and the Tax Shelter Industry.* MIT Press.
125 Pierce, L. and Snyder, J. 2008. "Ethical Spillovers in Firms: Evidence from Vehicle Emissions Testing." *Management Science* 54(11): 1891–1903.
126 Miller, C.B. 2018. *The Character Gap: How Good Are We?* Oxford University Press.
127 Dungan, J., Waytz, A. and Young, L. 2017. "Corruption in the Context of Moral Trade-offs." In *Thinking About Bribery: Neuroscience, Moral Cognition and the Psychology of Bribery,* Nichols, P. and Robertson, D. (eds.), 85–102. Cambridge University Press.
128 Latané, B. and Darley, J.M. 1970. *The Unresponsive Bystander: Why Doesn't He Help?* Prentice Hall.
129 Bandura, A. (2016).
130 Latané, B. and Darley, J. (1970).
131 Heffernan, M. 2012. *Willful Blindness: Why We Ignore the Obvious at Our Peril.* Walker & Co. (Italics added).

Chapter 6

132 Bazerman, M.H. and Tenbrunsel, A.E. 2011. *Blind Spots: Why We Fail to Do What's Right and What to Do about It.* Princeton University Press.
133 Johnson, D. 2004. *Overconfidence and War: The Havoc and Glory of Positive Illusions.* Harvard University Press.
134 Brooks, D. 2011. *The Social Animal: The Hidden Sources of Love, Character and Achievement.* Random House.
135 Ross, H.J. 2014. *Everyday Bias: Identifying and Navigating Unconscious Judgments in Our Everyday Lives.* Rowman & Littlefield.
136 Williams, S.H. 2014. "Probability Errors: Overoptimism, Ambiguity Aversion, and the Certainty Effect." In *The Oxford Handbook of Behavioral Economics and the Law,* Zamar, E. and Teichman, D. (eds.), 335–353. Oxford University Press.
137 Peterson, C.E. and Harris, S. 1965. "Psychology of Drivers in Traffic Accidents." *Journal of Applied Psychology* 49(4): 284–288.
138 Chabris, C. and Simons, D. 2010. *The Invisible Gorilla: How Our Intuitions Deceive Us.* Crown.
139 Shefrin, H. 2007. *Beyond Greed and Fear.* Oxford University Press.
140 Bazerman, M.H. 2002. *Judgment in Managerial Decision Making* (5th ed.). Wiley.

141 Cross, P. 1977. "Not Can but *Will* College Teaching Be Improved? *New Directions for Higher Education* 1977(17): 1–15.
142 Ross, H.J. (2014).
143 Bazerman, M.H. 1998. *Judgment in Managerial Decision Making* (4th ed.). Wiley.
144 Wegner, D.M. and Gray, K. 2016. *The Mind Club: Who Thinks, What Feels, and Why It Matters*. Viking.
145 Mlodinow, L. 2012. *Subliminal: How Your Unconscious Mind Rules Your Behavior*. Pantheon Books.
146 Alicke, M.D. 1985. "Global Self-Evaluation as Determined by the Desirability and Controllability of Trait Adjectives." *Journal of Personality and Social Psychology* 49(6): 1621–1630; Allison, S.T., Messick, D.M. and Goethals, G.R. 1989. "On Being Better but Not Smarter than Others: The Muhammad Ali Effect." *Social Cognition* 7(3): 275–295; Dunning, D., Meyerowitz, J.A. and Holzberg, A.D. 1989. "Ambiguity and Self-Evaluation: The Role of Idiosyncratic Trait Definitions in Self-Serving Appraisals of Ability." *Journal of Personality and Social Psychology* 57(6): 1082–1090; Goethals, G.R., Messick, D.M. and Allison, S.T. 1991. "The Uniqueness Bias: Studies of Constructive Social Comparison." In *Social Comparison: Contemporary Theory and Research*, Suls, J. and Will, T.A. (eds.), 149–176. Lawrence Erlbaum Associates.
147 Epley, N. and Dunning, D. 2000. "Feeling 'Holier Than Thou': Are Self-Serving Assessments Produced by Errors in Self- or Social Prediction?" *Journal of Personality and Social Psychology* 79(6): 861–875.
148 Chambliss, E. 2012. "Whose Ethics? The Benchmark Problem in Legal Ethics Research." In *Lawyers in Practice: Ethical Decision Making*, Levin, L. and Mather, L. (eds.), 47–60. University of Chicago Press.
149 Jennings, M.M. 2005. "Ethics and Investment Management: True Reform." *Financial Analysts Journal* 61(3): 45–58.
150 Pronin, E. and Schmidt, K. 2013. "Claims and Denials of Bias and Their Implications for Policy." In *The Behavioral Foundations of Public Policy*, Shafir, E. (ed.), 195–216. Princeton University Press.
151 Cohen, J.R., Pant, L.W. and Sharp, D.J. 1995. "An Exploratory Examination of International Differences in Auditors' Ethical Perceptions." *Behavioral Research in Accounting* 7: 37–64.
152 Messick, D. and Bazerman, M. 1996. "Ethical Leadership and the Psychology of Decision Making." *Sloan Management Review* 37(Winter): 9.
153 Halpern, D. 2010. *The Hidden Wealth of Nations*. Polity.
154 Staglin, D. 1997. "Oprah: A Heavenly Body?" *U.S. News and World Report*, Mar. 31.
155 Darley, J.M. 2005. "The Cognitive and Social Psychology of Contagious Organizational Corruption." *Brooklyn Law Review* 70(4): 1177–1194.
156 Kennedy, J. and Peecher, M. 1997. "Judging Auditors' Technical Knowledge." *Journal of Accounting Research* 35(2): 279–293.
157 McLean, B. and Elkind, P. 2003. *The Smartest Guys in the Room: The Amazing Rise and Scandalous Fall of Enron*. Portfolio.
158 Soltes, E. 2016. *Why They Do It: Inside the Mind of the White-Collar Criminal*. Public Affairs.
159 Anderson, M. and Escher, P. 2010. *The MBA Oath: Setting a Higher Standard for Business Leaders*. Portfolio.
160 Gentilin, D. 2016. *The Origins of Ethical Failures: Lessons for Leaders*. Routledge.
161 Soltes, E. (2016).
162 *Id.*
163 *Id.*
164 *Id.*
165 Baker, L.A. and Emery, R.E. 1993. "When Every Relationship Is Above Average: Perceptions and Expectations of Divorce at the Time of Marriage." *Law and Human Behavior* 17(4): 439–450.

166 Hanson, J.D. and Kysar, D.A. 1999. "Taking Behavioralism Seriously: Some Evidence of Market Manipulation." *Harvard Law Review* 112(7): 1420–1572.
167 Coopersmith, J.B. 1990. "Refocusing Liquidated Damages Law for Real Estate Contracts: Returning to the Historical Roots of the Penalty Doctrine." *Emory Law Journal* 39(1): 267–308.
168 Johnson, D. and Fowler, J. 2011. "The Evolution of Overconfidence." *Nature* 477: 317–320.
169 Sapolsky, R.M. 2017. *Behave: The Biology of Humans at Our Best and Worst*. Penguin Press.
170 Langevoort, D. 1997. "Organized Illusions: A Behavioral Theory of Why Corporations Mislead Stock Market Investors (And Cause Other Social Harms)." *University of Pennsylvania Law Review* 146(1): 101–172.
171 Libby, R. and Rennekamp, K.M. 2012. "Self-Serving Attribution Bias, Overconfidence, and the Issuance of Management Forecasts." *Journal of Accounting Research* 50(1): 197–231.
172 Renner, C.H. and Renner, M.J. 2001. "But I Thought I Knew That: Using Confidence Estimation as a Debiasing Technique to Improve Classroom Performance." *Applied Cognitive Psychology* 15(1): 23–32.
173 Hoch, S.J. 1985. "Counterfactual Reasoning and Accuracy in Predicting Personal Events." *Journal of Experimental Psychology: Learning, Memory, and Cognition* 11(4): 719–731.
174 Koriat, A., Lichtenstein, S. and Fischhoff, B. 1980. "Reasons for Confidence." *Journal of Experimental Psychology: Human Learning and Memory* 6(2): 107–118.
175 Williams, S.H. (2014).

Chapter 7

176 Bazerman, M.H. 2002. *Judgment in Managerial Decision Making* (5th ed.). John Wiley & Sons.
177 Langevoort, D. 1997. "Organized Illusions: A Behavioral Theory of Why Corporations Mislead Stock Market Investors (and Cause Other Social Harms)." *University of Pennsylvania Law Review* 146(1): 101–172.
178 Babcock, L. and Loewenstein, G. 1997. "Explaining Bargaining Impasse: The Role of Self-Serving Bias." *Journal of Economic Perspectives* 11(1): 109–126.
179 Farnsworth, W. 2003. "The Legal Regulation of Self-Serving Bias." *University of California Davis Law Review* 37(2): 567–603.
180 Quealy, K. 2017. "We Avoid News We Don't Like. Some Trump-Era Evidence." *New York Times*, Feb. 21. www.nytimes.com/interactive/2017/02/21/upshot/how-readers-react-to-political-news-they-dont-like-they-ignore-it.html.
181 Ross, C. 2005. "War Stories." *Financial Times*, Jan. 29–30. www.ft.com/content/cb9e8196-7032-11d9-b572-00000e2511c8.
182 Lord, C.G., Ross, L. and Lepper, M.R. 1979. "Biased Assimilation and Attitude Polarization: The Effects of Prior Theories on Subsequently Considered Evidence." *Journal of Personality and Social Psychology* 37(11): 2098–2109.
183 Hastorf, A.H. and Cantril, H. 1954. "They Saw a Game: A Case Study." *Journal of Abnormal and Social Psychology* 49(1): 129–134.
184 Cohen, G.L. 2003. "Party Over Policy: The Dominating Impact of Group Influence on Political Beliefs." *Journal of Personality and Social Psychology* 85: 808–822.
185 Kahan, D., Hoffman, D. Braman, B., Evans, D. and Rachlinski, J.J. 2012. "They Saw a Protest: Cognitive Illiberalism and the Speech-Conduct Distinction." *Stanford Law Review* 64(4): 851–906.
186 Koehler, J.J. 1993. "The Influence of Prior Beliefs on Scientific Judgments of Evidence Quality." *Organizational Behavior & Human Decision Processes* 56(1): 28–55.
187 Zhang, Y., Pan, Z., Li, K. and Guo, Y. 2018. "Self-Serving Bias in Memories." *Experimental Psychology* 65(4): 236–244.

188 Russell, D. and Jones, W.H. 1980. "When Superstition Fails: Reactions to Disconfirmation of Paranormal Beliefs." *Personality and Social Psychology Bulletin* 6(1): 83–88.
189 Pizarro, D. 2013. "The New Science of Morality: An Edge Conference." In *Thinking: The New Science of Decision-Making, Problem-Solving, and Prediction*, Brockman, J. (ed.), 356–369. Harper Collins.
190 Mlodinow, L. 2012. *Subliminal: How Your Unconscious Mind Rules Your Behavior*. Pantheon.
191 Bazerman, M.H. and Tenbrunsel, A.E. 2011. *Blind Spots: Why We Fail to Do What's Right and What to Do about It*. Princeton University Press.
192 Davies, M. 1997. "Belief Persistence After Evidential Discrediting: The Impact of Generated Versus Provided Explanations on the Likelihood of Discredited Outcomes." *Journal of Experimental Social Psychology* 33(6): 561–578.
193 Churchland, P.S. 2013. *Touching a Nerve: The Self as Brain*. W.W. Norton & Co.
194 Klayman, J. 1996. "Ethics as Hypothesis Testing, and Vice Versa." In *Codes of Conduct: Behavioral Research Into Business Ethics*, Messik, D. and Tenbrunsel, A. (eds.), 243–255. Russell Sage Foundation.
195 Bazerman, M.H. and Tenbrunsel, A.E. (2011).
196 Chait, J. 2013. "Rob Portman, Gay Marriage, and Selfishness." *New York Magazine*, Mar. 15. http://nymag.com/intelligencer/2013/03/rob-portman-gay-marriage-and-selfishness.html.
197 Paharia, N. and Deshpande, R. 2013. "Sweatshop Labor Is Wrong Unless the Jeans Are Cute: Motivated Moral Disengagement." *Organizational Behavior and Human Decision Processes* 121(1): 81–88.
198 Blaufus, K., Braune, M., Hundsdoerfer, J. and Jacob, M. 2015. "Self-Serving Bias and Tax Morale." *Economic Letters* 131(June): 91–93.
199 Soltes, E., 2016. *Why They Do It: Inside the Mind of the White-Collar Criminal*. Public Affairs (quoting David Solomon).
200 Harris, J. and Bromiley, P. 2007. "Incentives to Cheat: The Influence of Executive Compensation and Firm Performance on Financial Misrepresentation." *Organization Science* 18(3): 350–367.
201 Prentice, R. 2003. "Enron: A Brief Behavioral Autopsy." *American Business Law Journal* 40(2): 417–444.
202 Dana, J., Cain, D.M. and Dawes, R.M. 2006. "What You Don't Know Won't Hurt Me: Costly (But Quiet) Exit in a Dictator Game. *Organizational Behavior and Human Decision Processes* 100(2): 193–201.
203 Banaji, M.R., Bazerman, M.H. and Chugh, D. 2003. "How (Un)ethical Are You?" *Harvard Business Review* 81(12): 56–64.
204 Pronin, E. and Schmidt, K. 2013. "Claims and Denials of Bias and Their Implications for Policy." In *The Behavioral Foundations of Public Policy*, Shafir, E. (ed.), 195–216. Princeton University Press.
205 Shamis, G. 2000. Hearing on Auditor Independence (SEC, Sept. 13). www.sec.gov/rules/propose/s71300/testimony/shamis1.htm. (Italics added).
206 Moore, D.A., Telock, P.E., Tanlu, L. and Bazerman, M.H. 2006. "Conflicts of Interest and the Case of Auditor Independence: Moral Seduction and Strategic Issue Cycling." *Academy of Management Review* 31(1): 10–29.
207 Tenbrusel, A.E., Diekmann, K.A., Wade-Benzoni, K.A. and Bazerman, M.H. 2010. "The Ethical Mirage: A Temporal Explanation as to Why We Aren't as Ethical as We Think We Are." *Research in Organizational Behavior* 30: 153–173.
208 Pronin, E., Gilovich, T. and Ross, L. 2004. "Objectivity in the Eye of the Beholder: Divergent Perceptions of Bias in Self Versus Others." *Psychological Review* 111(3): 781–799.
209 Sah, S. and Fugh-Berman, A. 2013. "Physicians under the Influence: Social Psychology and Industry Marketing Strategies." *Journal of Law, Medicine & Ethics* 41(3): 665–672.
210 Pope, D.G., Price, J. and Walters, J. 2013. "Awareness Reduces Racial Bias." *Management Science* 64(11): 4988–4995.
211 Pronin, E., Gilovich, T. and Ross, L. (2004).

Chapter 8

212 Howard, R.A. and Korver, C.D. 2008. *Ethics for the Real World: Creating a Personal Code to Guide Decisions in Work and Life*. Harvard Business Press.
213 Palazzo, G., Krings, F. and Hoffrage, U. 2012. "Ethical Blindness." *Journal of Business Ethics* 109(3): 323–338.
214 Levin, I.P. and Gaeth, G.J. 1988. "How Consumers Are Affected by the Framing of Attribute Information Before and After Consuming the Product." *Journal of Consumer Research* 15(3): 374–378; Levin, I.P. 1987. "Associative Effects of Information Framing." *Bulletin of the Psychonomic Society* 25(2): 85–86.
215 Glenzer, F., Grundl, H. and Wilde, C. 2014. "'And Lead Us Not into Temptation': Presentation Formats and the Choice of Risky Alternatives." ICIR Working Paper Series No. 16/14 (June 17). http://ssrn.com/abstract=2455861.
216 Kahneman, D. and Tversky, A. 1979. "Prospect Theory: An Analysis of Decision under Risk." *Econometrica* 4(2): 263–291.
217 Benartzi, S. and Thaler, R. 1999. "Risk Aversion or Myopia? Choices in Repeated Gambles and Retirement Investments." *Management Science* 45(3): 364–381.
218 Durbach, I.N. and Stewart, T.J. 2011. "An Experimental Study of the Effect of Uncertain Representation on Decision Making." *European Journal of Operation Research* 214(2): 380–392.
219 Kahneman and Tversky are the subjects of a recent best seller. Lewis, M. 2017. *The Undoing Project: A Friendship that Changed Our Minds*. W.W. Norton & Co.
220 Tversky, A. and Kahneman, D. 1986. "Rational Choice and the Framing of Decisions." *Journal of Business* 59(4 pt.2): S251–S278.
221 Awasthi, V.N. 2008. "Managerial Decision-Making on Moral Issues and the Effects of Teaching Ethics." *Journal of Business Ethics* 78(1–2): 207–223.
222 Harris, S. 2010. *The Moral Landscape: How Science Can Determine Human Values*. Free Press.
223 Mitchell, J.M. and Yordy, E.D. 2010. "COVER It: A Comprehensive Framework for Guiding Students Through Ethical Dilemmas." *Journal of Legal Studies Education* 27(1): 35–60.
224 Kurzban, R. 2001. "The Social Psychophysics of Cooperation: Nonverbal Communication in a Public Goods Game." *Journal of Nonverbal Behavior* 25(4): 241–259.
225 Kuhberger, A. 1998. "The Influence of Framing on Risky Decisions: A Meta-Analysis." *Organizational Behavior and Human Decision Processes* 75(1): 23–55.
226 Gneezy, U. and Rustichini, A. 2000. "A Fine is a Price." *Journal of Legal Studies* 29(1): 1–17.
227 McDonald, A.J. and Hansen, J.R. 2009. *Truth, Lies, and O-Rings: Inside the Space Shuttle Challenger Disaster*. University Press of Florida.
228 Hoyk, R. and Hersey, P. 2008. *The Ethical Executive: Becoming Aware of the Root Causes of Unethical Behavior: 45 Psychological Traps That Everyone One of Us Falls Prey To*. Stanford Business Books.
229 Ewing, J. 2017. *Faster, Higher, Farther: The Volkswagen Scandal*. W.W. Norton & Co.
230 Bazerman, M.H. and Tenbrunsel, A.E. 2011. *Blind Spots: Why We Fail to Do What's Right and What to Do about It*. Princeton University Press.
231 Heffernan, M. 2011. *Willful Blindness: Why We Ignore the Obvious at Our Peril*. Walker & Co.
232 Moore, C. and Gino, F. 2013. "Ethically Adrift: How Others Pull Our Moral Compass from True North, and How We Can Fix It." *Research in Organizational Behavior* 33: 53–77.
233 Gibbs, J.C. 2001. *Moral Development & Reality: Beyond the Theories of Kohlberg, Hoffman, and Haidt* (3rd ed.). Oxford University Press (quoting Michel, L. and Herbeck, D. 2001. *American Terrorist: Timothy McVeigh and the Oklahoma City Bombing*. Harper.).
234 Sunstein, C.R. 2013. "The Storrs Lectures: Behavioral Economics and Paternalism." *Yale Law Journal* 122(7): 1826–1899.

235 Neale, M.A. and Bazerman, M.H. 1985. "The Effects of Framing and Negotiator Overconfidence on Bargaining Behaviors and Outcomes." *Academy of Management Journal* 28(1): 34–49.
236 Tenbrunsel, A.E., Diekmann, K.A., Wade-Benzoni, K.A. and Bazerman, M.H. 2010. "The Ethical Mirage: A Temporal Explanation as to Why We Aren't as Ethical as We Think We Are." *Research in Organizational Behavior* 30: 153–173.

Chapter 9

237 Seal, M. and Squillari, E. 2009. "'Hello, Madoff' What the Secretary Saw." *Vanity Fair*, June. www.vanityfair.com/news/2009/06/bernie-madoff-secretary-reveals-secrets.
238 Jensen, M.S., Yao, R., Street, W.N. and Simons, D.J. 2011. "Change Blindness and Inattentional Blindness." *WIREs Cognitive Science* 2(5): 529–546.
239 Simons, D.J. and Levin, D.T. 1998. "Failure to Detect Changes to People during a Real-World Interaction." *Psychonomic Bulletin & Review* 5(4): 644–649. A video of the experiment is available at www.youtube.com/watch?v=FWSxSQsspiQ.
240 Physical College. "AP Psychology Change Blindness Experiment at CHS." (Feb. 16). www.youtube.com/watch?v=INqDa0hv_lc.
241 Simons, D.J. 2010. "Gradual Change Test 1." www.youtube.com/watch?v=1nL5uIsWMYc.
242 Glover, J. 2012. *Humanity: A Moral History of the Twentieth Century* (2nd ed.). Yale University Press.
243 Tenbrunsel, A.E. and Messick, D.M. 2004. "Ethical Fading: The Role of Self-Deception in Unethical Behavior." *Social Justice Research* 17(2): 223–236.
244 Kelman, H.C. and Hamilton, V.L. 1989. *Crimes of Obedience*. Yale University Press.
245 Tenbrunsel, A.E. and Messick, D.M. (2004).
246 Babiak, B. and Hare, R. 2006. *Snakes in Suits: When Psychopaths Go to Work*. Harper.
247 Comer, D.R. and Vega, G. 2011. "The Personal Ethical Threshold." In *Moral Courage in Organizations: Doing the Right Thing*, Comer, C. and Vega, G. (eds.), 25–44. M.E. Sharpe.
248 Bandura, A. 2016. *Moral Disengagement*. Worth Publishers.
249 Welsh, D.T., Ordóñez, L.D., Snyder, D.G. and Christian, M.S. 2015. "The Slippery Slope: How Small Ethical Transgressions Pave the Way for Larger Future Transgressions." *Journal of Applied Psychology* 100(1): 114–127.
250 Garrett, N., Lazzaro, S.C., Ariely, D. and Sharot, T. 2016. "The Brain Adapts to Dishonesty." *Nature Neuroscience* 19(12): 1727–1735.
251 Olson, T. 2007. "'Slippery Slope' Led to Enron, CMU, Harvard Researchers Find." *Trib Live*, Aug. 29. https://archive.triblive.com/news/slippery-slope-led-to-enron-cmu-harvard-researchers-find/?printerfriendly=true.
252 Gino, F. and Bazerman, M.H. 2009. "When Misconduct Goes Unnoticed: The Acceptability of Gradual Erosion in Others' Unethical Behavior." *Journal of Experimental Psychology* 45(4): 708–719.
253 Schiltz, P. 1999. "On Being a Happy, Healthy, and Ethical Member of an Unhappy, Unhealthy, and Unethical Profession." *Vanderbilt Law Review* 52(4): 872–951.
254 Cooper, C. 2008. *Extraordinary Circumstances: The Journey of a Corporate Whistleblower*. Wiley.
255 Gourevitch, P. and Morris, E. 2008. "Exposure: The Woman Behind the Camera at Abu Ghraib." *New Yorker*, March 28. www.newyorker.com/magazine/2008/03/24/exposure-5. (Italics added).
256 Kren, G. and Rappoport, L. 1994. *The Holocaust and the Crisis of Human Behavior*. Holmes & Meier.
257 Lifton, R.J. 1986. *The Nazi Doctors: Medical Killing and the Psychology of Genocide*. Basic Books.
258 Dimsdale, J.E. 2016. *Anatomy of Malice: The Enigma of the Nazi War Criminals*. Yale University Press.

259 Gladwell, M. 2015. "The Engineer's Lament." *New Yorker*, May 4. www.newyorker.com/magazine/2015/05/04/the-engineers-lament.
260 Norris, F. 2014. "History Gives Other Cases of G.M.'s Behavior." *New York Times*, Mar. 14. www.nytimes.com/2014/03/28/business/history-offers-other-examples-of-gms-behavior.html.
261 Christensen, C.M. 2012. *How Will You Measure Your Life?* Harper Business.
262 Soltes, E. 2016. *Why They Do It: Inside the Mind of the White-Collar Criminal.* Public Affairs.
263 Suh, I., Sweeney, J.T., Linke, K. and Wall, J. 2018. "Boiling the Frog Slowly: The Immersion of C-Suite Financial Executives into Fraud." *Journal of Business Ethics* 1–29. https://link.springer.com/article/10.1007/s10551-018-3982-3.

Chapter 10

264 Cameron, J.S. and Miller, D.T. 2009. "Ethical Standards in Gain versus Loss Frames." In *Psychological Perspectives on Ethical Behavior and Decision Making*, De Cremer, D. (ed.), 91–106. Information Age Publishing.
265 Hastie, R. and Dawes, R.M. 2001. *Rational Choice in an Uncertain World: The Psychology of Judgment and Decision Making* (2nd ed.). Sage Publications.
266 Zamir, E. 2014. "Law's Loss Aversion." In *The Oxford Handbook of Behavioral Economics and the Law*, Zamir, E. and Teichman, D. (eds.), 268–299. Oxford University Press.
267 Bechara, A., Damasio, H., Damasio, A.R. and Lee, G.P. 1999. "Different Contributions of the Human Amygdala and Ventromedial Prefrontal Cortex to Decision-Making." *Journal of Neuroscience* 19(13): 5473–5481.
268 Kahneman, D. and Tversky, A. 1979. "Prospect Theory: An Analysis of Decision under Risk." *Econometrica* 47(2): 263–292.
269 Cai, Y. and Shefrin, H. 2014. "Bad Corporate Marriages: Waking Up in Bed the Morning After." https://papers.ssrn.com/sol3/papers.cfm?abstract_id=2372248.
270 Tversky, A. and Kahneman, D. 1991. "Loss Aversion in Riskless Choice: A Reference-Dependent Model." *Quarterly Journal of Economics* 106(4): 1039–1061.
271 Patel, M.S. et al. 2016. "Framing Financial Incentives to Increase Physical Activity among Overweight and Obese Adults: A Randomized, Controlled Trial." *Annals of Internal Medicine* 164(6): 385–394.
272 Fryer, Jr., R.G. 2012. "Enhancing the Efficacy of Teacher Incentives through Loss Aversion: A Field Incentive." NBER Working Paper No. 18237. www.nber.org/papers/w18237.
273 Hossain, T. and List, J.A. 2012. "The Behavioralist Visits the Factory: Increasing Productivity Using Simple Framing Manipulations." *Management Science* 58(12): 2151–2167.
274 Imas, A., Sadoff, S. and Samek, A. 2016. "Do People Anticipate Loss Aversion?" *Management Science* 63(5): 1271–1284.
275 Lane, M., Seiler, M. and Seiler, V. 2011. "Identifying Behavioral Explanations for a Subset of the Real Estate Shadow Market." *Journal of Housing Research* 20(2): 191–210.
276 Gros, L. 1982. *The Art of Selling Intangibles: How to Make Your Million($) by Investing Other People's Money*. Marketplace Books.
277 Margolis, J. and Molinsky, A. 2006. "Three Practical Challenges of Moral Leadership." In *Moral Leadership: The Theory and Practice of Power, Judgment and Policy*, Rhode, D. (ed.), 77–110. Jossey-Bass.
278 Cameron, J.S. and Miller, D.T. (2009).
279 Pinello, A. and Dusenbury, R. 2005. "The Role of Cognition and Ethical Conviction in Earnings Management Behavior." http://ssrn.com/abstract=711422.
280 Kern, M.C. and Chugh, D. 2009. "Bounded Ethicality: The Perils of Loss Framing." *Psychological Science* 20(3): 378–384.
281 Schweitzer, M.E., Ordóñez, L. and Douma, B. 2004. "Goal Setting as a Motivator of Unethical Behavior." *Academy of Management Journal* 47(3): 422–432.

282 Newberry, K.J., Reckers, P.M.J. and Wyndelts, R.W. 1993. "An Examination of Tax Practitioner Decisions: The Role of Preparer Sanctions and Framing Effects Associated with Client Condition." *Journal of Economic Psychology* 14(2): 439–452.
283 Mishina, Y., Dykes, B.J., Block, E.S. and Pollock, T.G. 2010. "Why 'Good' Firms Do Bad Things: The Effects of High Aspirations, High Expectations, and Prominence on the Incidence of Corporate Illegality." *Academy of Management Journal* 53(4): 701–722.
284 Harris, J. and Bromiley, P. 2007. "Incentives to Cheat: The Influence of Executive Compensation and Firm Performance on Financial Misrepresentation." *Organization Science* 18(3): 350–367.
285 Kessler, A. 2003. *Wall Street Meat*. Escape Velocity Press.
286 Maremont, M. 1996. "Anatomy of the Kurzweil Fraud." *Business Week*, Sept. 16. www.bloomberg.com/news/articles/1996-09-15/anatomy-of-the-kurzweil-fraud.
287 "Disgraced." 2017. Bat Bridge Entertainment. *See also* Wise, M. 2003. "College Basketball; Death and Deception." *New York Times*, Aug. 28. www.nytimes.com/2003/08/28/sports/college-basketball-death-and-deception.html?searchResultPosition=1.
288 Neumeister, L. 2013. "NY Insider Trading Cooperator Gets Year in Prison." *Washington Examiner*, Jan. 31. www.washingtonexaminer.com/ny-insider-trading-cooperator-gets-year-in-prison.
289 Gentilin, D. 2016. *The Origins of Ethical Failures: Lessons for Leaders*. Routledge.
290 Norris, F. 2014. "History Gives Other Cases of G.M.'s Behavior." *New York Times*, Mar. 14. www.nytimes.com/2014/03/28/business/history-offers-other-examples-of-gms-behavior.html.
291 Henriques, D. 2007. *The Wizard of Lies: Bernie Madoff and the Death of Trust*. Henry Holt and Company.
292 Rawnsley, J. 1995. *Total Risk: Nick Leeson and the Fall of the Barings Bank*. HarperCollins.
293 Gapper, J. 2011. "What Makes a Rogue Trader?" *Financial Times*, Dec. 2. www.ft.com/content/cbff2b02-1bcc-11e1-8647-00144feabdc0.
294 Parker, S. 2014. "Downfall: Tales of Rogue Traders." *EuropeanCEO*, Apr. 4. www.europeanceo.com/business-and-management/downfall-tales-of-rogue-traders/.

Chapter 11

295 Oregon State University. 2012. "Wearing Two Different Hats: Moral Decisions May Depend on the Situation." Oregon State University News and Research Communications, May 23. https://today.oregonstate.edu/archives/2012/may/wearing-two-different-hats-moral-decisions-may-depend-situation. See Leavitt, K. et al. 2012. "Different Hats, Different Obligation: Plural Occupational Identities and Situated Moral Judgments." *Academy of Management Journal* 55(6): 1316–1333.
296 Applbaum, A. 1999. *Ethics for Adversaries: The Morality of Roles in Public and Professional Life*. Princeton University Press.
297 Gibson, K. 2003. "Contrasting Role Morality and Professional Morality: Implications for Practice." *Journal of Applied Philosophy* 20(1): 17–29.
298 Radtke, R.R. 2008. "Role Morality in the Accounting Profession: How Do We Compare to Physicians and Attorneys?" *Journal of Business Ethics* 79(3): 279–297.
299 Armstrong, J.S. 1977. "Social Irresponsibility in Management." *Journal of Business Research* 5(Sept.): 187–213.
300 Id.
301 Jackall, R. 1988. *Moral Mazes: The World of Corporate Managers*. Oxford University Press.
302 Radtke, R.R. (2008).
303 Cohn, C., Fehr, E. and Marechal, M.A. 2014. "Business Culture and Dishonesty in the Banking Industry." *Nature* 516(Dec. 4): 86–89.
304 Schweigert, F.J. 2016. *Business Ethics Education and the Pragmatic Pursuit of the Good*. Springer International Publishing.
305 Leavitt, K. et al. (2012).

306 Bandura, A. 2016. *Moral Disengagement: How People Do Harm and Live with Themselves.* Worth Publishers.
307 Suh, I., Sweeney, J.T., Linke, K. and Wall, J. 2018. "Boiling the Frog Slowly: The Immersion of C-Suite Financial Executives into Fraud." *Journal of Business Ethics* 1–29. https://link.springer.com/article/10.1007/s10551-018-3982-3.
308 Houser, D. et al. 2015. "On the Origins of Dishonesty: From Parents to Children." NBER Working Paper No. 20897. www.nber.org/papers/w20897.
309 Medina, J., Benner, K. and Taylor, K. 2019. "College Admissions Scandal: Actresses, Business Leaders and Other Wealthy Parents Charged." *New York Times*, Mar. 12. www.nytimes.com/2019/03/12/us/college-admissions-cheating-scandal.html.
310 Ariely, D. 2012. *The (Honest) Truth About Dishonesty: How We Lie to Everyone–Especially Ourselves.* Harper Collins.
311 *Spaulding v. Zimmerman*, 116 N.W. 2d 704 (Minn. 1962).
312 Raghavan, A. 2017. "A Rogue Trader Blames the System, but Not All Are Persuaded." *New York Times*, Mar. 24. www.nytimes.com/2017/03/24/business/dealbook/ubs-trader-fraud-lessons.html.
313 Howard, R.A. and Korver, C.D. 2008. *Ethics for the Real World: Creating a Personal Code to Guide Decisions in Work and Life.* Harvard Business Review Press. (Italics added).
314 Lifton, R.J. 1986. *The Nazi Doctors: Medical Killing and the Psychology of Genocide.* Basic Books. (Italics added).

Chapter 12

315 Reeves, H. 2012. "Naturally Awful." *New York Times Magazine*, Sept. 2. See Erskine, K. 2012. "Wholesome Foods and Wholesome Morals? Organic Foods Reduce Prosocial Behavior and Harshen Moral Judgments." *Social Psychology and Personality Science* 4(2): 251–254.
316 Chugh, D. and Kern, M.C. 2016. "A Dynamic and Cyclical Model of Bounded Ethicality." *Research in Organizations* 36: 85–100.
317 Prentice, R. 2011. "Moral Equilibrium: Stock Brokers and the Limits of Disclosure." *Wisconsin Law Review* 2011(6): 1059–1107.
318 Mulder, L.B. and Aquino, K. 2013. "The Role of Moral Identity in the Aftermath of Dishonesty." *Organizational Behavior and Human Decision Processes* 121: 219–230.
319 Kotchen, M. and Moon, J.J. 2012. "Corporate Social Responsibility for Irresponsibility." *The B.E. Journal of Economic Analysis & Policy* 12(1): Article 55.
320 Zhong, C., Liljenquist, K.A. and Cain, D.M. 2009. "Moral Self-Regulation." In *Psychological Perspectives on Ethical Behavior and Decision Making*, De Cremer, D. (ed.), 75–89. Information Age Publishing.
321 Mullen, E. and Monin, B. 2016. "Consistency Versus Licensing Effects of Past Moral Behavior." *Annual Review of Psychology* 67: 363–385.
322 McMillen, D.L. and Austin, J.B. 1971. "Effect of Positive Feedback on Compliance Following Transgression." *Psychonomic Science* 24(2): 59–61.
323 Khan, U. and Dhar, R. 2006. "Licensing Effect in Consumer Choice." *Journal of Marketing Research* 43(May): 259–266.
324 Sachdeva, S., Iliev, R. and Medin, D.L. 2009. "Sinning Saints and Saintly Sinners: The Paradox of Moral Self-Regulation." *Psychological Science* 20(4): 523–528.
325 Jordan, J., Gino, F., Tenbrunsel, A. and Leliveld, M. 2011. "Moral Compensation and the Environment: Affecting Individuals' Moral Intentions Through How They See Themselves as Moral." *Advances in Consumer Research* 39: 196–197.
326 Dutton, D.G. and Lake, R.A. 1973. "Threat of Own Prejudice and Reverse Discrimination in Interracial Situations." *Journal of Personality & Social Psychology* 28(1): 94–100.
327 Monin, B. and Miller, D.T. 2001. "Moral Credentials and the Expression of Prejudice." *Journal of Personality and Social Psychology* 81(1): 33–43.
328 Mazar, N. and Zhong, C. 2010. "Do Green Products Make Us Better People?" *Psychological Science* 21(4): 494–498.

329 Brooks, D. 2011. *The Social Animal: The Hidden Sources of Love, Character, and Achievement*. Random House.
330 Hill, C.A. and Painter, R.W. 2015. *Better Bankers, Better Banks: Promoting Good Business Through Contractual Commitments*. University of Chicago Press.
331 DeSteno, D. and Valdesolo, P. 2011. *Out of Character: Surprising Truths about the Liar, Cheat, Sinner (and Saint) Lurking in All of Us*. Crown Publishing Group.
332 Id.
333 Sachdeva, S., Iliev, R. and Medin, D.L. (2009).
334 Lobel, T. 2014. *Sensation: The New Science of Physical Intelligence*. Atria Books.
335 Cornelissen, G. et al. 2013. "Rules or Consequences? The Role of Ethical Mindsets in Moral Dynamics." *Psychological Science* 24(4): 482–488.
336 Conway, P. and Peetz, J. 2012. "When Does Feeling Moral Actually Make You a Better Person? Conceptual Abstraction Moderates Whether Past Moral Deeds Motivate Consistency or Compensatory Behavior." *Personality & Social Psychology Bulletin* 38(7): 907–919.
337 Mullen, E. and Monin, B. (2016).

Chapter 13

338 Teresa, M. 1983. *Words to Love By*. Ave Maria Press.
339 Plous, S. 1993. *The Psychology of Judgment and Decision Making*. McGraw-Hill.
340 Harris, S. 2010. *The Moral Landscape: How Science Can Determine Human Values*. Free Press. (referring to studies by Paul Slovic).
341 Bandura, A. 2016. *Moral Disengagement: How People Do Harm and Live with Themselves*. Worth Publishers.
342 Glover, J. 2012. *Humanity: A Moral History of the Twentieth Century* (2nd ed.). Yale University Press.
343 Soltes, E. 2016. *Why They Do It: Inside the Mind of the White-Collar Criminal*. Public Affairs.
344 Gibbs, J.C. 2014. *Moral Development & Reality: Beyond the Theories of Kohlberg, Hoffman, and Haidt* (3nd ed.). Oxford University Press.
345 Damon, W. and Colby, A. 2015. *The Power of Ideals: The Real Story of Moral Choice*. Oxford University Press.
346 Jackall, R. 1989. *Moral Mazes*. Oxford University Press.
347 Soltes, E. 2017. "Teaching Versus Living: Managerial Decision Making in the Gray." *Journal of Management Education* 41(4): 455–468.
348 Id.
349 Id.
350 Bazerman, M.H. and Tenbrunsel, A.E. 2011. *Blind Spots: Why We Fail to Do What's Right and What to Do about It*. Princeton University Press.
351 Ewing, J. 2017. *Faster, Higher, Farther: The Volkswagen Scandal*. W.W. Norton & Co.
352 ASCE. 2015. "Piper Alpha: Ethics Case Study No. 2." www.youtube.com/watch?v=0DYHmpI20lI. (Italics added).
353 Darley, J.M. 1996. "How Organizations Socialize Individuals into Evildoing." In *Codes of Conduct*, Messick, D. and Tenbrunsel, A. (eds.). Russell Sage Foundation.
354 Ariely, D. 2012. *The (Honest) Truth About Dishonesty: How We Lie to Everyone–Especially Ourselves*. Harpers.
355 Sinek, S. 2014. *Leaders Eat Last: Why Some Teams Pull Together and Others Don't*. Portfolio/Penguin.
356 Id.
357 Sapolsky, R.M. 2017. *Behave: The Biology of Humans at Our Best and Worst*. Penguin Press.

Chapter 14

358 Tomasello, M. 2016. *A Natural History of Human Morality*. Harvard University Press.

359 Greene, J. 2013. *Moral Tribes: Emotion, Reason, and the Gap between Us and Them*. Penguin Press.
360 *Id.*
361 Sherif, M. et al. 1988. *The Robbers Cave Experiment: Intergroup Conflict and Cooperation*. Wesleyan University Press.
362 Shermer, M. 2015. *The Moral Arc: How Science and Reason Lead Humanity Toward Truth, Justice and Freedom*. Henry Holt.
363 Bargh, J. 2017. *Before You Know It: The Unconscious Reasons We Do What We Do*. Touchstone.
364 Tomasello, M. (2016).
365 Stout, L.A. 2008. "Taking Conscience Seriously." In *Moral Markets*, Zak, P. (ed.), 157–172. Princeton University Press.
366 Alexander, R.D. 1987. *The Biology of Moral Systems*. AldineTransaction.
367 Valdesolo, P. and DeSteno, D. 2007. "Moral Hypocrisy: Social Groups and the Flexibility of Virtue." *Psychological Science* 18(8): 689–690.
368 Banaji, M. and Greenwald, A. 2009. *Blindspot: Hidden Biases of Good People*. Delacorte Press.
369 Sapolsky, R.M. 2017. *Behave: The Biology of Humans at Our Best and Worst*. Penguin Press.
370 Wegner, D. and Gray, K. 2016. *The Mind Club: Who Thinks, What Feels, and Why It Matters*. Penguin Books.
371 Cohen, T.R. and Morse, L. 2014. "Moral Character: What It Is and What It Does." *Research in Organizational Behavior* 34: 43–61.
372 Narvaez, D. 2014. *Neurobiology and the Development of Human Morality*. W.W. Norton & Co.
373 DiTomaso, N. 2013. *The American Non-Dilemma: Racial Inequality Without Racism*. Russell Sage Foundation.
374 Messick, D.M. 2009. "What Can Psychology Tell Us About Business Ethics?" *Journal of Business Ethics* 89(Supp.1): 73–80.
375 Sapolsky, R.M. (2017).
376 Diekmann, K.A., Samuels, S.M., Ross, L. and Bazerman, M.H. 1997. "Self-Interest and Fairness in Problems of Resource Allocation: Allocators versus Recipients." *Journal of Personality and Social Psychology* 72(5): 1061–1074.
377 Zak, P.J. 2012. *The Moral Molecule: The Source of Love and Prosperity*. Dutton.
378 Gibbs, J.C. 2014. *Moral Development & Reality: Beyond the Theories of Kohlberg, Hoffman, and Haidt* (3nd ed.). Oxford University Press.
379 Shermer, M. (2015).
380 Grant, A. 2013. *Give and Take: A Revolutionary Approach to Success*. Penguin Books.
381 Hildreth, A.J., Gino, F. and Bazerman, M.H. 2016. "Blind Loyalty? How Group Loyalty Makes Us See Evil or Engage in It." *Organizational Behavior and Human Decision Processes* 132: 16–36.
382 Hume, D. 1738/1985. *A Treatise of Human Nature*. Penguin Books.
383 Bandura, A., Underwood, B. and Fromson, M.E. 1975. "Disinhibition of Aggression through Diffusion of Responsibility and Dehumanization of Victims." *Journal of Research in Personality* 9(4): 253–269.
384 Smith, D.L. 2011. *Less Than Human: Why We Demean, Enslave, and Exterminate Others*. St. Martin's Press.
385 Damon, W. and Colby, A. 2015. *The Power of Ideals: The Real Story of Moral Courage*. Oxford University Press.
386 Ross, H.J. 2014. *Everyday Bias: Identifying and Navigating Unconscious Judgments in Our Everyday Lives*. Rowman & Littlefield.
387 Baron, J. 2014. "Moral Judgment." In *The Oxford Handbook of Behavioral Economics and the Law*, Zamir, E. and Teichman, D. (eds.), 61–89. Oxford University Press.
388 Goldstein, R.N. 2010. *Does Moral Action Depend on Reasoning?* (June) (John Templeton Foundation Symposium). www.rebeccagoldstein.com/files/rgoldstein/files/goldstein.pdf.

Chapter 15

389 Payne, K., Niemi, L. and Doris, J.M. 2018. "How to Think about 'Implicit Bias'." *Scientific American*, Mar. 27.
390 Kristof, N. 2008. "What? Me Biased?" *New York Times*, Oct. 29. www.nytimes.com/2008/10/30/opinion/30kristof.html.
391 Bertrand, M., Chugh, D. and Mullainathan, S. 2005. "Implicit Discrimination." *American Economic Review* 95(2): 94–98.
392 Eberhardt, J.L. 2019. *Biased: Uncovering the Hidden Prejudice That Shapes What We See, Think, and Do.* Viking.
393 Banaji, M. and Greenwald, A. 2013. *Blind Spot: Hidden Biases of Good People.* Delacorte Press.
394 Singal, J. 2017. "Psychology's Favorite Tool for Measuring Racism Isn't Up to the Job." *New Yorker*, Jan. 11. www.thecut.com/2017/01/psychologys-racism-measuring-tool-isnt-up-to-the-job.html.
395 Nosek, B. and Greenwald, A. 2007. "The Implicit Association Test at Age 7: A Methodological and Conceptual Review." *Automatic Processes in Social Thinking and Behavior*, Bargh, J.A. (ed.), 265–292. Psychology Press.
396 Greenwald, A., Banaji, M.R. and Nosek, B.A. 2015. "Statistically Small Effects of the Implicit Association Test Can Have Societally Large Effects." *Journal of Personality and Social Psychology* 108(4): 553–561.
397 Bertrand, M. and Mullainathan, S. 2004. "Are Emily and Greg More Employable Than Lakisha and Jamal? A Field Experiment on Labor Market Discrimination." *American Economic Review* 94: 991–1013.
398 Libgober, B. 2020. "Getting a Lawyer While Black: A Field Experiment." *Lewis and Clark Law Review* 24(1).
399 Ayres, I., Vars, F.E. and Zakariya, N. 2005. "To Insure Prejudice: Racial Disparities in Taxicab Tipping." *Yale Law Journal* 114(7): 1613–1674.
400 Lynn, M. et al. 2008. "Consumer Racial Discrimination in Tipping: A Replication and Extension." *Journal of Applied Social Psychology* 38(4): 1045–1060.
401 Green, A.R. et al. 2007. "Implicit Bias among Physicians and its Prediction of Thrombolysis Decisions for Black and White Patients." *Journal of General Internal Medicine* 22(9): 1231–1238.
402 Cintron, A. and Morrison, R.S. 2006. "Pain and Ethnicity in the United States: A Systematic Review." *Journal of Palliative Medicine* 9(6): 1454.
403 Glaser, J. and Knowles, E. 2008. "Implicit Motivation to Control Prejudice." *Journal of Experimental Social Psychology* 44(1): 164–172.
404 Beckett, K. and Sasson, T. 2004. *The Politics of Injustice: Crime and Punishment in America.* Sage.
405 Eberhardt, J.L. et al. 2006. "Looking Deathworthy: Perceived Stereotypicality of Black Defendants Predicts Capital Sentencing Outcomes." *Psychological Science* 17(5): 383–386.
406 Milkman, K.L., Akinola, M. and Chugh, D. 2012. "Temporal Distance and Discrimination: An Audit Study in Academia." *Psychological Science* 23(7): 710–717.
407 Glaser, J. and Knowles, E. (2008).
408 Baker, A. 2018. "Confronting the Implicit Bias in the New York Police Department." *New York Times*, July 15. www.nytimes.com/2018/07/15/nyregion/bias-training-police.html.
409 Dasgupta, N. and Asgari, S. 2004. "Seeing Is Believing: Exposure to Counterstereotypic Women Leaders and Its Effect on the Malleability of Automatic Gender Stereotyping." *Journal of Experimental Social Psychology* 40: 642–658.
410 Blair, I., Ma, J.E. and Lenton, A.P. 2001. "Imagining Stereotypes Away: The Moderation of Implicit Stereotypes through Mental Imagery." *Journal of Personality and Social Psychology* 81(5): 828–841.
411 Dasgupta, N. and Rivera, L.M. 2006. "From Automatic Antigay Prejudice to Behavior: The Moderating Role of Conscious Beliefs about Gender and Behavioral Control." *Journal of Personality and Social Psychology* 91(2): 268–280.

412 Lai, C. et al. 2016. "Reducing Implicit Racial Preferences: II. Intervention Effectiveness across Time." *Journal of Experimental Psychology* 145(8): 1001–1016.

Chapter 16

413 Fanon, F. 1952. *Black Skin, White Masks*. Grove Press.
414 Moser, W. 2011. "Apocalypse Oak Park: Dorothy Martin, The Chicagoan Who Predicted the End of the World and Inspired the Theory of Cognitive Dissonance." *Chicago Magazine*, May 20. www.chicagomag.com/Chicago-Magazine/The-312/May-2011/Dorothy-Martin-the-Chicagoan-Who-Predicted-the-End-of-the-World-and-Inspired-the-Theory-of-Cognitive-Dissonance/.
415 Festinger, L., Riecken, H.W. and Schachter, S. 1956. *When Prophecy Fails: A Social and Psychological Study of a Modern Group That Predicted the Destruction of the World*. Harper & Row.
416 Festinger, L. 1957. *A Theory of Cognitive Dissonance*. Row, Peterson & Co.
417 Lowell, J. 2012. "Managers and Moral Dissonance: Self Justification as a Big Threat to Ethical Management?" *Journal of Business Ethics* 105(1): 17–25.
418 Gentilin, D. 2016. *The Origins of Ethical Failures: Lessons for Leaders*. Routledge.
419 Aronson, E. 1972. *The Social Animal*. W.H. Freeman.
420 Engelberg, J., Parsons, C.A. and Tefft, N. 2013. "First, Do No Harm: Financial Conflicts in Medicine." http://citeseerx.ist.psu.edu/viewdoc/download?doi=10.1.1.643.8605&rep=rep1&type=pdf.
421 Ariely, D. 2012. *The (Honest) Truth About Dishonesty: How We Lie to Everyone–Especially Ourselves*. HarperCollins.
422 Luban, D. 2006. "Making Sense of Moral Meltdowns." In *Moral Leadership: The Theory and Practice of Power, Judgment, and Policy*, Rhode, D. (ed.), 57–75. Jossey Bass.
423 Godsey, M. 2017. *Blind Injustice: A Former Prosecutor Exposes the Psychology and Politics of Wrongful Conviction*. University of California Press.
424 Prentice, R. 2017. *Cognitive Dissonance and the Case of the Unindicted Co-ejaculator*. https://ethicsunwrapped.utexas.edu/cognitive-dissonance-case-unindicted-co-ejaculator.
425 Ewing, J. 2017. *Faster, Higher, Farther: The Volkswagen Scandal*. W.W. Norton & Co.
426 Kouchaki, M. and Gino, F. 2016. "Memories of Unethical Actions Become Obfuscated Over Time." *PNAS* 113 (May 31): 6166–6171.
427 Irwin, J., Reczek, R. and Zane, D. 2017. "Untrustworthy Memories Make It Hard to Shop Ethically." *The Conversation*, Dec. 20. http://theconversation.com/untrustworthy-memories-make-it-hard-to-shop-ethically-87572.
428 Akerlof, G. and Dickens, W. 1982. "The Economic Consequences of Cognitive Dissonance." *American Economic Review* 72(3): 307–319.
429 Samuel, A. 2017. "Cognitive Dissonance, Ethical Behavior, and Bribery." In *Thinking About Bribery: Neuroscience, Moral Cognition and the Psychology of Bribery*, Nichols, P. and Robertson, D. (eds.), 103–119.
430 Anand, V., Ashforth, B.E. and Joshi, M. 2004. "Business as Usual: The Acceptance and Perpetuation of Corruption in Organizations." *Academy of Management Executive* 18(2): 39–55.
431 Soltes, E. 2016. *Why They Do It: Inside the Mind of the White-Collar Criminal*. Public Affairs.
432 Lowell, J. (2012).
433 Comer, D.R. and Vega, G. 2011. "The Personal Ethical Threshold." In *Moral Courage in Organizations: Doing the Right Thing at Work*, Comer, D. and Vega, G. (eds.), 25–44. M.E. Sharpe.
434 Lehrer, J. 2009. *How We Decide*. Mariner Books.
435 Bazerman, M.H. and Tenbrunsel, A.E. 2011. *Blind Spots: Why We Fail to Do What's Right and What to Do about It*. Princeton University Press.

Chapter 17

436 Doris, J.M. 2002. *Lack of Character: Personality and Moral Behavior*. Cambridge University Press.

437 Isen, A. and Levin, P. 1972. "Effect of Feeling Good on Helping: Cookies and Kindness." *Journal of Personality and Social Psychology* 21: 384–388.
438 Baron, R.A. 1997. "The Sweet Smell of . . . Helping: Effects of Pleasant Ambient Fragrance on Prosocial Behavior in Shopping Malls." *Personality and Social Psychology Bulletin* 23(5): 498–503.
439 Damon, W. and Colby, A. 2015. *The Power of Ideals: The Real Story of Moral Choice.* Oxford University Press; Colby, A. and Damon, W. 1992. *Some Do Care.* Free Press, Oxford University Press.
440 Doris, J.M. 2015. *Talking to Our Selves: Reflection, Ignorance, and Agency.* Oxford University Press; Doris, J.M. 2002. *Lack of Character: Personality and Moral Behavior.* Cambridge University Press.
441 Houser, D. et al. 2015. "On the Origins of Dishonesty: From Parents to Children." NBER Working Paper No. 20897. https://papers.ssrn.com/sol3/papers.cfm?abstract_id=2558949.
442 Miller, C.B. 2018. *The Character Gap: How Good Are We?* Oxford University Press.
443 Darley, J.M. and Batson, C.D. 1973. "'From Jerusalem to Jericho': A Study of Situational and Dispositional Variables in Helping Behavior." *Journal of Personality and Social Psychology* 27(1): 100–108.
444 Fine, C. 2005. *A Mind of Its Own: How Your Brain Distorts and Deceives.* W.W. Norton & Co.
445 Coram, P., Ng, J. and Woodliff, D.R. 2004. "The Effect of Risk of Misstatement on the Propensity to Commit Reduced Audit Quality Acts Under Time Budget Pressure." *Auditing: A Journal of Practice & Theory* 23(2): 159–167.
446 Margolis, J. and Molinsky, A. 2006. "Three Practical Challenges of Moral Leadership." In *Moral Leadership: The Theory and Practice of Power, Judgment, and Policy*, Rhode, D. (ed.), 77–93. Jossey-Bass.
447 Plato. 1946. *The Republic* (Benjamin Jowett, trans.). The World Publishing Co.
448 Brandeis, L. 1913. "What Publicity Can Do." *Harper's Weekly*, Dec. 20. http://3197d6d14b5f19f2f440-5e13d29c4c016cf96cbbfd197c579b45.r81.cf1.rackcdn.com/collection/papers/1910/1913_12_20_What_Publicity_Ca.pdf.
449 Lieberman, M.D. 2013. *Social: Why Our Brains Are Wired to Connect.* Crown Publishers.
450 Miller, G. 2014. "Using Smartphones to Track Our Everyday Moral Judgments." *Wired*, Sept. 11. www.wired.com/2014/09/smartphone-study-moral-psychology/ (quoting Jonathan Haidt).
451 Tomasello, M. 2016. *A Natural History of Human Morality.* Harvard University Press.
452 Priks, M. 2014. "Do Surveillance Cameras Affect Unruly Behavior? A Close Look at Grandstands." *Scandinavian Journal of Economics* 116(4): 1160–1179.
453 Covey, M., Saladin, S. and Killen, P.J. 1989. "Self-Monitoring, Surveillance, and Incentive Effects on Cheating." *Journal of Social Psychology* 129(5): 673–679.
454 Di Tella, R. and Schargrodsky, E. 2003. "The Role of Wages and Auditing During a Crackdown on Corruption in the City of Buenos Aires." *Journal of Law & Economics* 46(1): 269–292.
455 Anonymous. 2010. "Manager's Best Friend: Dogs Improve Office Productivity." *The Economist* 396(8695): 66. www.economist.com/science-and-technology/2010/08/12/managers-best-friend.
456 van Rompay, T., Vonk, D.J. and Fransen, M.L. 2009. "The Eye of the Camera: Effects of Security Camera on Prosocial Behavior." *Environment and Behavior* 41(1): 60–74.
457 Ernest-Jones, M., Nettle, D. and Bateson, M. 2011. "Effects of Eye Images on Everyday Cooperative Behavior: A Field Experiment." *Evolution and Human Behavior* 32(3): 172–178.
458 Bateson, M., Nettle, D. and Roberts, G. 2006. "Cues of Being Watched Enhance Cooperation in a Real-World Setting." *Biology Letters* 2(3): 412–414.
459 Burnham, T. and Hare, B. 2007. "Engineering Human Cooperation-Does Involuntary Neural Activation Increase Public Goods Cooperation?" *Human Nature* 18(2): 88–108.

460 Haley, K. and Fessler, D. 2005. "Nobody's Watching? Subtle Cues Affect Generosity in an Anonymous Economic Game." *Evolution and Human Behavior* 26(3): 245–256.
461 Bateson, M. et al. 2013. "Do Images of 'Watching Eyes' Induce Behaviour That Is More Pro-Social or More Normative? A Field Experiment on Littering." *PLoS One* 8(12): e82055.
462 Francey, D. and Bergmuller, R. 2012. "Images of Eyes Enhance Investments in a Real-Life Public Good." *PLoS One* 7(5): e37397.
463 Powell, K., Roberts, G. and Nettle, D. 2012. "Eye Image Increases Charitable Donations: Evidence from an Opportunistic Field Experiment in a Supermarket." *Ethology* 118(11): 1096–1101.
464 Gervais, G. and Norenzayan, A. 2012. "Like a Camera in the Sky? Thinking about God Increases Public Self-Awareness and Socially Desirable Responding." *Journal of Experimental Social Psychology* 48(1): 298–302.
465 Greenberg, J. 1983. "Overcoming Egocentric Bias in Perceived Fairness through Self-Awareness." *Social Psychology Quarterly* 46(2): 152–156.
466 Diener, E. and Wallbom, M. 1976. "Effects of Self-Awareness on Antinormative Behavior." *Journal of Research in Personality* 10(1): 107–111.
467 Beaman, A.L., Klentz, B., Diener, E. and Svanum, S. 1979. "Self-Awareness and Transgression in Children: Two Field Studies." *Journal of Personality and Social Psychology* 37(10): 1835–1846.
468 Miller, C.B. 2014. *Character & Moral Psychology*. Oxford University Press.
469 Zhong, C., Bohns, V.K. and Gino, F. 2010. "Good Lamps Are the Best Police: Darkness Increases Dishonesty and Self-Interested Behavior." *Psychological Science* 21(3): 311–314.
470 Diener, E., Fraser, S.C., Beaman, A.L. and Kelem, R.T. 1976. "Effects of Deindividuation Variables on Stealing Among Halloween Trick-or-Treaters." *Journal of Personality and Social Psychology* 33(2): 178–183.
471 Zhong, C., Bohns, V.K. and Gino, F. (2010).
472 de Waal, F. 2013. *The Bonobo and the Atheist: In Search of Humanism among the Primates*. W.W. Norton & Co. (quoting psychologist Ara Norenzayan).
473 Bloom, P. 2018. *Against Empathy: The Case for Rational Compassion*. ECCO.
474 Baumeister, R., Vohs, K.D. and Tice, D.M. 2007. "The Strength Model of Self-Control." *Current Directions in Psychological Science* 16(6): 351–355.
475 Langevoort, D. 2018. "Behavioral Ethics, Behavioral Compliance." In *Research Handbook on Corporate Crime and Financial Misdealing*, Arlen, J. (ed.), 263–281. Edward Elgar.
476 Christian, M. and Ellis, A. 2011. "Examining the Effects of Sleep Deprivation on Workplace Deviance: A Self-Regulatory Perspective." *Academy of Management Journal* 54(5): 913–934.
477 Danziger, S., Levav, J. and Avnaim-Pesso, L. 2011. "Extraneous Factors in Judicial Decisions." *PNAS* 108(17): 6889–6892.
478 Kouchaki, M. and Smith, I. 2014. "The Morning Morality Effect: The Influence of Time of Day on Ethical Behavior." *Psychological Science* 25(1): 95–102.
479 Gino, F., Schweitzer, M.E., Mead, N.L. and Ariely, D. 2011. "Unable to Resist Temptation: How Self-Control Depletion Promotes Unethical Behavior." *Organizational Behavior and Human Decision Processes* 115(2): 191–203; Mead, N. et al. 2009. "Too Tired to Tell the Truth: Self-Control Resource Depletion and Dishonesty." *Journal of Experimental Social Psychology* 45(3): 594–597; Muraven, M., Pogarsky, G. and Shmueli, D. 2006. "Self-Control Depletion and the General Theory of Crime." *Journal of Quantitative Criminology* 22(3): 263–277.
480 DeWall, C.N., Baumeister, R.F., Gailliot, M.T. and Maner, J.K. 2008. "Depletion Makes the Heart Grow Less Helpful: Helping as a Function of Self-Regulatory Energy and Genetic Relatedness." *Personality and Social Psychology Bulletin* 34(12): 1653–1662.
481 Mischel, W. 2014. *The Marshmallow Test: Mastering Self Control*. Little, Brown & Co.
482 Vohs, K., Mead, N.L. and Goode, M.R. 2008. "Merely Activating the Concept of Money Changes Personal and Interpersonal Behavior." *Current Directions in Psychological Science* 17(3): 208–212.

483 Vohs, K., Mead, N.L. and Goode, M.R. 2006. "The Psychological Consequences of Money." *Science* 314(5802): 1154–1156.
484 Mogilner, C. 2010. "The Pursuit of Happiness: Time, Money, and Social Connection." *Psychological Science* 21(9): 1348–1354.
485 Powdthavee, N. and Oswald, A.J. 2014. "Does Money Make People Right-Wing and Inegalitarian? A Longitudinal Study of Lottery Winners?" IZA Discussion Paper No. 7934. https://papers.ssrn.com/sol3/papers.cfm?abstract_id=2396429.
486 Kouchaki, M., Smith-Crowe, K., Brief, A.P. and Sousa, C. 2013. "Seeing Green: Mere Exposure to Money Triggers a Business Decision Frame and Unethical Outcomes. *Organizational Behavior and Human Decision Processes* 121(1): 53–61.
487 Vohs, K.D. 2015. "Money Priming Can Changes People's Thoughts, Feelings, Motivations, and Behaviors: An Update on 10 Years of Experiments." *Journal of Experimental Psychology: General* 144(4): e86–e93.
488 Hendry, J. 2013. *Ethics and Finance: An Introduction.* Cambridge University Press.
489 Brink, D.O. 2013. "Situationism, Responsibility, and Fair Opportunity." *Social Philosophy and Policy* 30(1–2): 121–149.
490 Lewis, M. 2014. "Occupational Hazards of Working on Wall Street." *Bloomberg View*, Sept. 24. www.bloombergview.com/articles/2014-09-24/occupational-hazards-of-working-on-wall-street.
491 Soltes, E. 2016. *Why They Do It: Inside the Mind of the White-Collar Criminal.* Public Affairs.
492 Wegner, D.M. and Gray, K. 2016. *The Mind Club: Who Thinks, What Feels, and Why It Matters.* Penguin Books.
493 Edmonds, D. 2014. *Would You Kill the Fat Man?* Princeton University Press.
494 Bicchieri, C. and Ganegoda, D. 2017. "Determinations of Corruption: A Sociopsychological Analysis." In *Thinking About Bribery: Neuroscience, Moral Cognition and the Psychology of Bribery*, Nichols, P. and Robertson, D. (eds.), 179–205.
495 Houser, D. et al. (2015).
496 Cohen, T.R. and Morse, L. 2014. "Moral Character: What It Is and What It Does." *Research in Organizational Behavior* 34: 43–61.
497 Glover, J. 2012. *Humanity: A Moral History of the Twentieth Century* (2nd ed.). Yale University Press.

Chapter 18

498 Payne, J.W., Bettman, J.R. and Johnson, E.J. 1993. *The Adaptive Decision Maker.* Cambridge University Press.
499 Tenbrunsel, A.E., Diekmann, K.A., Wade-Benzoni, K.A. and Bazerman, M.H. 2010. "The Ethical Mirage: A Temporal Explanation as to Why We Aren't as Ethical as We Think We Are." *Research in Organizational Behavior* 30: 153–173.
500 Loewenstein, G. and Prelec, D. 1992. "Anomalies in Intertemporal Choice: Evidence and Interpretation." *Quarterly Journal of Economics* 107(2): 573–597.
501 Prentice, R. 2013. "Beyond Temporal Explanations of Corporate Crime." *Virginia Journal of Criminal Law* 1(2): 397–422.
502 Kirby, K.N. and Herrnstein, J.R. 1995. "Preference Reversals Due to Myopic Discounting of Delayed Reward." *Psychological Science* 6(2): 83–88.
503 Milkman, K.L., Rogers, T. and Bazerman, M.H. 2009. "Highbrow Films Gather Dust: Time-Inconsistent Preferences and Online DVD Rentals." *Management Science* 55(6): 1047–1059.
504 Paxton, J.M., Ungar, L. and Greene, J.D. 2012. "Reflection and Reasoning in Moral Judgment." *Cognitive Science* 36(1): 163–177.
505 Da Silveira, A.D.M. 2018. *The Virtuous Barrel: How to Transform Corporate Scandals into Good Businesses via Behavioral Ethics.* Alexandre Di Miceli Da Silveira.
506 Utset, M.A. 2007. "Hyperbolic Criminals and Repeated Time-Inconsistent Misconduct." *Houston Law Review* 44(3): 609–677.

507 Kirby, K.N., Petry, N.M. and Bickel, W.K. 1999. "Heroin Addicts Have Higher Discount Rates for Delayed Rewards than Non-Drug-Using Controls." *Journal of Experimental Psychology: General* 128(1): 78–87.
508 Wilde, O. 1892/1999. *Lady Windermere's Fan*. W.W. Norton & Co.
509 Sharot, T. 2012. *The Optimism Bias: A Tour of the Irrationally Positive Brain*. Vintage.
510 Gilbert, D. 2013. "Affective Forecasting . . . Or . . . The Big Wombassa: What You Think You're Going to Get, and What You Don't Get, When You Get What You Want." In *Thinking: The New Science of Decision-Making, Problem-Solving and Prediction*, Brockman, J. (ed.), 55–68. Harper Collins.
511 Swanson, A. 2016. "What Your New Gym Doesn't Want You to Know." *Washington Post*, Jan. 5. www.washingtonpost.com/news/wonk/wp/2016/01/05/what-your-new-gym-doesnt-want-you-to-know/?utm_term=.89aa3d91ea86.
512 Matousek, M. 2011. *Ethical Wisdom: The Search for a Moral Life*. Anchor Books.
513 Bargh, J. 2017. *Before You Know It: The Unconscious Reasons We Do What We Do*. Touchstone.
514 Chabris, C.F. and Simons, D.J. 2014. "Why Our Memory Fails Us." *New York Times*, Dec. 2. www.nytimes.com/2014/12/02/opinion/why-our-memory-fails-us.html.
515 Bandura, A. 2016. *Moral Disengagement: How People Do Harm and Live with Themselves*. Worth Publishers.
516 Kouchaki, M. and Gino, F. 2016. "Memories of Unethical Actions Become Obfuscated Over Time." *PNAS* 113 (May 31): 6166–6171.
517 Shu, L., Gino, F. and Bazerman, M.H. 2011. "Dishonest Deed, Clear Conscience: When Cheating Leads to Moral Disengagement and Motivated Forgetting." *Personality and Social Psychology Bulletin* 37(3): 330–349.
518 Reczek, R.R., Irwin, J., Zane, D. and Ehrich, K. 2017. "That's Not How I Remember It: Willfully Ignorant Memory for Ethical Product Attributes." *Journal of Consumer Research* 45(1): 185–207.
519 Escobedo, J.R. and Adolphs, R. 2011. "Becoming a Better Person: Temporal Remoteness Biases Autobiographical Memories for Moral Events." *Emotion* 10(4): 511–518.
520 Tenbrunsel, A.E., Diekmann, K.A., Wade-Benzoni, K.A. and Bazerman, M.H. (2010).
521 Woodzicka, J.A. and LaFrance, M. 2001. "Real Versus Imagined Gender Harassment." *Journal of Social Science* 57(1): 15–30.
522 Hofling, C.K. et al. 1966. "An Experimental Study in Nurse-Physician Relationships." *Journal of Nervous and Mental Disease* 143(2): 171–180.
523 Gupta, S., Swanson, N.J. and Cunningham, D.J. 2009. "A Study of the Effect of Age, Gender, & GPA on the Ethical Behavior of Accounting Students." *Journal of Legal, Ethical and Regulatory Issues* 12(2): 103.
524 Bocchiaro, P., Zimbardo, P.G. and Van Lange, P. 2011. "To Defy or Not to Defy: An Experimental Study of the Dynamics of Disobedience and Whistleblowing." *Social Influence* 7(1): 35–50.
525 Myers, D.G. 2004. *Intuition: Its Powers and Perils*. Yale University Press.
526 Epley, E. and Dunning, D. 2000. "Feeling 'Holier Than Thou': Are Self-Serving Assessments Produced by Errors in Self- or Social Prediction?" *Journal of Personality and Social Psychology* 79(6): 861–875.
527 Tenbrunsel, A.E., Diekmann, K.A., Wade-Benzoni, K.A. and Bazerman, M.H. (2010).

Chapter 19

528 Gentilin, D. 2016. *The Origins of Ethical Failures: Lessons for Leaders*. Routledge.
529 Ross, L. 1977. "The Intuitive Psychologist and His Shortcomings: Distortions in the Attribution Process." *Advances in Experimental Social Psychology* 10: 173–220.
530 Gino, F. 2013. *Sidetracked: How Our Decisions Get Derailed and How We Can Stick to the Plan*. Harvard Business Review Press.
531 Doris, J.M. 2002. *Lack of Character: Personality and Moral Behavior*. Cambridge University Press.

532 Sabini, J., Siepmann, M. and Stein, J. 2001. "The Really Fundamental Attribution Error in Social Psychological Research." *Psychological Inquiry* 12(1): 1–15.
533 Hopthrow, T. et al. 2016. "Mindfulness Reduces the Correspondence Bias." *Quarterly Journal of Experimental Psychology* 70(3): 351–360.
534 Friedman, H.H. 2017. "Cognitive Biases that Interfere with Critical Thinking and Scientific Reasoning: A Course Module." https://papers.ssrn.com/Sol3/papers.cfm?abstract_id=2958800.
535 McPherson, M.B. and Young, S.L. 2004. "What Students Think When Teachers Get Upset: Fundamental Attribution Error and Student-Generated Reasons for Teacher Anger." *Communication Quarterly* 52(4): 357–369.
536 Gilbert, D.T. and Malone, P.S. 1995. "The Correspondence Bias." *Psychological Bulletin* 117(1): 21–38.
537 Zimbardo, P. 2007. *The Lucifer Effect*. Random House.
538 Ross, L., Amabile, T.M. and Steinmetz, J.L. 1977. "Social Roles, Social Control, and Biases in Social-Perception Processes. *Journal of Personality and Social Psychology* 35(7): 485–494.
539 Jones, E.E. and Harris, V.A. 1967. "The Attribution of Attitudes." *Journal of Experimental Social Psychology* 3(1): 1–24.
540 Kelsey, D.M. et al. 2004. "College Students' Attributions of Teacher Misbehaviors." *Communication Education* 53(1): 40–55.
541 Heider, F. 1958. *The Psychology of Interpersonal Relations*. Wiley.
542 Gilbert, D.T. and Malone, P.S. (1995).
543 Kunda, Z. and Nisbett, R.E. 1986. "The Psychometrics of Everyday Life." *Cognitive Psychology* 18(2): 195–224.
544 Hartshorn, H. and May, M. 1928. *Studies in Deceit*. MacMillan.
545 O'Sullivan, M. 2003. "The Fundamental Attribution Error in Detecting Deception: The Boy-Who-Cried Wolf Effect." *Journal of Personality and Social Psychology* 29(10): 1316–1327.
546 Pronin, E. 2008. "How We See Ourselves and How We See Others." *Science* 320(5880): 1177–1180.
547 Gentilin, D. (2016).
548 Shermer, M. 2015. *The Moral Arc*. Henry Holt and Company.
549 Piff, P.K. 2013. "Does Money Make You Mean?" *TED Talk*. www.ted.com/talks/paul_piff_does_money_make_you_mean?language=en.
550 Piff, P.K. 2014. "Wealth and the Inflated Self: Class, Entitlement, and Narcissism." *Personality and Social Psychology Bulletin* 40(1): 34–43.
551 Krull, D.S. et al. 1999. "The Fundamental Attribution Error: Correspondence Bias in Individualist and Collectivist Cultures." *Personality and Social Psychology Bulletin* 25(10): 1208–1219.
552 Bauman, C.W. and Skitka, L.J. 2010. "Making Attributions for Behaviors: The Prevalence of Correspondence Bias in the General Population." *Basic and Applied Social Psychology* 32(3): 269–277.
553 Id.

Part II

554 Rest, J.R. 1994. *Moral Development: Advances in Research and Theory*. Praeger.
555 Prentice, R. 2015. "Behavioral Ethics: Can It Help Lawyers (and Others) Be Their Best Selves?" *Notre Dame Journal of Law, Ethics & Public Policy* 29(1): 35–85.
556 Drumwright, M.E. and Murphy, P.E. 2004. "How Advertising Practitioners View Ethics: Moral Muteness, Moral Myopia, and Moral Imagination." *Journal of Advertising* 33(2): 7–24.

Chapter 20

557 Fuller, J.G. 1962. *The Gentleman Conspirators: The Story of the Price-Fixers in the Electrical Industry*. Grove Press (quoting the *New York Herald Tribune* regarding one of the greatest antitrust scandals of all time).

558 Wrangham, R. 2019. *The Goodness Paradox: The Strange Relationship between Virtue and Violence in Human Evolution.* Pantheon.
559 *Id.*
560 May, J. 2016. *Regard for Reason in the Moral Mind.* Oxford University Press.
561 May, J. 2018. "The Limits of Emotion in Moral Judgment." In *The Many Moral Rationalisms,* Jones, K. and Schroeter, F. (eds.), 286–306. Oxford University Press.
562 Wrangham, R. (2019).
563 *Id.*
564 Klein, G., Shtudiner, Z. and Kantor, J. 2019. "Judging Ethical Behavior in the Workplace: The Role of Attractiveness and Gender." https://papers.ssrn.com/sol3/papers.cfm?abstract_id=3122277.
565 Cullity, G. 2018. "Stupid Goodness." In *The Many Moral Rationalisms,* Jones, K. and Schroeter, F. (eds.), 227–246. Oxford University Press.
566 *Id.*
567 Sauer, H. 2019. *Moral Thinking, Fast and Slow.* Routledge Focus.
568 *Id.*
569 Feldman, Y. 2019. "Companies Need to Pay More Attention to Everyday Unethical Behavior." *Harvard Business Review,* Mar. 1. https://hbr.org/2019/03/companies-need-to-pay-more-attention-to-everyday-unethical-behavior.
570 Reynolds, S.J. 2008. "Moral Attentiveness: Who Pays Attention to the Moral Aspects of Life?" *Journal of Applied Psychology* 93(5): 1027–1041.
571 Agapakis, C. 2014. "Ring Ritual Reminds Engineers of Their Responsibility." *Scientific American* (blog), May 7. https://blogs.scientificamerican.com/oscillator/ring-ritual-reminds-engineers-of-their-responsibility/?redirect=1.
572 Milgram, S. 1974. *Obedience to Authority.* Harper & Row.
573 Mayer, D.M. et al. 2013. "Encouraging Employees to Report Unethical Conduct Internally: It Takes a Village." *Organizational Behavior and Human Decision Processes* 121(1): 89–103.
574 Kahneman, D. 2011. *Thinking, Fast and Slow.* Farrar, Straus & Giroux.
575 Neale, M.S. and Bazerman, M.H. 1985. "The Effects of Framing and Negotiator Overconfidence on Bargaining Behaviors and Outcomes." *Academy of Management Journal* 28(1): 34–49.
576 Moore, F.C., Obradovich, N., Lehner, F. and Baylis, P. 2019. "Rapidly Declining Remarkability of Temperature Anomalies May Obscure Pubic Perception of Climate Change." *PNAS* 116(11): 4905–4910.
577 Ariely, D. 2012. *The (Honest) Truth About Dishonesty: How We Lie to Everyone–Especially Ourselves.* Harper.
578 Johnson, M. 1993. *Moral Imagination: Implication of Cognitive Science for Ethics.* University of Chicago Press.
579 Werhane, P. 1999. *Moral Imagination and Management Decision-Making.* Oxford University Press.
580 Cook, K. 2014. *Kitty Genovese: The Murder, the Bystanders, the Crime That Changed America.* W.W. Norton & Co. (Italics added).
581 Fink, S. 2013. *Five Days at Memorial: Life and Death in a Storm-Ravaged Hospital.* Crown Publishers.(Italics added).
582 Gibbs, J.C. 2014. *Moral Development & Reality: Beyond the Theories of Kohlberg, Hoffman, and Haidt 2003* (3rd ed.). Oxford University Press.
583 Miller, C.B. 2018. *The Character Gap: How Good Are We?* Oxford University Press.
584 Reed, A. and Aquino, K.F. 2003. "Moral Identity and the Expanding Circle of Moral Regard toward Out-Groups." *Journal of Personality and Social Psychology* 84: 1270–1286.
585 Reynolds, S.J. and Ceranic, T.L. 2007. "The Effects of Moral Judgment and Moral Identity on Moral Behavior: An Empirical Examination of the Moral Individual." *Journal of Applied Psychology* 92: 1610–1624.
586 Aquino, K. and Becker, T.E. 2005. "Lying in Negotiations: How Individual and Situational Factors Influence the Use of Neutralization Strategies." *Journal of Organizational Behavior* 26: 661–679.

587 McFerran, B., Aquino, K. and Duffy, M. 2010. "How Personality and Moral Identity Relate to Individuals' Ethical Ideology." *Business Ethics Quarterly* 20: 35–56.
588 Reynolds, S.J. 2008. "Moral Attentiveness: Who Pays Attention to the Moral Aspects of Life?" *Journal of Applied Psychology* 93(5): 1027–1041.
589 Smith, I. and Kouchaki, M. 2018. "Moral Humility: In Life and at Work." *Research in Organizational Behavior* 38: 77–94.
590 Damon, W. and Colby, A. 2015. *The Power of Ideals: The Real Story of Moral Choice*. Oxford University Press.
591 Colby, A. and Damon, W. 1994. *Some Do Care: Contemporary Lives of Moral Commitment*. Free Press.
592 Hallie, P. 1994. *Lest Innocent Blood Be Shed: The Story of the Village of Le Chambon and How Goodness Happened There*. Harper Perennial.

Chapter 21

593 May, J. 2018b. *Regard for Reason in the Moral Mind*. Oxford University Press.
594 "Rationalize." *Dictionary.com*. 2020. www.dictionary.com/browse/rationalization?s=t.
595 Hall, K. and Holmes, V. 2009. "The Power of Rationalisation to Influence Lawyers' Decisions to Act Unethically." *Legal Ethics* 11(2): 137–153.
596 Id.
597 Anand, V., Ashforth, B.E. and Joshi, M. 2004. "Business as Usual: The Acceptance and Perpetuation of Corruption in Organizations." *Academy of Management Executive* 18(2): 39–55.
598 The Trial of Adolf Eichmann, Session 95, July 13, 1961. Goo.gl/YghtTS.
599 Lewis, M. 1989. *Liar's Poker*. Penguin Books.
600 Stone, P.H. 2006. *Casino Jack and the United States of Money*. Melville House Publishing.
601 Norris, F. 2013. "After Fraud, The Fog Around Libor Hasn't Lifted." *New York Times*, Nov. 1. www.nytimes.com/2013/11/01/business/after-fraud-the-fog-around-libor-hasnt-cleared.html.
602 Vandivier, K. 1972. "The Aircraft Brake Scandal." *Harper's Magazine*. https://harpers.org/archive/1972/04/the-aircraft-brake-scandal/.
603 Abramoff, J. 2011. *Capitol Punishment: The Hard Truth about Washington Corruption from America's Most Notorious Lobbyist*. WND Books.
604 Bandura, A. 2016. *Moral Disengagement: How People Do Harm and Live with Themselves*. Worth Publishers.
605 Anderson, M. and Escher, P. 2010. *The MBA Oath: Setting a Higher Standard for Business Leaders*. Portfolio.
606 Bandura, A. (2016).
607 Cressey, D.R. 1965. "The Respectable Criminal." *Criminologica* 3(1): 13–16.
608 Bandura, A. (2016).
609 Lee, D. 1985. *Sergeant York: An American Hero*. University Press of Kentucky.
610 Bandura, A. (2016).
611 Kelman, H. 1973. "Violence without Moral Restraint: Reflections on the Dehumanization of Victims and Victimizers." *Journal of Social Issues* 29(4): 25–61.
612 Vandivier, K. (1972).
613 Bandura, A. (2016).
614 Id.
615 Larsen, K., Coleman, D., Forbes, J. and Johnson, R. 1972. "Is the Subject's Personality or the Experimental Situation a Better Predictor of a Subject's Willingness to Administer Shock to a Victim?" *Journal of Personality and Social Psychology* 22(3): 287–295.
616 Id.
617 Harris, L.T. and Fiske, S.T. 2011. "Perceiving Humanity or Not: A Social Neuroscience Approach to Dehumanized Perception." In *Social Neuroscience: Toward Understanding the Underpinnings of the Social Mind*, Todorov, A., Fiske, S. and Prentice, D. (eds.), 123–134. Oxford University Press.

618 Bandura, A. (2016).
619 *Id.*
620 Gambino, R. 1973. "Watergate Lingo: A Language of Non-Responsibility." *Freedom at Issue* 22: 7–9, 15–17.
621 Da Silveira, A.D.M. 2018. *The Virtuous Barrel: How to Transform Corporate Scandals into Good Businesses via Behavioral Ethics.* Alexandre Di Miceli Da Silveira.
622 Moore, C. and Gino, F. 2013. "Ethically Adrift: How Others Pull Our Moral Compass from True North, and How We Can Fix It." *Research in Organizational Behavior* 33: 53–77.
623 Tavris, C. and Aronson, E. 2007. *Mistakes Were Made (But Not By Me): Why We Justify Foolish Beliefs, Bad Decisions, and Hurtful Acts.* Houghton Mifflin Harcourt.
624 Bandura, A. (2016).
625 *Id.*

Chapter 22

626 Bandura, A. 2016. *Moral Disengagement: How People Do Harm and Live with Themselves.* Worth Publishers.
627 And you can. She is on the ethics speaker circuit: https://helensharkey.info/.
628 Monteiro, M. 2017. "Ethics Can't Be a Side Hustle." *Designer News*, Mar. 19. https://deardesignstudent.com/ethics-cant-be-a-side-hustle-b9e78c090aee.
629 Gentile, M.C. 2010. *Giving Voice to Values: How to Speak Your Mind When You Know What's Right.* Yale University Press.
630 McCombs School of Business. 2013. *Intro to Giving Voice to Values (GVV).* https://ethicsunwrapped.utexas.edu/video/introduction-to-giving-voice-to-values.
631 Darden School of Business. 2020. *Giving Voice to Values.* www.darden.virginia.edu/ibis/initiatives/giving-voice-to-values/.
632 Gentile, M.C. (2010).
633 *Id.*
634 Hall, T. 2019. *Writing to Persuade.* Liveright Publishing Corp.
635 Nelson, T.E. and Garst, J. 2005. "Values-Based Political Messages and Persuasion: Relationships among Speaker, Recipient, and Evoked Values." *Political Psychology* 26(4): 489–515.
636 Druckman, J.N. 2001. "The Implications of Framing Effects for Citizen Competence." *Political Behavior* 23(3): 225–256.
637 Seligman, M. 2004. *Authentic Happiness: Using the New Positive Psychology to Realize Your Potential for Lasting Fulfillment.* Atria Books.
638 Kidder, R.M. 2005. *Moral Courage: Taking Action When Your Values Are Put to the Test.* William Morrow.
639 Gentile, M.C. (2010).
640 Press, E. 2012. *Beautiful Souls: Saying No, Breaking Ranks, and Heeding the Voice of Conscience in Dark Times.* Farrar, Straus & Giroux.
641 Asch, S.E. 1951. "Effects of Group Pressure upon the Modification and Distortion of Judgment." In *Groups, Leadership and Men*, Guetzkow, H.S. (ed.), 177–190. Russell & Russell.
642 Staub, E. 1974. "Helping a Distressed Person: Social, Personality, and Stimulus Determinants." *Advances in Experimental Psychology* 7: 293–341.
643 Gentile, M.C. (2010).
644 *Id.*
645 *Id.*
646 Damon, W. and Colby, A. 2015. *The Power of Ideals: The Real Story of Moral Choice.* Oxford University Press.
647 Gentile, M.C. (2010).
648 *Id.*
649 McCarthy, M. 1961. "Characters in Fiction." *Partisan Review*, March/April. www.theparisreview.org/interviews/4618/mary-mccarthy-the-art-of-fiction-no-27-mary-mccarthy.

650 Gentile, M.C. (2010).
651 Dees, G. and Crampton, P. 1991. "Shrewd Bargaining on the Moral Frontier: Toward a Theory of Morality in Practice." *Business Ethics Quarterly* 1(2): 135–167.
652 Prentice, R. 2015. "Behavioral Ethics: Can It Help Lawyers (and Others) Be Their Best Selves?" *Notre Dame Journal of Law, Ethics & Public Policy* 29(1): 35–85.
653 Gentile, M.C. (2010).
654 Id.
655 Guffey, M.E. and Loewy, D. 2008. *Business Communication: Process and Product* (7th ed.). Southwestern/Cengage.
656 Hall, T. (2019).
657 Gentile, M.C. (2010).
658 Roghanizad, M.M. and Bohns, V.K. 2017. "Ask in Person: You're Less Persuasive than You Think over E-mail." *Journal of Experimental Social Psychology* 69(March): 223–226.
659 Gentile, M.C. (2010).
660 Miller, S. 2019. "Kendrick Castillo, Hero in Colo. School Shooting, Told His Dad He Would Act If Confronted with a Gunman." *USA Today*, May 9. www.usatoday.com/story/news/nation/2019/05/08/colorado-school-shooting-kendrick-castillo-student-dead-rampage/1140182001/.
661 Vaughn, D. 1982. "Toward Understanding Unlawful Organizational Behavior." *Michigan Law Review* 80(7): 1377–1402.
662 Stoknew, P.E. 2015. *What We Think About When We Try Not to Think About Global Warming*. Chelsea Green Publishers.
663 Gentile, M.C. (2010).
664 Id.

Chapter 23

665 Ashworth, B., Gioia, D., Robinson, S. and Trevino, L. 2008. "Introduction to Special Topic Forum: Reviewing Organizational Corruption. *Academy of Management Review* 33(3): 670–684.
666 Hirsh, J.B., Lu, J.G. and Galinsky, A.D. 2018. "Moral Utility Theory: Understanding the Motivation to Behave (Un)ethically." *Research in Organizational Behavior* 38: 43–59.
667 Haugh, T. 2019. "The Power Few of Corporation Compliance." *Georgia Law Review* 53: 129–195.
668 Treviño, L. and den Nieuwenoe, N. 2019. "How to Avoid Becoming the Next Wells Fargo." *Ethical Systems Blog*, Jan. 14. www.ethicalsystems.org/content/how-avoid-becoming-next-wells-fargo.
669 Epley, N. and Kumar, A. 2019. "How to Design an Ethical Organization." *Harvard Business Review* 97(3): 144–150.
670 Thaler, R.H. and Sunstein, C.R. 2008. *Nudge: Improving Decisions about Health, Wealth, and Happiness*. Penguin.
671 Sunstein, C.R. 2013. "The Storrs Lectures: Behavioral Economics and Paternalism." *Yale Law Journal* 122(7): 1826–1899.
672 Madrian, B.C. and Shea, D.F. 2001. "The Power of Suggestion: Inertia in 401(k) Participation and Savings Behavior." *Quarterly Journal of Economics* 116(4): 1149–1187.
673 *EthicalSystems.org*. 2020. www.ethicalsystems.org/.
674 Khan, A. 2018. "A Behavioral Approach to Financial Supervision, Regulation, and Central Banking." IMF Working Paper No. 18/178. www.imf.org/en/Publications/WP/Issues/2018/08/02/A-Behavioral-Approach-to-Financial-Supervision-Regulation-and-Central-Banking-46146.
675 Engler, H. 2018. *Remaking Culture on Wall Street: A Behavioral Science Approach for Building Trust from the Bottom Up*. Palgrave MacMillan.
676 Engler, H. 2018. "Bank Culture Forum: Big Banks Gain More Understanding of Staff Conduct; Lack Common Standards." *Reuters Financial Regulatory Forum*, Apr. 24. www.reuters.com/article/bc-finreg-bank-culture-forum-understandi/

bank-culture-forum-big-banks-gain-more-understanding-of-staff-conduct-lack-common-standards-idUSKBN1HV27P.
677 May, J. 2018. *Regard for Reason in the Moral Mind.* Oxford University Press.
678 Treviño, L.K. and Nelson, K.A. 2007. *Managing Business Ethics: Straight Talk About How To Do It Right* (4th ed.). Wiley.
679 Toffler, B.L. 2003. *Final Accounting: Ambition, Greed, and the Fall of Arthur Andersen.* Crown Business.
680 Mayer, D.M. et al. 2013. "Encouraging Employees to Report Unethical Conduct Internally: It Takes a Village." *Organizational Behavior and Human Decision Processes* 121(1): 89–103.
681 Owens, B.P. et al. 2019. "The Impact of Leader Moral Humility on Follower Moral Self-Efficacy and Behavior." *Journal of Applied Psychology* 104(1): 146–163.
682 Ariely, D. 2012. *The (Honest) Truth About Dishonesty: How We Lie to Everyone–Especially Ourselves.* Harper.
683 DeSombre, E.R. 2018. *Why Good People Do Bad Environmental Things.* Oxford University Press.
684 Valentine, S. and Fleischman, G. 2004. "Ethics Training and Businesspersons' Perceptions of Organizational Ethics." *Journal of Business Ethics* 41(4): 391–400.
685 Delaney, J.T. and Sockell, D. 1992. "Do Company Ethics Training Programs Make a Difference? An Empirical Analysis." *Journal of Business Ethics* 11(9): 719–727.
686 Haugh, T. 2017. "The Criminalization of Compliance." *Notre Dame Law Review* 92(3): 1215–1269.
687 Gino, F. 2013. *Sidetracked: Why Our Decisions Get Derailed, and How We Can Stick to the Plan.* Harvard Business Review Press.
688 Mazar, N., Amir, O. and Ariely, D. 2008. "The Dishonesty of Honest People: A Theory of Self-Concept Maintenance." *Journal of Marketing Research* 45(6): 633–644.
689 Gino, F. and Margolis, J.D. 2011. "Bringing Ethics into Focus: How Regulatory Focus and Risk Preferences Influence (Un)ethical Behavior." *Organizational Behavior and Human Decision Processes* 115(2): 145–156.
690 Zhang, S., Cornwell, J.F.M. and Higgins, E.T. 2014. "Repeating the Past: Prevention Focus Motivates Repetition, Even for Unethical Decisions." *Psychological Science* 25(1): 179–187.
691 Welsh, D.T., Ordóñez, L.D., Snyder, D.G. and Christian, M.S. 2015. "The Slippery Slope: How Small Ethical Transgressions Pave the Way for Larger Future Transgressions." *Journal of Applied Psychology* 100(1): 114–127.
692 Dungan, J., Waytz, A. and Young, L. 2017. "Corruption in the Context of Moral Trade-offs." In *Thinking About Bribery: Neuroscience, Moral Cognition and the Psychology of Bribery*, Nichols, P. and Robertson, D. (eds.), 85–102. Cambridge University Press.
693 Barnett, T. and Vaicys, C. 2000. "The Moderating Effect of Individuals' Perceptions of Ethical Work Climate on Ethical Judgments and Behavioral Intention." *Journal of Business Ethics* 27(4): 351–362.
694 Kahneman, D. 2011. *Thinking, Fast and Slow.* Farrar, Straus & Giroux.
695 Shalvi, S., Eldar, O. and Bereby-Meyer, Y. 2012. "Honesty Requires Time (and Lack of Justifications)." *Psychological Science* 23(10): 1264–1270.
696 Gentilin, D. 2016. *The Origins of Ethical Failures: Lessons for Leaders.* Routledge.
697 Margolis, J. and Molinsky, A. 2006. "Three Practical Challenges of Moral Leadership." In *Moral Leadership: The Theory and Practice of Power, Judgment, and Policy*, Rhode, D. (ed.), 77–93. Jossey-Bass.
698 Gawande, A. 2011. *The Checklist Manifesto: How to Get Things Right.* Picador.
699 Broadcat. 2020. *We Are Compliance Design.* www.thebroadcat.com/.
700 Haugh, T. (2017).
701 Ketzer, K., Lindenberg, S. and Steg, L. 2008. "The Spreading of Disorder." *Science* 322(5908): 1681–1685.

702 Zhong, C., Bohns, V.K. and Gino, F. 2010. "Good Lamps Are the Best Police: Darkness Increases Dishonesty and Self-Interested Behavior." *Psychological Science* 21(3): 311–314.
703 Gladwell, M. 2005. *Blink: The Power of Thinking Without Thinking.* Little Brown and Company.
704 Banaji, M.R. and Greenwald, A.G. 2013. *Blind Spot: Hidden Biases of Good People.* Delacorte Press.
705 Office for Inclusion and Equity, Division of Diversity and Community Engagement, University of Texas at Austin. 2015. *Inclusive Search and Recruitment Toolkit.* University of Texas at Austin.
706 Fisher, L.M. 1992. "Accusation of Fraud at Sears." *New York Times*, June 12. www.nytimes.com/1992/06/12/business/accusation-of-fraud-at-sears.html.
707 Bicchieri, C. and Ganegoda, D. 2017. "Determinants of Corruption: A Sociopsychological Analysis." In *Thinking About Bribery: Neuroscience, Moral Cognition and the Psychology of Bribery*, Nichols, P. and Robertson, D. (eds.), 179–205. Cambridge University Press.
708 Treviño, L.K. and Youngblood, S.A. 1990. "Bad Apples in Bad Barrels: A Causal Analysis of Ethical Decision-Making Behavior." *Journal of Applied Psychology* 75(4): 378–385.
709 Haugh, T. 2018. "*Caremark's* Behavioral Legacy." *Temple Law Review* 90: 611–646.
710 Hannah, S.T., Avolio, B.J. and May, D.R. 2011. "Moral Maturation and Moral Conation: A Capacity Approach to Explaining Moral Thought and Action." *Academy of Management Review* 36(4): 663–685.
711 Gonzales, M.H., Aronson, E. and Costanzo, M.A. 1988. "Using Social Cognition and Persuasion to Promote Energy Conservation: A Quasi-Experiment." *Journal of Applied Social Psychology* 18(12): 1049–1066.
712 Diener, E., Fraser, S.C., Beaman, A.L. and Kelem, R.T. 1976. "Effects of Deindividuation Variables on Stealing Among Halloween Trick-or-Treaters." *Journal of Personality and Social Psychology* 33(2): 178–183.
713 Priks, M. 2014. "Do Surveillance Cameras Affect Unruly Behavior? A Close Look at Grandstands." *The Scandinavian Journal of Economics* 116(4): 1160–1179.
714 Zhong, C., Bohns, V.K. and Gino, F. (2010).
715 Miller, C.B. 2014. *Character & Moral Psychology.* Oxford University Press.
716 Bateson, M. et al. 2013. "Do Images of 'Watching Eyes' Induce Behavior That Is More Pro-Social or More Normative? A Field Experiment on Littering." *PLoS One* 8(12): e82055–e82064.
717 Langevoort, D. 2018. "Behavioral Ethics, Behavioral Compliance." In *Research Handbook on Corporate Crime and Financial Misdealing*, Arlen, J. (ed.), 263–281. Edward Elgar.
718 Ewing, J. 2017. *Faster, Higher, Farther: The Volkswagen Scandal.* W.W. Norton & Co.
719 Oc, B., Bashshur, M.R. and Moore, C. 2015. "Speaking Truth to Power: The Effect of Candid Feedback on How Individuals with Power Allocate Resources." *Journal of Applied Psychology* 100(2): 450–463.
720 Mayer, D.M. et al. (2013).
721 Bard, J. 2012. "What to Do When You Can't Hear the Whistleblowing: A Proposal to Protect the Public's Health by Providing Whistleblower Protection for Medical Researchers." *Indiana Health Law Review* 9(1): 1–67.
722 Hess, D. 2007. "A Business Ethics Perspective on Sarbanes-Oxley and the Organizational Sentencing Guidelines." *Michigan Law Review* 105(8): 1781–1816.
723 Weng, H.Y., Fox, A.S. and Shackman, A.J. 2013. "Compassion Training Alters Altruism and Neural Responses to Training." *Psychological Science* 24(7): 1171–1180.
724 Gneezy, A. et al. 2012. "Paying to Be Nice: Consistency and Costly Prosocial Behavior." *Management Science* 58(1): 179–187.

INDEX

Note: Page numbers in *italics* refer to illustrations.

Abramoff, Jack 190–191
absolving ourselves from responsibility 41
academic dishonesty 47
acceptability heuristic 41
actor-observer bias 165–166
addiction 177
Adoboli, Kweku 101
agency locus 193–194
allies 181, 206–207
altruism *184*
altruistic cheating 100
ambiguity and complexity 65–66
Anand, Vikas 188–191, 194, 196–197
Andersen, Arthur 48, 221
anger 22, 192
antisocial behavior 22
Aquinas, Thomas 177
Ariely, Dan 117, 137
Aristotle 177
Armstrong, Lance 47, 100
Aronson, Elliot 137, 197
Asch, Solomon 46, 49, 206
Asch experiment 46
Ashforth, Blake 188
attractiveness bias 176
attributing blame 196
audiences, selection and sequencing of 207
Auschwitz 101
Authority foundation 15
automatic norm following 16

Bandura, Albert 100, 113, 158, 187, 192–198
Bandura's four categories 192–193
Banning Burkas *126*
Bentley, Robert *111*
Bargh, John 122
Barings Bank collapse 85, 93–94, *95*
Baron, Jonathan 124
Bazerman, Max 53, 61, 63, 83, 140, 155
behavioral ethics *8*, 31, 219; business practices 2; definition 1, 7; influences 2; in practice 6–7, *8*
behavioral locus 193
behavioral nudges 220–221
behavioral psychology 5, 170
belief persistence 63–64
belligerence 54
Bentham, Jeremy 146, 177
Berns, Gregory 46
best self 175; character 182–183; enlist allies 180; ethical antennae 178–179; guard against biases and influences 179–180; moral action decisions 177–178; moral imagination 180–182; moral judgments 175–177
B.F. Goodrich Company 191, 194
Biased (Eberhardt) 130
Big Short, The (Lewis) 189
binding values 34
Blair, Tony 129
"blame the victim" mentality 34

Blind Injustice (Godsey) 137–138
Bliss, Dave 92
Bloom, Paul 23
bounded ethicality *8*, 158, 169, *171*, 180
brain scans 26, 46
Brooks, David 53
buying green *111*
bystander effect 49

Cameron, Jessica 90
Candid Camera (TV Series) 45
Care foundation 14
Castro, Fidel 164
causal attribution bias 64
Challenger, The 73–74
change blindness 81–82, 179
character 56, 97, 143, 148, 150–152, 164–165, 178–179, 182–183
cheating 6, 47, 91, 146–147, 222
choice 206, *215*
choice architecture 220
Chugh, Dolly 105
Climate Change & the Paris Deal *118*
Clinton, Bill 148
codes of conduct 67, 99, 227
cognitive bias 53
cognitive dissonance 135–136, *141*; corporate cognitive dissonance 139; law enforcement 137–139; mitigating moral dissonance 139–140; moral dissonance 136–137
cognitive heuristics 53, 56
cognitive science 5
Cohen, Taya 152
Colby, Anne 183
collective action 195
Comer, Debra 83
community values 16
compassion 23
compensatory ethics 105
compounding illness *118*
confabulation 24
confirmation bias 32–33, 63
conformity bias 23, 32, 45–46, *50*, 122, 131, 136, 169, 179; Asch experiment 46; and ethics 47–48; good and bad 49; in real world 46–47
considerateness 54
contempt 22, 192
Cooper, Cynthia 84
cooperativeness 54
corporate cognitive dissonance 139
correspondence bias 163
Costco Model *230*
Cressey, Donald 193

Cullity, Garrett 176
cyberbullying 117

Damon, William 183
Daraprim Price Hike *199*
Darley, John 49, 55, 116–117
deceitfulness 54
Dees, Gregory 210
dehumanization 124, 196
denial of injury 140, 189
denial of responsibility 188–189, 194, 198
denial of victim 139, 189–190, 198
deontological approach 26, 109, 156
deontology *28*
DeSteno, David 34
de Waal, Frans 147
dialoguing 211
Diekmann, Kristina 148, 161
diffusion of responsibility 49, *50*, 194–195
disgust 12–13, 22, 25, 27, 192
displacement of responsibility 194
dispositional bias 163
divine punishment 192
division of labor 195
Dodd-Frank Act 227
The Door Study 81–82
Doris, John 129, 143
dot-com boom 1990 40
Dunning, David 161
dyadic completion 34
Dynegy 203

Eberhardt, Jennifer 130
Ebola & American Intervention *118*
Edmonds, David 151
effects locus 193, 195
ego depletion 147
Ehrlichman, John 40
Eichmann, Adolf 41, 188
Elsass, Priscilla 2, 12
embarrassment 22, 146, 192
emotionism *see* sentimentalism
empathetic bias 115
empathy 23, 114, 123, 147, 180, 183
employee behavior 48, 232
Enron rewards systems 65
Enron scandal 32, 39, 48, 55, 65, 74, 83, 108, 191
Epley, Nick 220
Equifax's Breach of Trust *95*
ethical amnesia 139, 159
ethical blindness 140
ethical coloration 83
ethical errors 6, 225

ethical fading 41, *42*, 77, 169, 204; and framing 73; victim of 161
ethical leadership *229*
ethical traps 6
ethics 1–2, *4*; and framing 72–73; improvement 2; moral humility 12; overconfidence bias 54–55; training 222; *see also specific terms*
euphemisms 75–76
euphemistic language 196–197
evolutionary biology 5
Ewing, Jack 139

FAE *see* fundamental attribution error (FAE)
Fair, Eric 41
fairness 15, 34, 54, 129, 205
Fairness foundation 14
fake accounts 219
False Claims Act 227
familiarity bias 115
Fanon, Frantz 135
fear 23
Feldman, Yuval 178
Festinger, Leon 136
Filabi, Azish 221
Flynn, Michael *167*
Ford 39, 85, 116
Foreign Corrupt Practices Act 99, 224
forgiveness 23
framing 71–72, 77, 100, *102*, 131, 157, 196, 179, 208, *216*; and ethical fading 73; and ethics 72–73; euphemisms 75–76; loss aversion 74; in real world 73–74; and role morality 74–75, 98–99
Freedom of Speech on Campus *216*
Freedom vs. Duty in clinical social work *102*
fundamental attribution error (FAE) 163–164, *167*; actor-observer bias 165–166; causes 165; ethics and 165; studies 164–165; third base effect 166
Funt, Alan 45

Galinsky, Adam 161
Gambino, Richard 196
Garfinkel, Steven 56
Gebhard, Helen Sharkey 203–204, 210
General Motors 85, 93
general situational factors 143–144; lack of transparency 145–147; money 150; money changes everything 148–150; self-control 151; self-control exhaustion 147–148; situational influences, minimizing 150; time 150; time pressure 144–145; transparency 150–151
generosity 54
genocide 124
Gentile, Mary 170, 181, 204–214
Gentilin, Dennis 92, 163
Gibbs, John 75
Gilbert, Dan 164
Gino, Francesca 75, 83, 123, 222
Giving voice to values (GVV) 17, 181, 203–205, *215*; allies 206–207; audiences, Selection and sequencing of 207; choice 206; framing 208; information, critical importance of 207; normalization 208–209; purpose 209; reasons and rationalizations 211–213; self-knowledge and alignment 209–210; values 205; voice 210–211
Giving Voice to Values: How to Speak Your Mind When You Know What's Right (Gentile) 170
Glaucon 22, 145
Global Crossing 91
Glover, Jonathan 41, 152
Gneezy, Uri 227
Godsey, Mark 137–138
Goldilocks incentive system 225
Goldstein, Rebecca 125
Grass, Martin 92
gratitude 23
Greene, Joshua 121
Gretzinger, Ralph 191, 194
group-decision making 195
groupthink 32, 123, *126*
Grubbe, Deb 116
guilt 21–22, 152, 195, 219
gut feelings 24, 34, 115
Gyges 145

Haidt, Jonathan 12, 14, 22, 31–32, 146, 221
Hallie, Philip Paul 183
Harman, Sabrina 85
Harrington, Noreen 116
Harvey, William 64
Hendry, John 149
Hess, David 227
higher loyalties, appeal to 191, 194
Hippocratic Oath violation 101
Houser, Daniel 144
Howard, Ronald 71
Hubbard, L. Ron 135
human experimentation 38

human inclination to divide ourselves into tribes 122
humanization 113
human moral decision making 31; confirmation bias 32–33; indelible victim effect 34; just world hypothesis 34; Knobe effect 33; moral judgments *versus* moral action decisions 31–32; moral luck 33; moral reasoning flaws 32; omission bias 33
human rationality 6
Hume, David 124

illusion of hope 57
Implicit Association Test (IAT) 130–131
implicit bias 32, 66, 123, *126*, 129–130, *133*, 224–225, *229*; disconcerting story 130; evidence of 131–132; IAT 130–131
implicit social cognition 129
impoliteness 54
incentive gaming *229*
incrementalism 32, 81, *86*, 93, 101, 131, 156, 179–180, 223; change blindness 81–82; in real world 84–85; varieties of 82–83
indelible victim effect 34, 176
individualizing values 34
in-group bias 121, 180; minimizing 124–125; moral action decisions 123–124; moral implications of our tribal sorting 122–123; sorting ourselves into tribes 121–122
in-group/out-group *126*
In It To Win: The Jack Abramoff Story *199*
integrity 149, 183, *184*, 227, *229*
integrity tests 219
invisibility problem 165
irrational optimism 57
irrational overconfidence 53, 57
Irwin, Julie 139

Jackall, Robert 99
Jack & Rationalizations *141*, *199*
Jack & Role morality *102*
Jennings, Marianne 54, 181
Johnson, Dominic 53
Johnson, Mark 180
Joshi, Mehendra 188
justice 24, 205, *216*
justified harm 97
Just World Hypothesis 34, 176–177

Kaepernick, Colin 14–15
Kahneman, Daniel 6, 12, 72–74, 89, 156, 177

Kant, Immanuel 11–12, 34
Keillor, Garrison 53
Kelly, Daniel 25, 27
Keltner, Dacher 47
Kern, Mary 105
Khan, Roomy 92
kindness 23, 54, 183
Knobe, Joshua 33
Knobe effect 33, 176
Korver, Clinton 71
Kouchaki, Maryam 6
Kozlowski, Dennis 56
Krogh, Egil "Bud" 40
Krogh & the Watergate Scandal 40, *43*
Kumar, Amit 220

Laden, Osama bin 123
Lance Armstrong cycling scandal 47, 100
Langevoort, Donald 57
Latané, Bibb 49
Lauper, Cindy 148
law enforcement 137–139
Lay, Kenneth 48, 55
lay dispositionism 163
laziness 54
Leeson, Nick 85, 93
Lest Innocent Blood Be Shed (Hallie) 183
Levin, Daniel 81
Levy, Neil 11
Lewis, Michael 150, 189–190
Liar's Poker (Lewis) 189–190
Liberty foundation 14
LIBOR scandal 190
Lifton, Robert Jay 39
Limbaugh on Drug addiction *167*
Liu, Lucy 129
Lobel, Thalma 109
Lockheed-Martin 225
loss aversion 74, 77, 89, *95*, 101, 226; academic studies 90–91; and ethics 90; failure to own our mistakes 92–94; in real world 91–92; studies of 89–90
loyalty 34, 54, 191
Loyalty foundation 15
Luban, David 137
Luhrmann, Tanya Marie 15

Madoff, Bernie 81, 93
Malone, Patrick 164
Malti, Tina 21
Margolis, Joshua 145
Martin, Dorothy 134–135
masturbation 11, 34
May, Joshua 13, 26, 187

McVeigh, Timothy 75
meanness 54
Meet Me At Starbucks *133*
Mein Kampf (Hitler) 194
mental shortcuts (internal biases) 3, 6, 53
metaphor of ledger 191–192, 224
#Me Too *230*
Milgram, Stanley 37–39, 41, 55, 179, 206
Milgram experiment 37–39, 55, 124, 206
Milgram "shock" experiment 55
Miller, Christian 144, 147
Miller, Dale 90–91
Mischel, Walter 148
Miss Saigon Controversy *133*
Mistakes Were Made (Tavris and Aronson) 197
mitigating moral dissonance 139–140
moderating overconfidence 57–58
Molinsky, Andrew 145
money 148–150
Moneyball, The Blind Side (Lewis) 189
money-oriented environments 149
money priming experiments 149
Moody's 40
Moore, Celia 75
moral, social, and economic justification 193–194
moral action 24, 170, *171*
moral action decisions 31–32, 123–124, 177–178
moral attentiveness 179
moral awareness 169, *171*
moral awe 23
moral balancing 105
moral character 5, 109, 158, 221
moral cleansing 109
moral code 97
moral cognition *35*
moral compensation 105–106, 108, 140
moral consistency 110
moral credentialing 108
moral decision making 169, *171*
moral decisions 12, 175
moral dilemmas 1–2
moral disengagement 34, 56, 83, 99–100, 140, 170, 183, 187, 192; advantageous comparison 197; agency locus 194–195; Bandura's four categories 192–193; behavioral locus 193; denial of injury 189; denial of responsibility 188–189; denial of victim 189–190; effects locus 195; euphemistic language 196–197; higher loyalties, appeal to 191; metaphor of ledger 191–192; moral, social, and economic justification 193–194; by observers 197–198; rationalizations 187–188; role morality 99–100; social weighting 190; victim locus 196
moral dissonance 136–137
moral dumbfounding 24–26, 176
moral elevation 23
moral emotions 12, *17*, 21, *28*, 123, 146, 192; impact of 32; moral dumbfounding 24–25; other-condemning emotions 22–23; other-praising emotions 23; other-suffering emotions 23; role of 23–24; self-conscious emotions 21–22; trolley problem 25–27
moral equilibrium 32, 105, *111*; moral cleansing 109; moral compensation 105–106; moral credentialing 108; moral licensing 106, 109–110; outside the laboratory 108; studies of 106–107
moral equilibrium theory 107
moral fallibility 6
moral fiber 182
moral foul play 27
moral humility 6, 12, 222
moral identity 106, 109, 152, 183
moral imagination 180–182, *184*
moral intent 170, *171*, *199*
moral intuitions 12, 14, 23–24, 33
morality 5, 11, 14, 24, 55, 66, 147, 177
moral judgments 11–13, 24, 31, 175–177; *versus* moral action decisions 31–32; moral intuitions 12; moral socialization 16; rationalism 13–14; sacred values 15; sentimentalism 12–13; values 14–15
moral licensing 105–109
moral luck 33, 175
moral muscle 147, 183
moral muteness *42*
moral myopia 169
moral philosophy *4*, 11
moral psychology *35*, 146, 177
moral reasoning 11–12, 16, *17*, 23–24, 31–32, 175–176, *184*
moral reasoning flaws 32
moral relativism 16, *17*, 177
moral self-esteem 158
moral self-licensing 105
moral self-regulation 105
moral self-sanctions 192
moral sentiments 12
moral socialization 16
moral standards 6, 16, 21–22, 24, 66, 82–83, 122, 192
moral worth *126*

morality surplus 109
Morse, Lily 152
mortgage-backed securities crisis 117
Mother Teresa 55, 113, 158, 182
motivated forgetting 159
motivated reasoning 63
My Lai Massacre 82

Niemi, Laura 129
Nixon, Richard 40
noncontact bias 176
normalization 208–209, *215*
Norris, Floyd 93

Obama, Barack 129
obedience studies 38–39
obedience to authority 32, 37, *42*, 131, 178–179, 191, 221; absolving ourselves from responsibility 41; Milgram experiment 37–39; outside the lab 39–41
obedience to orders 41
Oberlechner, Thomas 45
Ohio Innocence Project (OIP) 138
omission bias 33, 175
organizational pressures 6, 32, 37, 56, 143, 180, 182, 198
ostracism 49
other-condemning emotions 21–23
other-praising emotions 21, 23
other-suffering emotions 21, 23
overconfidence bias 32, 53–54, *59*, 158, 166, 179; ethical overconfidence in action 55; ethics 54–55; moderating overconfidence 57–58; overoptimism 57; reason 56–57
overoptimism 57–58

Packing Peanuts for Profit Scandals *118*
Pao & Gender Bias *216*
Park, Rand 2, 12
Payne, Keith 129
peer pressure 37, 46
Pentagon Papers 40
Piëch, Ferdinand 74
Pierce, Lamar 48, 219
Piff, Paul 166
Ponzi scheme 93, 115–116
Portman, Rob 64
POS (pieces of you-know-what) 40
Power of Ideals, The (Damon and Colby) 183
primatology 5
prosocial behavior 23, *28*, 147, 228, *229*
psychic pain 89

psychological biases 6, 32, 53, 56, 63, 129, 132, 158, 166, 180, 198
purpose 209, *215*

Qwest 91

racial discrimination 14
Rajaratnam, Raj 92, *95*
ratings agencies 40
rationalism 13–14
rationalists 13
rationalizations *17*, 32, 34, *35*, 41, 90, 100, *102*, 139, *141*, 170, 187–188, 194–198, *199*, 211–213, 224, *216*; appeal to higher loyalties 191; classification 188, 192; for decisions 12, *17*; defined 187–188; denial of injury 189; denial of responsibility 188–189; denial of victim 196; metaphor of the ledger 191–192; self-narrative 188; social weighting 190
reason & rationalizations *215*
Reeves, Hope 105
regulatory focus theory 223
remorse 23
replication crisis 7
resist authority 179, 206
Rest, James 169
RICE (Respect, Integrity, Communication, Excellence) code 48, 55
righteous anger 23
Rite-Aid 92
role morality 32, *42*, 74–75, *78*, 97–100, *102*, 178; altruistic cheating 100; and framing 98–99; moral disengagement 99–100; in real world 100–101
Roosevelt, Theodore 1
routinization 83
rule violators 22

Sabini, John 163
sacred values 15
Sanctity or Purity foundation 15
Sander, Fritz 101
Sapolsky, Robert 22
Sarbanes-Oxley Act 227
Sauer, Hanno 13–14, 31, 177
Schiltz, Patrick 84
Schwartz, Janet 137
Schwartz, Mark 2
Schweigert, Francis 99
selective social comparison 190, 197–198
self-conscious emotions 21–22

self-control 146–148, 151
self-deception 139
self-knowledge and alignment 209–210, *215*
selflessness 54
self-monitoring 76
self-serving bias 32, 61–63, *68*, 166, 178, 180, 195; ambiguity and complexity 65–66; complicating factors 64; conflating what is good 64; factors reinforcing 63–64; magnitude 65; subconscious influences 66–67
sentimentalism 12–13
sentimentalists 13
sermonizing 211
shame 22, 32, 34, 92, 146, 195
Shermer, Michael 21, 24, 123, 166
side effect bias 176
Siepmann, Michael 163
Simons, Daniel 81
sincerity 54
Sinek, Simon 117
situational attribution bias 165–166
situational forces (circumstances) 6, 39, 143, 182
situationalists 144
situationists 144
Skilling, Jeff 39, 48
Smith, Isaac 6
Snyder, Jason 48
social and organizational pressures (external pressures) 6, 32, 37, 56, 43, 180, 182, 198
social contract theory *17*
social identity theory 121
social intuitionist model 31
social norms 21, 25, 47, 146
social pressures 37, 56
social weighting 188, 190, 197
Solomon, David 64
Soltes, Eugene 56, 115, 151
Some Do Care (Damon and Colby) 183
sorting ourselves into tribes 121–122
Spitzer, Eliot 108
Stalin, Joseph 182
Standard & Poor's 40
Stein, Julia 163
Stout, Lynn 37
Strohminger, Nina 24
subconscious influences 66–67
subject of moral worth *126*, 179
Suer, Oral 108
Sullenberger, Sully 182
Sunstein, Cass 47, 220

sympathy 23
System 1 thinking 12, 177, 223
System 2 thinking 12, 14, 177

tangible and abstract 113, *118*, 165, 178, 195; examples 114–117; tangible ethics 114
Tavris, Carol 197
temporal factors 155; about time 156; act less ethically 159–161; inaccurate memory about 158–159; mismatch 157–158; poor predictors 157; of two minds 156–157
Tenbrunsel, Ann 53, 63, 66, 140, 155–156, 161
Thaler, Richard 220
Thiokol, Morton 73
third base effect 166
time pressure 145, 155–156, 178, 223
Tomlin, K.A. 2
transparency 146, 158, 226
transparency, lack of 145–147, 158, 226
tribal sorting 122–123
triple-process moral psychology 177
trolley problem 25–27, 31, 114
trust 23
Tversky, Amos 6, 12, 72–74, 89

unconscious influences 6, 13
us-against-them 223
utilitarian 26, 109, 156
utilitarianism *28*

Valdesolo, Piercarlo 34
values 14–15, *17*, 34, 122, 180, 205, *215–216*
Varsity Blues college admissions scandal of 2019 22, *50*, 100, 224–225
Vega, Gina 83, 140
vengeance 23
victim locus 193, 196
Vietnam War 40, 82, 113
virtue ethics 183, *184*
voice *215*
Volkswagen "Dieselgate" scandal 39, 74, 116, 139, 226–227

Wade-Benzoni, Kimberly 155
Waksal, Sam 151
Wasendorf, Russell 139–140
Watergate burglars 40
Watergate scandal 40, 197
Watson, Mark 55
Welfare Reform *126*
Wells Fargo 219, 225–227

Welsh, David 223
Werhane, Patricia 180
What Do You Say to a Naked Lady? 45
When Prophecy Fails (Festinger) 136
whistle-blowing 226–227
white-collar criminals 56, 115, 178
Why They Do It: Inside the Mind of the White-Collar Criminal 56
Wilde, Oscar 157
willful blindness 140

Williams, Robin *102*
Winfrey, Oprah 47
Winslet, Kate 129
WorldCom 91
WorldCom's bankruptcy 84
Wrangham, Richard 175

York, Alvin 193

Zak, Paul 123

Printed in Great Britain
by Amazon